Enhancing Competency
of teachers

A Teaching-and-Learning Enhancement Guide

(With Test Banks in "Jose Rizal" and "Philippine History" Subjects)

DR. MARCELINO D. CATAHAN, PhD

authorHOUSE®

AuthorHouse™
1663 Liberty Drive
Bloomington, IN 47403
www.authorhouse.com
Phone: 1 (800) 839-8640

Published by AuthorHouse   05/27/2015

ISBN: 978-1-5049-0794-1 (sc)
ISBN: 978-1-5049-0929-7 (e)

Library of Congress Control Number: 2015906578

Print information available on the last page.

Any people depicted in stock imagery provided by Thinkstock are models, and
such images are being used for illustrative purposes only.
Certain stock imagery © Thinkstock.

This book is printed on acid-free paper.

ACKNOWLEDGMENT

I wish to thank ALL my former students—in about 10 Social/Political Science subjects that I taught from 1997-2004—at the College of St. Benilde (CSB-DLSU), 2544 Taft Avenue, Manila; and, at the AMA Computer College (AMACC), Sta. Mesa, also in Manila. They inspired me to think, conceptualize and write a comprehensive "Teaching-and-Learning Enhancement Guide" to facilitate teaching-and-learning of significant skill, method and social competencies on learners for their professional career developments.

My heartfelt gratitude goes to three of my most beloved sisters and their families, i.e. *Conchita C. Lestones, Nieves C. Villamin* and *Amelia C. Reyes.* Their respect, love, empathy and compassion have greatly influenced my professional career development; and, have provided me also with the needed inspiration and support during my years of post graduate studies at the Pacific Western University in Los Angeles, CA, USA.

My lasting appreciation is due also to *Col. J. Sergio Labbe*; Commander of the Canadian Joint Forces—a UN Military Contingent in war-torn Somalia in 1993-94—who was my chief cooperating-partner in the mission of reactivating the Primary Education System in Hiran Province, Somalia. Despite the occasional rain of bullets from the Somali rebels, Colonel Labbe courageously built, with his military contingent, a number of primary schools in Hiran Province; and thereafter, this writer did the remaining jobs to complete the primary education reactivation process.

Finally, a million thanks to the Lord God, Almighty—Who has always made every load of mine lighter and productive.

To my family, especially my children, I hope I make you proud as you have made me.

To all my former students who are now in different parts of the world,
I hope you continue making a difference in somebody's lives.

ON REVERENCE

"OUR LORD'S SAVING GRACE"

Oh, life's so sweat and full of joy
Living in this world,
Where all material things abound
Endowed by our Lord;

Because of this, sometimes we fail
To thank—Lord Jesus,
We got entrapped unknowingly
At evil's dark world!

When later on. . .
We realized—we're on a way lost,
Our hearts dictate to hurry back
To Pious Fold;

Oh, we're really human:
Weak—in spirit and flesh,
We easily forsake our Lord's Saving Grace. . .
We easily forsake—our Lord's Saving Grace!

Note: This poem is also a song. It can be sung to the tune of Mr. Rico Puno's (i.e. the "Singer," and *not* the "U-Sec.") famous song, entitled: *"Ang Tao'y Marupok."*

CONTENTS

REFERENCES

APPENDICES

LIST OF TABLES

LIST OF FIGURES

SEC. JESSE M. ROBREDO
(8.18.2012)

Leader-Managers are all passersby (*We—all—are passersby*).
The depth of the footprints we left behind, determines. . .
the ETHICO-MORAL STANDARD ***we'd served,*** and
the way ***how people loved us***—after we'd died!

MODULE 1
THE TLEP PROTOCOLS

> As teachers, there are two extremes that we normally associate our memories in remembering students. We permanently recall the *best* ones and the *bad* ones. The same basic principle applies among the learners! Now. . . would you like to be remembered as a *bad educator*?

The Demand for Change in Education

Preview.   Today, a pressing demand for change in education is taking place locally in the General Education System. Teaching-and-learning is being taken more seriously after many long years of criticisms and loud calls for reforms. Nowadays, many colleges and universities are reviewing their commitment to teaching-and-learning process to discover ways to improve overall educational standard. School Administrators are becoming more rigid in the selection of teachers today. Perhaps, this is an outcome of the negative reports from personnel placement and promotion committees that curriculum vitae (CV)—being submitted by teacher-applicant during application period—is *not* sufficient to guarantee a competent and effective classroom teaching performance. They argued that CV indicates *only* such qualifications, e.g. master's degree, publications, research and other scholarly achievements; and, reveals very little information about the actual teaching competencies. Hence, the teacher is being held accountable for low institutional performance rating.

Focus of the Blame.   At a glance, it is seemingly *fair* to blame the teachers for the low performances of student graduates, e.g. during the Annual Nursing Board Examination. The teachers are expected to be the best enhancers of effective *skill, method* and *social* (SMS) competencies in learners to become more competitive. However, there are other factors to consider for the low performances of graduates, e.g. the proper selection of students and the provision of adequate facilities and equipment for teaching-and-learning activities. Moreover, it is the function of every school institution to maintain a continuous teaching-and-learning enhancement program for their faculty members in order to keep abreast with the technological trends of modern time.

Unfortunately, the case of low institutional performance is blamed mainly against the poor teachers. It is to no surprise today, that school administration committee members are even trying to find out what instructors are teaching inside the classroom—and how they are doing it. They think that without SMS competencies, the teachers cannot give the teaching profession its rightful value. They assume that: "the school institution cannot produce competitive graduates with productive SMS competencies, if the instructors are *not* fully competent themselves." This negative assumption prompted a number of school administrators to interfere very often with the daily teaching-and-learning activities being done inside the classroom. And on the part of the teachers, they do not welcome this kind of interference. Teachers usually feel embarrassed whenever the College Dean or an Area Coordinator seats inside the classroom (outside regularly scheduled Annual Performance Review). This condition results to a serious confusion in a number of school institutions. Teachers begin to complain against certain school administrators resulting to chaos—that deters the flow of peaceful organizational operations; and thus, impeding the productive development of the young learners.

The Need for TLEP.   Considering the crisis in current educational situation, is there a way for the colleges and universities to respond seriously to clamor for the innovative pedagogical changes? Is it justified to enhance the teaching competencies by applying pressures to faculty members—to accept standards of professional responsibility and accountability? Personally, this writer would answer "yes." For verily, the instructor's competency is a primary factor in honing the students' learning to an excellent level for eventual competition in various fields of endeavor. As such, the measurement criteria for hiring teachers should be done rigidly to ensure the proper personnel selection.

For instructors who have worked with the institution for years already and who failed meeting the set standards, the recourse should *not* be to dismiss them right away. They should be given a chance to enhance their competencies through locally-organized formal *Teaching-and-Learning Enhancement Program* (TLEP). Verily, the TLEP is a part of the administrative function in any educational institution. If instructors do not measure up accordingly to institutional standard after a series of staff development training program and activities—then, that is the time when they should be removed or replaced from the service. They can find other jobs somewhere else, where they can be more productive.

Enhancing instructors' teaching-and-learning competencies is a continuous process. There is a need to maintain a reserve of competent and productive teachers to realize the noble vision-mission of the educational institution. In addition, instructors should also be informed accordingly on school matters, e.g.: recently-adopted technology; new rules and regulations; revised working conditions; newly-installed facilities and equipment; newly-introduced teaching methods; recently-retired faculty members; and, other organizational changes. All these are valid reasons for the need of a continuous TLEP.

Concept within the TLEP.   *Teaching-and-Learning Enhancement Program* (TLEP) is a planned program of activities for faculty members—done locally in a particular school institution through organized training workshops or seminars—to enhance or broaden their skill, method and social competencies in instructional performances. In essence, TLEP is synonymous to *Staff Development and Training Program* (SDTP). Other authors mostly call it this way, but there is a slight technical difference between the two.

In SDTP, readers may have the impression that competencies of teacher-participants could be of *lower grade* and underdeveloped—hence, the need for staff development and training. In TLEP however, faculty members are generally presumed to be in possession of *higher grade* teaching-and-learning qualities, although there is a need for *continuous* enhancement of teaching-and-learning competencies to become totally productive despite new advancements in the modern time. For the purpose of this book, this writer is calling this exercise as: "Teaching-and-Learning Enhancement Program (TLEP)."

In general, TLEP is an actual educational innovation that aims to *advance, increase, improve, elaborate, enhance, raise, heighten, elevate, enrich* and *refine* the instructor's professional ethico-moral standard and competencies in teaching-and-learning process. It includes the studies of various reference books, documents and materials that suggest the function and quality of an instructor in productive teaching and performance deliveries. In addition, TLEP is an appropriate venue for sharing the quality experiences in teaching-and-learning. Learning is a life-long process and professionals must consider sharing and enhancing previously-acquired competencies to keep abreast with the new trends.

Verily, productive teachers are the vital *change agents* in the high percentage results of board-passers in an Annual National Board Examination and *not* the famous name of the school institution. The high passing average of graduates in Annual National Board Examination is an absolute indicator of the acquired quality ethico-moral values and SMS competencies of faculty members in any particular institution.

Why should a school institution spend resources continuously in conducting a taxing and expensive Teaching-and-Learning Enhancement Program? The School Management is obligated to do so, to give time to low-performing instructors to develop; and, to gather specific data on instructors' teaching competencies for records and promotion basis.

Again, why should every full-time occupied faculty members join and participate in the TLEP? The instructors should participate to have an honest self-assessment on the specific weak areas of teaching-and-learning where improvements are necessary. They should participate in the TLEP to be able to:

1. Record for themselves how their teaching competency has evolved over time;
2. Learn more about the ideal characteristics of a good instructor;
3. Follow the logical instructional process and principles of instructions;
4. Refine their skill, method and social competencies in presenting lessons with the use of good training aids/materials for teaching effectiveness;
5. Improve the arts of questioning and speech techniques during lesson presentation;
6. Avoid comical mannerisms and distractions when presenting lessons;
7. Use the proper evaluation and assessment techniques;
8. Share their expertise and experience with the younger faculty members, e.g. providing teaching tips about a specific course to a new faculty;
9. Seek promotion, teaching awards or grants relative to teaching; and,
10. Leave a written legacy for the school so that future generations of teachers will benefit from retired instructors—in knowledge and experience.

TLEP: A Strategy in Educational Innovation

Logical Approach.   The logical approach in the process of educational, industrial and organizational innovations utilizes the standard *management concept*. First, the problem is *identified*. Then, possible solutions to identified problems are *planned* and *organized*. Out-of-the noted solutions to the problem, the best possible one is selected and is put into trial/ *implementation*. The implementation period is then closely *monitored* and *controlled* by the School Training Committee (STC) and followed by the *evaluation* of results.

If the solution on trial is promising and is solving the problem—the solution is then implemented on a wider scale. If it continuously gives productive results, the solution is absorbed into the system and is formally *institutionalized*.[1]

---

[1] Bishop, G. Innovation in Education. Hong Kong. Macmillan Publishers Ltd. 1986.

Enhancing competencies of faculty members in a school setting is an innovation more critical in scope—compared to skill and knowledge upgrading of the workers in industrial companies. Both innovations however identify the existing operational problems; find suitable solutions; implement best solutions; and, evaluate the enhancement results.

As part of identifying the various teaching-and-learning enhancements needs, the particular School Training Committee may distribute simple survey questionnaires to teachers—inquiring as to what particular area of instruction the teachers feel they need improvement. From there, the STC members may continue selecting the main priority areas where the teaching-and-learning discussions will concentrate during the TLEP.

A Prescribed Teaching Standard.   During the past few years, educational managers and administrators in many parts of the United States have defined precisely as to *what* specific knowledge and skills a productive teacher should *know* and be able to *do*. After conducting researches and considering education experiences—they drew-up their own standard elements of teaching in order to get the job done. The elements of teaching however, were *not* the same in all the states. The teaching standard elements *vary* from one state to another, depending on particular needs.

The North Carolina Teacher Performance Evaluation System had identified eight elements in teaching, which were prescribed as the state's standard on what a teacher should *know* and be able to *do*. The eight elements mentioned are:[2]

1. Management of instructional time
2. Management of student behavior
3. Instructional presentation
4. Instructional monitoring of student performance
5. Instructional feedback
6. Facilitating instruction
7. Communicating with the educational environment
8. Performing non-instructional duties

The above-listed elements in teaching are the measurement basis in determining the adequacy of performances of a teacher in North Carolina. But there is more to productive teaching. There are other subsidiary factors to consider in effective teaching-and-learning. The *context*, for example, is a major influence on the teacher's performances and on the student's achievement. According to Edelfelt, the context includes the social and psychological climate of the school; teaching resources available; the way how resources are used; quality of management; physical environment; life-style of the student body; school setting; and, the quality of school life.[3]

In the mind of Edelfelt, *learning develops over time.* How well knowledge and skills are learned by the student in school depends on many factors. In essence, the teacher should *not* be held strictly accountable when a student does not learn. Edelfelt further argues that there are *no* standard techniques to ensure the productive learning of every student in all situations. He says that, "A teacher often does not know that he or she helped a particular student until the student returns years later to say so."[4] Moreover, the learning gained by

---

[2] Edelfelt, Roy A.. <u>Careers in Education</u>. Chicago, U.S.A. National Textbook Company. 1988.

[3] Ibid.

[4] Ibid. Edelfelt, R. A.

the student may not be within the subject matter taught in school, but out-of-the inspiration derived from the teacher, as a role model.

The eight elements in teaching—prescribed as standard in North Carolina, USA—are the basic elements in teaching-and-learning process. Using these elements as basis, this writer is presenting, in the succeeding discussions, a list of more significant teaching-and-learning priorities, considering the local educational conditions and needs.

Selecting TLEP Priorities.   Every educational institution should have a working School Training Committee (STC). This School Training Committee should conduct teaching-and-learning enhancement program according to the training needs of the instructors. In doing this, the STC should consider the areas which need most attention and that the time and resources allocated to the program are justified by the expected results. All problems identified should be studied systematically. Some problems may only require simple technical-organizational solutions, e.g. change in the work assignments, improved human relations or adjusting the working time schedules.

Considering the fundamental SMS competencies required of an instructor in order to become effective and productive in classroom performance delivery, this TLEP guide has identified and developed 12 significant modules in teaching-and-learning enhancement program. These basic modules are selected by this writer based on his long experience in human resource development and training (locally and abroad). In doing so, the present local educational condition and needs are also considered. The implementation of the TLEP workshop can be conducted during school breaks for a period of at least five consecutive days. Below are the 12 modules this writer is recommending for coherent, simple, clear and effective discussions during the TLEP workshop, i.e.:

1. Teaching-and-Learning Enhancement Protocols
2. The Learning Process
3. Teaching Methods, Techniques and Strategies
4. Characteristics of a Good Instructor
5. Preparing a Daily Lesson
6. Sequence of Instruction
7. Selection and Use of Teaching Aids
8. Speech Techniques
9. Questioning Techniques
10. Learning Distractions
11. Evaluation Techniques
12. Review/ Summary/Reinforcement

STC Management of the TLEP

Planning Stages.   After the School Training Committee is through with selection of TLEP training modules (i.e. the 12 items listed on previous page), the next step the STC should do is to plan and organize the actual TLEP. The planning procedure is basically consists of six stages, which are summarized and discussed separately below, i.e.:

1. Design a "Modular Training Schedule" (MTS)
2. Design a Modular Training Content (MTC)
3. Draw-up a Training Syllabus

4. Prepare Overall Training Requirements
5. Implement, Monitor and Control the TLEP
6. Evaluate the Enhancement Results.

1. **Design a "Modular Training Schedule" (MTS).** The Modular Training Schedule should contain a sequential list of priority *modules*, with enough number of *training hours* assigned for each module and the specific *dates* when such a module should be laid on the table for discussion. The allotment of training hours per module is dependent on the *performance objectives* to be met; the *content/discussion points* for each module; and, the *related learning activities/experience* to be done by the TLEP participants. Remember that the MTS is only tentative and is subject to revision. It can be finalized later after working on various needed requirements. Below is an example of typical MTS.

TLEP MODULAR TRAINING SCHEDULE

MODULES:	TRAINING HOURS:	DATES:
1) Teaching-and-Learning Enhancement Protocols	2x hr.	May 7, 2013
2) The Learning Process	2x hr.	" " "
3) Teaching Methods, Techniques and Strategies	4x hr.	" " "
4) Characteristics of a Good Instructor	8x hr.	May 8, 2013
5) Preparing a Daily Lesson	4x hr.	May 9, 2013
6) Sequence of Instruction	4x hr.	" " "
7) Selection and Use of Teaching Aids	4x hr.	May 10, 2013
8) Speech Techniques	2x hr.	" " "
9) Questioning Techniques	2x hr.	" " "
10) Learning Distractions	2x hr.	May 11, 2013
11) Evaluation Techniques	4x hr	" " "
12) Review/Summary/Reinforcement	2x hr.	" " "

Total Hours: 40x hr. **Days:** Five (5) days

Table 1. TLEP Modular Training Schedule

2. **Design a "Modular Training Content" (MTC).** The second stage in planning and designing the TLEP is to work on a tentative MTC, containing the *performance objectives;* the vital *contents;* related learning *activities;* and, the relevant *discussion points.* This has to be done in all the identified 12-TLEP learning modules. Below is a typical MTC example, i.e.:

Module 2. "THE LEARNING PROCESS"

1) **Performance Objectives.** After covering this module, TLEP participants should be able to:

    a. Define "Learning Process" and outline the basic strategies used in learning;

    b. Explain why hospitality and friendliness are considered as *negative* values;

    c. Discuss the importance of instilling the primary core values, e.g. *reverence, discipline, character* and *individuality* (RDCI) among learners;

    d. Understand the guidelines/rules for productive learning; and,

    e. Explain the Conceptual Paradigm: "Rules in Teaching-and-Learning."

2) **Contents:**

    a. Learning Process

    b. The Human Brain/Memory; Channels for Individual Stimulation

    c. Requirements for Effective Learning

    d. Value Enhancement: A Key Requirement in Teaching-and-Learning

    e. A Flashback: Filipino Native Character Traits

    f. Concept: "Hospitality and Friendliness are Negative Traits"

    g. The "Ethico-Moral Theory" in Learning

    h. Rules in Teaching-and-Learning: RDCI/ SMS/ PDRC/ RLEC/ PIA

    i. RDCI: Significant Primary Core Values for Learning

    j. Conceptual Summary: "Rules in Teaching-and-Learning"

3) **Related Learning Activities:**

    a. Talk about the Topic

    b. Teamwork

    c. Discussion

    d. Question and Answer

    e. Review/Summary/Reinforcement

4) **Discussion Points.** Note: The major highlights of discussion points to be tabled on *Day-1 Workshop* are significant contents covered under TLEP Modules 1-2: "Teaching-and-Learning Enhancement Protocols" and "The Learning Process."

Figure 1. TLEP Modular Training Contents

3. **Draw-up a Training Syllabus.** The Modular Training Schedule (MTS) and the Modular Training Contents (MTC), as shown on the previous pages respectively are exactly the training syllabus or guide that can be used to conduct an effective TLEP. As necessary, the School Training Committee may draw-up its own training syllabus to suit the local ideas and needs.

    As already explained, MTS contains the sequenced priority *modules*; the number of *training hours* assigned for each module; and the specific *dates* when such a module should be laid on the table for discussion. The assignment of the number of training hours per module is dependent on the contents of specific training modules.

The MTC outlines the training coverage for each module, containing the training *objectives*, vital *contents*, related learning *activities* and the relevant *discussion points*. The MTS and the aggregates of 12 Modular Training Contents—as recommended in this guide—are sufficient training syllabus or guide for a productive TLEP.

4. **Prepare Overall Training Requirements.** The preparation of the overall training requirements for the TLEP should be done cautiously to ensure success in the desired innovation or change. At this juncture, the teaching-and-learning *problems* are already identified—i.e. the enhancement of teaching competencies of teachers' in their daily performance deliveries. The suitable *solution* is noted—i.e. through the TLEP, to be conducted locally in the form of training workshop. The 12 basic areas, where TLEP should concentrate in reviewing/enhancing instructors' competencies are also established. As part of TLEP planning and organizing, the MTS and MTC for Modules1-2 are already designed to serve as training syllabus for use in the intended teaching-and-learning enhancement workshop.

There are still other training requirements to prepare before conducting the actual TLEP workshop. The physical facilities, e.g. *venue* for the workshop and needed training *materials/equipment* should be made ready with the consent of the local School Administration. The *food/snack services* for the participants should also be arranged, including possible *financial expenses* during the TLEP workshop. Other needs may arise depending on the school setting and ongoing regulations.

The selection of teacher-participants for the TLEP workshop should be made compulsory as possible. Other teachers may truly be competent enough in their daily classroom teaching performances, but they should also be required to attend the scheduled training workshop to share their valuable inputs to other instructors. The scheduling of the TLEP workshop should also be planned carefully. The workshop can be scheduled for at least one whole week and can be done during school vacation when majority of the faculty members is free.

The resource persons for every discussion topics, under each module, shall be selected and be notified accordingly. The School Training Committee shall assign also various TLEP Workshop Committees, e.g.: Committee for Venue Preparation; Committee for Food and Refreshment; Committee for Training Materials/Aids and Equipment; and, other technical supports. The designated Workshop Facilitator shall draw up the Daily Workshop Program (DWP) of activities for the duration of TLEP and shall guide the daily workshop training procedures. A typical example of the DWP is shown on the next page.

WANG-WANG UNIVERSITY (WWU)
0210 San Miguel, Manila

DAILY WORKSHOP PROGRAM
Module 1: "Teaching-and-Learning Enhancement Protocols"
Module 2: "The Learning Process"
Day-1: May 7, 2013

Ang kahoy na liko at baluktot—hutukin habang malambot. Pag lumaki at tumayog, mahirap na ang paghutok! . . . Old Filipino Adage	The world is getting too advanced and complicated. The technology today is **not** the same technology tomorrow. Life evolves! We, too, **must** evolve to survive in the changes of time!

TIME:	ACTIVITIES:	METHODS/AIDS:
08h00 – 08h30	*Opening of the Workshop* **Rene C. Cordova, Ph.D.** Dean, College of Education, WWU	Plenary; P/P, OHP
08h30 – 09h00	*TLEP: A Strategy in Educational Innovation* **Jose F. Bolador, D.Ed.** Dean, College of Agriculture, WWU	Plenary; P/P, OHP
09h00 – 10h00	*Learning Process with Value Enhancement* **Vergel Garcia, Ph.D.** Commissioner, Values Education, DepEd.	Plenary; P/P, OHP
10h00 – 10h15	COFFEEBREAK	
10h15 – 11h15	*Requirements for Effective Learning* **Glorita M. Arceo, D.Ed.** Secretary, Department of Education	Plenary; P/P, OHP
11h15 – 12h00	*Learning Rules: RDCI/ SMS/ PDRC/ RLEC/ PIA* **Ben G. Abao, Ph.D.** Project Commissioner, CHED	Plenary; P/P, OHP
12h00 – 13h00	LUNCHBREAK	
13h00 – 14h00	Case Study 1. *Reactivating the Primary Education System of Somalia* **Romualdo Neron, M.Ed.** (Workshop Facilitator)	Teamwork; P/P, OHP
14h00 – 15h00	*Team Reporting*	Plenary; P/P, OHP
15h00 – 15h15	COFFEEBREAK	
15h15 – 16h15	*Workshop Evaluation Procedures* **Ed Ermano, M.Ed.** Project Coordinator, DepEd.	Plenary; P/P, OHP
16h15 – 17h00	*Summary/Feedback* (Workshop Facilitator)	Question and Answer

Table 2. Day-1 Workshop Program

5. **Implement/Monitor/Control the TLEP.** The TLEP implementation, monitoring and control can commence once the Daily Workshop Program is completed; handouts and training materials are made readily available; various workshop committees are designated; and, financial arrangement secured.

   During implementation period, the input of Workshop Facilitator is very critical toward the success of the daily training program. Ideally, he/she should also be assigned as the Master of Ceremonies in the workshop. The succeeding presentation below outlines significant hints on how a *Workshop Facilitator* must discipline or prepare himself/herself for the training workshop.

   Note: These suggested hints below can also be adopted and applied by all teachers in their daily performance of classroom duties for more productive teaching-and-learning deliveries and outcomes.

   a. *Be neat and respectable in front of workshop participants.* The participants will respect you better and may adopt you as a model if you conduct yourself as a professional Workshop Facilitator.

   b. *Set the workshop venue conducive to teaching-and-learning activities.* The venue should be kept clean every day. The tables and chairs should always be arranged. The training materials/aids should be strategically accessible. The light and ventilation in the venue should be adequate. The venue should be free from unnecessary noises and interruptions. The DWP and other workshop records should be kept intact in your possession.

   c. *Take pride in yourself as a designated Workshop Facilitator.* Exert optimum competencies to your mission. As an educator, your success is not measured mainly in the forthcoming job level promotions—but in your valuable inputs in enhancing the competencies of faculty members.

   d. *Be inside the venue before the teacher-participants come in.* The workshop participants are matured professionals. They would be ashamed to come late when they see you at your post—well ahead of time.

   e. *As the bell rings, place yourself in front of the podium.* Wait for the coming workshop participants. Start the day meeting the participants with a happy and genial face. Be the first to greet them for the day, e.g. *"Hello; good morning, how are you this morning?"* Show them your genuine human concern. The participants will feel comfortable when they see you with a smile in your lips. Inversely, they will feel nervous when you show them an ugly *un-glorified* countenance.

   f. *Keep a daily workshop record.* Let participants seat first before passing the attendance checklist. Keeping daily workshop record is very important. It shows participants that you are recording the workshop progress religiously.

   g. *Assess condition of teacher-participants before starting the day's program.* Some of them may be sluggish yet in the early morning. If so, crack a clean funny joke to enliven their spirit to prepare them for the day's activities.

   h. *Start the day's program with a short invocation to the Almighty.* *Reverence* for God is a vital primary *discipline* that everybody must learn—to form a good moral *character*, in order to achieve *individuality* (RDCI).

6. **Evaluation of TLEP Results.**   Evaluation of TLEP workshop is very critical in line with the intention to introduce positive changes in ongoing classroom teaching-and-learning activities. The *Workshop Daily Evaluation Sheet* (WDES) should be done at the end of each day's session to assess effectiveness of the workshop and the corresponding impacts to teacher-participants. Below is an example of a WDES. (Note: *Workshop Final Evaluation Sheet* is on the next page).

WANG-WANG UNIVERSITY (WWU)
0210 San Miguel, Manila

WORKSHOP DAILY EVALUATION SHEET
Module 1: "Teaching-and-Learning Enhancement Protocols"
Module 2: "The Learning Process"
Day-1: May 7, 2013

Team Leader:_____ Team No.:_____
Team Members: _____
_____

1. Give your team's rating/comment on the effectiveness of the day's session (e.g. overall session was excellent; various topics discussed were boring; presentation methods were dull; time allotment for each subject was too short; etc.).

    _____
    _____
    _____
    _____

2. Comment about your team-working (e.g. team members were interested; team members were not serious; team leader was not helpful; etc.).

    _____
    _____
    _____
    _____

3. Write your suggestions to improve the forthcoming sessions considering Performance Objectives; Modular Contents; Related Learning Activities; Discussion Points; Presentation Method; Duration of the Workshop, etc.

    _____
    _____
    _____
    _____

Figure 2. Workshop Daily Evaluation Sheet

WANG-WANG UNIVERSITY (WWU)
0210 San Miguel, Manila

WORKSHOP FINAL EVALUATION SHEET

Name: _____ Team No.: _____
Team Leader: _____ Date: _____

Direction: Please answer the following questions on separate sheets of pad paper. This will serve as your feedback information in order to improve forthcoming workshops of this nature.

1. As an educator, what competencies did you learn from this workshop, which you can possibly apply in your daily classroom performances relative to teaching-and-learning deliveries? How would you apply the *skill, method* and *social* (SMS) competencies that you have learned from the recently concluded workshop? Discuss.

2. What possible constraints might hamper you in applying the newly-acquired SMS competencies during daily teaching-and-learning classroom sessions? Will RDCI value formation help you to overcome those constraints? How?

3. How well the workshop was planned, organized, implemented, monitored, controlled and evaluated (POIMCE)? Make your suggestion on how to productively manage this type of workshop.

4. Give your comments on the overall modular coverage and contents of the TLEP workshop. Any suggestion to improve the modular coverage and contents?

5. Write your comments on the overall methodologies used during the workshop. Any suggestion to enhance the delivery methodologies for future TLEP workshops?

6. Criticize the training aids/materials used during the workshop. Write your suggestion to improve the preparation of training aids/materials for future workshops.

7. Examine the time allotments given for the 12 modules covered during the workshop? Make your suggestion pertaining to appropriate time allotments.

8. Overall, how valuable is the recently concluded TLEP workshop for you—being an educator? Are you sure it will help you in improving your daily teaching-and-learning activities? Cite particular case or example.

9. List down further suggestions or comments that you would like to make relative to TLEP being done locally here in the school.

Figure 3. Final Workshop Evaluation Sheet

Case Study-1: "Reactivating the Primary Education System of Somalia"

Preview. In January 1993, Dr. John Doe (not his real name) was hired by UNICEF-Somalia as an Education Consultant. His mission was to reactivate Somalia's Primary Education System—disrupted for about 10 years due to ongoing civil war. Dr. Doe was a fresh graduate of PhD, Major in Educational Administration, at the Pacific Western University, LA, CA, USA. He had no previous experience in solving difficult problems such as this one. He accepted the post, because it was a high-paying job and he wanted to prove that Filipinos have SMS competencies in solving acute educational problems.

During his initial situational survey of Somalia's Education, Doe noted the deplorable conditions of the *Nine Building Blocks of Education,*[5] as follows:

1. *School Children.* There were thousands and thousands of Somali school children who were out-of-school for many years—a *sad* result of the ongoing civil strife. Without proper education, their futures were at stake.
2. *School Teacher.* There were very few certified school teachers available. Many school teachers joined the rebellion and had died. Some teachers migrated to more peaceful African countries nearby, e.g. Kenya, Djibouti and Ethiopia.
3. *Time.* The time for Somali children's education was swiftly passing by. There was an urgent need to reactivate the Primary Education System for the children's psychological, emotional, mental and sociological developments.
4. *School Buildings.* Most school buildings were burned to the ground because of the civil war. A few schools stood the ongoing violence, but were very dilapidated and needing major repairs.
5. *Parents and Community.* Despite varying political beliefs, the Somali parents and community were very willing to provide their children with good formal education. They firmly believed that education was the best legacy they could leave to their offspring.
6. *School Curriculum.* There were *no* available copies of the standard school curriculum. Most records pertaining to school curriculum were razed by fire and some were destroyed in the middle of the conflict.
7. *Pedagogy.* Pedagogy, which is "the act or practice of teaching,"[6] desperately needed upgrading and redevelopment. If Primary Education System were to be reactivated, retraining of new teacher-recruits was critical in order to achieve a good level of educational standard.
8. *Administration and Management.* Only very few school administrators and managers were available. Like many school teachers, some of them had died and had migrated to neighboring countries for survival.
9. *Financial Support.* Since the existing political government was unstable, there was *no* fund allotted for education. Although the UN Agencies had come in, they could afford to share a very limited assistance only.

---

[5] Anderson, M. B. Education For All: What are We Waiting? N. Y., USA. UNICEF New York. September 1992.
[6] Barnhart & Barnhart, Eds. The World Book Dictionary. Chicago. Doubleday & Company, Inc. 1979.

Conceptual Pattern. Applying the standard management concept in innovating educational, industrial and other organizational set-ups, Dr. Doe *identified* the extent of the problem first. Then, the possible solutions to identified problems were *planned* and *organized.* The best solutions were selected and put into trial/*implementation.* The implementation period was closely *monitored* and *controlled,* followed by *evaluation* of results. The solutions proved successful and were implemented later on a wider scale in 10 provinces of Somalia. Below is a conceptual representation of Doe's intervention:

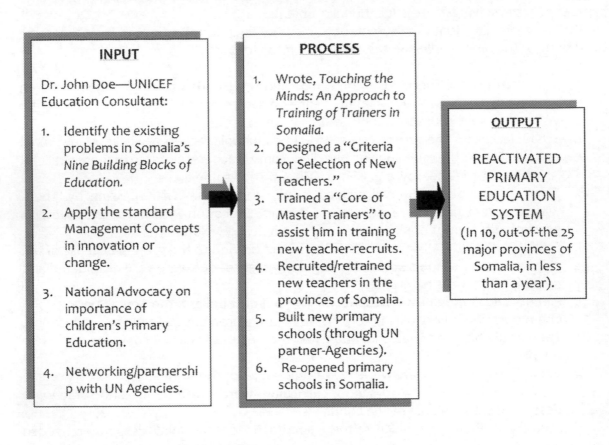

Figure 4. Conceptual Pattern

Questions for Case Study-1. The following questions shall be answered by the team participants during Teamwork Reporting in the plenary sessions of the training workshop.

1. Explain the initial step that Dr. John Doe conducted to identify existing problems relative to reactivation of Primary Schools in Somalia. What were his findings?
2. Outline the standard management concepts that Doe applied (as pattern) to trigger the reactivation of Somalia's Primary Education.
3. In your opinion, how were *advocacy, networking* and *partnerships* (with other UN Agencies) done by Doe in connection with his mission? Discuss.
4. Enumerate the various *processes* that Doe planned, organized and implemented in reactivating Somalia's Primary Education System.
5. In your opinion, did Doe fulfill his noble mission in Somalia? How? Explain.

The Honorable Admiral Howe (right)—the *Special UN Representative* to Somalia, designated by UN Secretary General—posed with Marcelino D. Catahan, Ph.D., near an original epigraphic expression (which caught the admiration of Admiral Howe), saying: "*A lesson delivered with lack of speech techniques is like a lullaby song that puts the children to sleep.*" The Admiral visited the Teachers' Training Workshop organized and implemented by Dr. Catahan at Belet Uen, Hiran, Somalia on March 2–5, 1993.

Catahan posed here with selected members of the *Regional Education Management Committee* in Hiran Province, Somalia during the Teachers' Training Workshop, held on March 2–5, 1993. It was unfortunate that the Somali Teacher, whom Dr. Catahan asked the favor to take the shot, was a non-experienced photographer. Admiral Howe (from the right) appeared just partially in the picture.

The Filipino Educator (standing at the middle) was on lunch break with teacher-participants during the *Hiran Teachers' Training Workshop.*

Col. J. S. Labbe (fourth from left)—Commander of Canadian Forces in Somalia—was the chief cooperating partner of Dr. Catahan in reactivating the Primary Education System in Hiran Province, Somalia. Colonel Labbe became a close ally of the *hospitable* and *friendly* Filipino. Colonel Labbe built a number of primary schools in Hiran with his military contingent and the Filipino did the rest. Colonel Labbe is shown in the picture with Lt. General Bir (first from left—Commander of UNOSOM-II); General Baril (second from left—Adviser to UNOSOM-II); and, Colonel Peck (third from left—of UNITAF, PAFFO). They visited Dr. Catahan to provide security and moral support during the course of *Hiran Teachers' Training Workshop.*

Dr. Catahan (left) was presenting a session on Learning Process/Methods in the Teachers' Training Workshop at Baidoa Province, held on October 23–28, 1993. To the right was his Somali interpreter named *Osman*, who helped him a lot in upgrading the skill, method and social (SMS) competencies of the newly-hired teachers.

In the picture were the teacher-participants during the *Baidoa Teachers' Training Workshop*—listening to the Filipino Consultant during his discussion of learning process and learning methods in Education. Dr. Catahan's cooperating partner in this region was the AMURT—a religious/sectarian denomination.

This picture shows participants of the *Workshop for the Core of Master Trainers*, which Dr. Catahan organized and implemented in Hargeisa Province of Somalia (March 1–7, 1994). Most of the participants were former school administrators. Catahan guided them in systematic school administration and management—and prepared them to train and upgrade the primary school teachers in the region.

A Somali School Principal was presenting a session in Module 9, i.e. "Challenge for the Future." This was the last module of the training guide, which Dr. Catahan wrote for *Capacity Building of Educational Administrators* (January 25, 1994).

This picture shows three primary school pupils being tested by Dr. Catahan inside one of the improvised tent-classrooms in Mogadiscio, Somalia. The Filipino Teacher visited the school to monitor the operation of Primary Education System in the Capital Region, sometime in March 1994.

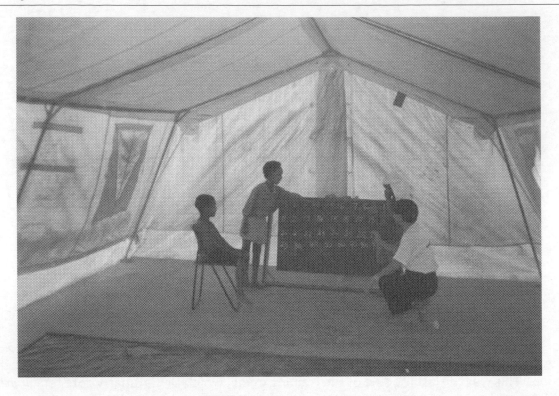

This photo exposes a wider view of the inner part of a tent-classroom. Take note that there were *no* desks or chairs, where the children could seat during class instructions. The children were sitting on the floor--covered neatly by pieces of mats/rags.

MODULE 2
THE LEARNING PROCESS

Ang kahoy na liko at baluktot—hutukin habang malambot. Pag lumaki at tumayog, mahirap na ang paghutok! . . . Old Filipino Adage	The world is getting too advanced and complicated. The technology today is *not* the same technology tomorrow. Life evolves! We, too, *must* evolve to survive in the changes of time!

A Systematic TLEP

Introduction.   Systematic Teaching-and-Learning Enhancement Program is a critical strategy when introducing innovations to any educational set-up. This is done through the application of standard *management* principles to enhance the skill, method and social competencies of teachers in order to become more productive in their daily functions. The TLEP follows basic management concepts in solving educational problems, e.g.:

1. *Identifying* the problems.
2. *Planning* and *organizing* the possible solutions to identified problems, e.g.:
   a. Designing a Modular Training Schedule (MTS);
   b. Designing a Modular Training Content (MTC);
   c. Drawing-up a Training Syllabus;
   d. Preparing Overall Training Requirements; and,
   e. Final agreement by the School Training Committee (STC) regarding all the TLEP preparation formalities.
3. *Implementing* best possible solution to the problems through a workshop/seminar.
4. *Monitoring* and *controlling* the implementation of TLEP by the STC.
5. *Evaluating* the TLEP results. If TLEP gives productive results, it is absorbed into the system and is finally institutionalized.

Modular Contents.   The modular contents designed for daily workshop are important guidelines in effective teaching-and-learning activities. The Daily Workshop Program (Page 9) for Day-1 covers Modules 1-2. Under Module 1, "Strategy for Educational Innovations" and "Teaching-and Learning Enhancement Protocols" are highlighted while under Module 2, the following topics are selected for major discussion points, i.e.:

1. The Learning Process
2. The Human Brain
3. Requirements for Effective Learning
4. Value Enhancement: A Key Requirement in Learning
5. "Hospitality and Friendliness are Negative Traits"
6. Guidelines for Productive Learning
7. Value Enhancement Levels
8. Rules in Productive Teaching-and- Learning

The Learning Process

Learning Defined.   Learning is an active life-long process. According to Barnhart & Barnhart, learning is "the gaining of knowledge and skills."[7] Knowledge means *knowing, understanding* or a mental perception. Skill is the ability *to do* things well with hands using appropriate tools. Besides knowing and doing, there is more to learning. The learners should also possess the *social* abilities to work together as a group. For the purpose of this training guide, *learning* is simply defined as the process of acquiring new *skill, method* and *social* (SMS) competencies that will enable an individual (e.g. a teacher or student) to do productive things, which he/she is not capable to do before.

Learning process is normally based on *memorizing* information that leads to the level of understanding and followed by practical applications until specific learning becomes permanent. There is also that kind of learning by *doing,* where an individual learns SMS competencies faster by performing the actual work. Whatever strategy is applied, if learning occurs, it will show a positive change in the behavior of the learner—which can be observed, measured and evaluated.

Theories of Learning.   Scientists and educators have *not* agreed completely on the number of standard theories on *how* a learner learns. Modern Psychology however had advanced suggestions based on previous studies—dividing the theories of learning into three main groups. All these formative groupings try to explain how learners can best achieve productive learning by applying different learning techniques and strategies. The following presentation discusses three main groups of the *theories of learning*.[8]

1. *"Behavior Modification Theory."*   This theory of learning is also known as *stimulus-response* theory, which states that learning results from formed habits. According to this theory, a learner forms habit when what he/she does is self-satisfying and rewarding. For example, a child may easily learn that 5 + 5 = 10, if the parents or teacher praises him/her for the correct answer; but, withholding the praise if the answer is wrong. The same rule applies when a child throws a ball or draws a simple figure. These acts need praises to the child and approval from parents or elders, done in the proper way, to influence good learning habit formation. And when all these simple, yet satisfying and rewarding habits are fashioned as learning foundation—the learner can go on forming more complicated learning habits, e.g. reading books or operating various home appliances.

    Behavior modification works best when the teacher is present during learning situations—observing the learner's operations—and is always ready to make prompt evaluation or measurement of the act being performed. In other words, the learning that results from habit performance must always be measured and evaluated. The solution to problem must be explained and reinforced. This is how a learner acquires ability in solving mathematical problems or learns to speak local/foreign languages.

2. *"Cognitive/Problem-Solving Theory."*   This theory stresses the vital significance of thought processes in learning, e.g. "understanding relationships between things and deciding

---

[7] Ibid.

[8] Nault, W. H. et al., Eds. The World Book Encyclopedia. Chicago, USA. World Book–Childcraft International, Inc. 1979.

which solution to a problem is the best one."[9] Unlike behavior modification theory, cognitive theory believes that a problem may be solved in two or more ways or in several solutions. Cognitive theory adopts the *discovery technique* in learning, where a teacher helps the learners to select each own problem to solve. In the process, the teacher guides the learners; provides needed materials and information; and, asks questions to encourage them to think.

3. *"Humanistic Theory."* Humanistic theory emphasizes the importance of emotions in learning. This theory considers emotional development as important instrument in any learning situation. It advances that each individual is different from one another and therefore each one should be allowed to develop in his/her own way. The teacher should be able to determine the emotional needs of the learners and encourage them to acquire the skill, method and social competencies needed to achieve those needs.

The Human Brain

The Human Brain. The human brain is a major organ of the nervous system located in the skull or *cranium*. It registers, arranges and interprets sensations; and, initiates or coordinates the motor output involved in activities, e.g. movement and speech. In general, the brain is "the organ of thought, speech and emotion, but its primary role in humans—just as in animals—is as the body's control center."[10]

Considering the delicate functions of the brain in total human development, the child's brain must be trained or conditioned with *reverence* for God, good *discipline, character* and *individuality* (RDCI). The brain must be prepared to receive, sort and interpret *idealistic sensations* only, so that it will mainly initiate and coordinate righteous motor output towards *right, just* and *fair* productive activities. *This is learning through the use of **ideally formed, enhanced** and **righteous morals.*** For verily, a righteous brain will surely result to further formation of exemplary moral character in a person, enabling him/her to learn SMS competencies very easily; and, to think, act or do extraordinary things that are not done normally by everyone. Value formation is critically significant in developing a healthy and productive human brain—a brain with immunity to any form of evils, including graft and corruption.

The common saying that, *practice makes perfect* is very true in learning, or in brain development. By memorizing information and practicing the actual operations involved, permanent learning becomes possible. Also, as humans grow older, it has been noted that brain power or ability to learn increases—if the brain is used constantly for learning. Medical studies suggest that, there is no such thing as *mental fatigue* in humans. Physical tiredness occurs in human body but it does not categorically happen in the brain.

According to medical research, the portion of the brain called, *frontal lobe* is the one associated with learning abstract thought, creativity, conscience and personality.[11] Further, it was suggested that only about 15% of the capacity to learn is used by the brain—even by the most intelligent human being. From this theory, it is evident that there is an ample capacity left for the learners to increase their SMS competencies through continued systematic learning.

---

[9] Ibid. Nault, W. H. et. al.

[10] Smith, T., Ed. Complete Family Heath Encyclopedia. Great Britain. Dorling Kindersley Limited, London. 1990.

[11] Ibid. Smith, T.

In addition, experience had shown too that when the body muscles are not used, they will fail to develop accordingly. The same principle applies to the brain; it also deteriorates when not used for productive learning.

The Human Memory.   *Memory is the ability to remember.* A person with good memory is someone who has the capacity to remember, recall and use vital information, as and when required. Remembering is the opposite of forgetting and forgetting is *not* always a bad thing to do. There are cases when some information we receive through our senses are trivial and insignificant. We need to disregard such unimportant information and remember only the more important ones.

It is the responsibility of the teacher to decide what information is most significant to be taught and to plan the structure of the lesson accordingly. In general, the students depend on the teaching competency of the teacher in guiding and encouraging them to remember important information. And when such information is learnt by the learners, positive changes occur within their brains. The information is stored in the brain memory—categorized as learning—ready for use, as and when needed. With the constant application or practice of this learning, it becomes a productive ability on the part of the learner. There are three stages in human memory associated with the process of learning information. They are discussed in the succeeding presentation below, i.e.:[12]

1. *Surface Memory.*   The students are normally occupied daily with plenty of activities in and outside the classroom, generating diverse information that competes for their attention. Because of the variety of information received at one time, very few are retained in their memory. However, unless followed by constant repetition, the information—no matter how relevant—is stored in the *surface memory* only and is forgotten within in 15 to 30 seconds.

2. *Transitory/Short-Term Memory.*   Selected items or pieces of information that are stored temporarily in the brain—and which are forgotten in two days or a week's time— are considered to have stayed in the *transitory/short term memory* only. This stage in memory storage allows the learner to remember information today or tomorrow, but *not* next week or next month. This case happens especially if the information registered is insignificant and has no impact or further use for the daily life of the learner. A learner, for example, who joins an educational tour to a strange place for the first time—and who thinks he/she will never visit that place ever again—can forget previous information about the place that is registered earlier in his/her brain, since it is going to be of *no* further use.

3. *Permanent/Long-Term Memory.*   Significant information that is useful to the life of the learner is believed to be staying in the brain's *permanent/long term memory*. The permanency of storage and recall for use however, is influenced by the long-term application, repetition and experience. Constant practical application of information enables such to reach the channels of the brain's permanent/long-term memory—thus allowing recall of said information long time after it is registered. In this stage, "the

---

[12] City & Guilds Examiners, Ed. Instructor Training Course 1: Theoretical Part. Austria. 1989.

process of storage involves associations with words or meanings, with the visual imagery evoked by it, or with other experiences, such as smell or sound."[13]

Channels for Individual Stimulation.   There are various channels through which an individual is stimulated resulting to a change in the activities of the body as a whole. The five senses— i.e. *hearing, sight, smell, touch* and *taste* (HSSTT)—enable the learner to make contact with surrounding things; generating stimulation on the central nervous system which is consists of the *brain* and the *spinal cord*.

Authors of medical books write that certain nerve cells—known as *receptors*—are specialized to collect information and respond to specific stimuli. They contend that receptors are "attuned to a particular stimulus, such as light of a particular wavelength, chemical molecules of a certain shape, vibration, or temperature."[14] When a receptor is excited, it sends an electrical signal passing along the appropriate nerve fiber to the spinal cord or the brain. As the signal reaches the sensory area of the brain's cerebral cortex, the information is consciously perceived.

A receptor allows only one specific chemical (e.g. a hormone or a neurotransmitter substance, which has the fitting configuration) to bind to it. This chemical binding to the receptor "alters the outer cell membrane and triggers a change—such as contraction by a muscle cell or increased activity in an enzyme-producing cell."[15]

The receptor cells for the eyes are found in the retina. In the ears, it is in the auditory apparatus. In the tongue, the receptor cells are the taste-buds; while in the nose, they are the apparatus for smell. The receptors for the sense of touch are found mostly in the skin. For a particular stimulation example—the mere sight, smell or taste of a delicious food stimulates receptors cells resulting to heavy salivation.

In the classroom setting, the teacher should assume the responsibility of providing various learning situations that would stimulate the maximum use of the individual's five senses. As a rule, lessons should appeal to the various senses as much as possible. Lesson information should call the full *contact, interest* and *attention* (CIA) of the learner. Vital information that appeals to majority of the cell surface or receptors of the five senses reaches the brain easily and are mostly retained or learned by the individual. This is the main reason why most modern teachers are usually giving and emphasizing on practical related exercises and actual demonstrations as their major activities in daily classroom meetings. In general, using this strategy enables stimulation of majority of the five senses, influencing signal of vital information to the brain via designated receptor cells, which eventually becomes a part of the individual's permanent learning.

---

[13] Op. Cit. Smith, T.
[14] Ibid.
[15] Ibid.

Requirements for Effective Learning

Essential Conditions.   Arden N. Frandsen (1961) suggests seven essential conditions for effective learning to be "present in every instance of good teaching."[16] These conditions however, do not come naturally or are possessed just so easily by a learner during the teaching-and-learning process. The teacher has yet to play a major role in developing the learner's abilities by observing and maintaining the essential learning conditions in the classroom. The seven essential conditions for effective learning are:

1. *Readiness.*   This condition pertains to learner's preparedness, considering various variables, i.e. level of maturity, pattern of abilities and an appropriate background of generalizations from his/her previous experience. When these elements are present within the learner during classroom teaching, there is a greater chance for him/her to progress and succeed in the total learning activities.

2. *Motivation.*   Motivation in learning is the process of providing the learner with an incentive or inducement to learn. Frandsen argues that motivational processes arouse, sustain, direct, determine the intensity of learning effort and in conjunction with perception of the effects, define and evaluate the consequences of provisional acts. There are many ways in motivating learner; the best way to do it is to provide moral supports to learner's natural desire for creative and productive use of talents.

3. *Structured Approaches to Problems.*   The teacher should provide guidance and structure approaches to learning problems "by explaining, demonstrating, correcting the pupil's provisional trials and by arrangement of learning sequences and leading questions which encourage pupil self-discoveries."[17] Teacher's guidance is critical.

4. *Repeated Trials.*   This condition for effective learning needs repetition of provisional trials or goal-directed self-activity towards discovery, differentiation and integration of more effective patterns of behavior.

5. *Perception of Effects.*   Learning is achieved through repeated trials, which is then improved upon perception of effects on provisional trials. When the learner's effort is perceived as inadequate or incorrect during provisional trial, he/she makes the needed adjustments to correct the mistakes.

6. *Transfer.*   In order to hasten learning transfer, the learner should possess previously mastered generalizations and skills, able to unify principles in complicated and multi-element tasks, thus developing further generalizations for subsequent applications.

7. *Mental Health.*   Most important condition for effective learning is the mental health of the learner. Good mental health is indicated when the learner is feeling secured, i.e. accepted by his/her teacher and classmates and confident of his/her learning abilities.

---

[16] Frandsen, A. N. Educational Psychology. New York, USA. McGraw-Hill Book Company, Inc. 1961.
[17] Ibid.

Teachers' Mandate in Teaching.   In actual fact, everyone is a whole-life learner. However one *thinks, talks* and *does* things is the product of learning in itself. Teachers are mandated to act as role-models in teaching-and-learning. They are required to possess a very strong professional commitment to help the youngsters—especially the deprived, abused, neglected and disillusioned ones. As such, the teachers must be equipped emotionally and intellectually with outstanding ethico-moral values and appropriate competencies to become effective and efficient molders of the youth. Teachers must remember: *"they are inside the classroom daily, **not** for the monetary remunerations, but to facilitate the process of learners' total developments."* Therefore, the teachers must understand themselves constantly and be susceptible to changes, as and when needed.

The teachers must adapt themselves continuously to the dynamic process of the learners. They must monitor and evaluate keenly how the learners deal, react or accept the daily teaching-and-learning activities in the classroom. As need arises, teachers must guide the learners to achieve learners' ideal development and progress. Teachers must bear in minds that when they give lessons to the learners, this process is of extreme significance—*not* on the activity alone, but on the positive impact to the recipients.

Students' Responsibilities in Learning.   The students have personal responsibilities also for the quality of learning they deserve. The effectiveness of a teaching-and-learning cannot be achieved simply in terms of the challenge, facilitation, support and resources provided by the teaching staff and local educational institution. The students must also contribute complementary responsibilities for their development progress—manifested through their level of desire, commitment, efforts and time devoted to study. They have significant obligations to share in the creation and maintenance of an effective teaching-and-learning environment. The basic obligations that must be impressed by the teachers unto their students in daily classroom meetings are:

1. Learn, develop and practice the core moral values, i.e. *reverence* for God, *discipline, character* and *individuality* (RDCI) to gain competencies faster.
2. Learn, develop and practice the vital skill, method and social competencies that are needed for personal and professional development.
3. Learn, develop and practice cooperative team-working with other students in learning activities and constantly assume the role of a good team member.
4. Prepare study homework and daily lesson religiously and seriously with keen perception on effects—correcting discovered deficiencies from previous trials.
5. Maintain contact, interest and attention in daily classroom discussions/debates.
6. Respect the teachers' viewpoints, as well as the viewpoints of others.
7. Join community activities—be productive beyond the confines of classroom.
8. Be creative, open-minded and receptive to new ideas.
9. Consult the teaching staff for support and guidance, when necessary.
10. Respect and comply with the rules of the academic institution.
11. Provide honest feedback to the institutional staff on the quality of teaching and learning services.
12. Practice professionalism, dedication, responsibility and commitment (PDRC) to learning and work hardest to achieve intellectual and economic success.

Value Enhancement: The Main Key to Learning

Filipino Native Character Traits: A Flashback.   Value enhancement is the *main key* to productive learning. A lengthy review of the inherent Filipino character traits is being presented herein this section to support the idea that value enhancement is truly the main key that will open the gate to effective and productive teaching-and-learning process.

Similar to other races, Filipinos have inherent good and bad traits as well. Despite the worldwide recognition to Filipinos as the most *hospitable* and *friendly* people, a few foreigners still had come up with negative views concerning Filipino native character. With those negative comments received, this writer thinks that it is not bad to *look back* and reinvestigate ourselves and be open-minded to innovative changes as necessary.

Jason Vann—a former U.S. Marine turned journalist—must have had bad experiences in the Philippines, having seen mostly "misery, despair and harshness in everyday life"[18] in the country for a long thirty years. In his book about the Philippines (1991), Vann observed that, "the major problem of the Filipinos is the system that allows intolerable levels of corruption to continue unabated." Vann hopes though that *credibility, honesty* and *justice* may one day find its way into the main stream of government. He writes his personal impression on the Filipinos, thus:

> The Filipinos are friendly; they make you feel at home. They are warm, outgoing people, polite, patient and have endless tolerance, but don't let that fool you completely. It can be a bittersweet affair. That beautiful and unsuspecting rose can close up and swallow you. . . . The Spanish culture is very much alive in the Philippines. The manana [*sic*] attitude is a way of life for a Filipino. As a result, doing business in the Philippines can be a very frustrating experience for foreigners. There is a lot of red tape and bureaucratic hurdles. The Spanish culture in the Filipinos is very strong and being the case the traditional problems go with it.

If one has to interpret Vann's description without reading between the lines, the final impression would be negative. Vann's warning that, the beautiful rose can *close up and swallow you* is very true. In general, when someone fools around a Filipino, he does not forget it—not until after he has exacted revenge or has gotten even. The idea of putting the blame to the Spaniards for the red tapes and bureaucracy happening in the public service however is *questionable*. The Spaniards might be corrupt during colonial era; but, it does not mean Filipinos learned corruption from them. Filipinos have their own inherent culture. The succeeding cultural review starts with the *positive* Filipino traits, based on a local history book, as follows:[19]

1. *Hospitality.*   This is a trademark for Filipinos all over the world. Filipinos are very hospitable, generous and friendly people even to strangers who chance to visit their homes during unholy hours. Visitors are normally given the most cordial and amiable reception; extended the best comfort; given the most respect; and, offered the best food even this may mean for homeowners to miss meals on the succeeding days.

---

[18] Vann, J. The Philippines and Its Public Enemy No. 1. Manila. Ten Star Books. 1991.

[19] Agoncillo, T. A. History of the Filipino People. Quezon City, Philippines. Garotech Publishing. 1990.

2. *Respect for the Elders.*   This trait is being imbued earlier by parents to their children from the tender age. Filipino parents commonly exercise absolute authority over the children. They do not allow the children to answer back to them, even to elder brothers and sisters and to other elder members of the family. They teach the children to respect, by kissing their hands or putting their hands on the children's forehead. This practice is done even to other people who are not related to the clan. They ensure that the children grow respectful and polite—in thoughts, in words and in deeds. Even in everyday conversations, children are obliged to show a high degree of respect, by using the Filipino Language particle *po* and the second person plural number words e.g. *kayo, inyo* and *ninyo.*

3. *Collective Responsibility.*   Generally, the elders believe and demand that—they must be obeyed whether right or wrong. Elders think that, even if the children may have string of degrees to their credit, such accomplishments do not warrant the children to impose regulations in family affairs. They opine that the academic degrees cannot compare well with experiences. The children possess knowledge *only*—and theirs is wisdom. They assert that, they have *drunk more water* than the children have.

4. *Close Family Ties.*   Filipinos are famous for their close family ties and extended family structures. Apart from being loyal to blood relatives, Filipinos adopt new kinfolks, i.e. *kumpadre* and *kumadre*, through having male and female sponsors called *ninong* and *ninang* during baptism and wedding. This type of family extension guarantees an effective support system (or *damayan*) to a particular family especially during time of distress. For example, when a particular family member dies—all family relatives give financial and moral supports, including ninongs and ninangs.

5. *Friendliness/Loyalty to a Friend.*   This trait is very strong amongst Filipinos up to the present. For a Filipino, friendship is sacred and implies mutual help under any circumstance. A friend is expected to come to the aid—not only of a personal friend, but also of the latter's family. A man's friend is considered a member of the family and is expected to share its tribulations as well as prosperity and happiness.

6. *Gratitude.*   Do a good deed to a Filipino and he won't forget you for the rest of his life. He will remain loyal and grateful to you even to the extent of giving his life, as and when necessary. To him, the favor you gave him is a debt of honor, which even if compensated later, would continuously bind him loyally and gratefully to you. Gratitude or *utang-na-loob* is a gesture of camaraderie or *mabuting pakikisama*.

7. *Cooperative.*   The Filipinos value the virtue of helping each other and even other unknown people. This was manifested in the ancestral trait of *bayanihan,* which can mean helping a rural family move their small hut to another place or helping in plowing/planting the rice field at no cost charged.

8. *Brave.*   The Filipinos rank among the bravest peoples on earth. They believe that whatever happens to them is a work of fate or *tadhana*. For Filipinos, courage is a badge of manhood—proven by Filipino soldiers in many battles and wars.

9. *Passionately Romantic and Artistic.*   Filipino people are passionately romantic and artistic. This is manifested in the rural traditional moonlight *harana*, where young men normally sing love songs in front of the house of the girl they love. They are ardent in love and are born musicians, singers, artists and poets.

10. *Highly Intelligent.*   According to Dr. David P. Barrows, an American Educator, the Filipinos possess quick perceptions, retentive memory, aptitude and extraordinary docility making them the most teachable persons. This is one reason why rich countries around the world prefer to hire Filipinos in domestic and technical fields.

11. *Adaptable, Enduring and Resilient.*   Throughout the ages, Filipinos have been lashed out by multiple sufferings, e.g. invasions, revolts, revolutions, wars, earthquakes, typhoons, volcanic eruptions and epidemics. Yet, the Filipinos continuously survive. They can assimilate in any civilization and thrive in any climate. Filipinos working in the hottest desert of the Middle East attest to this.

12. *Religious.*   The Filipinos have a deep spiritual yearning and a gift of faith. Most Filipinos perform their spiritual obligations with utmost devotion and faithfulness.

Filipino Negative Character Traits.   Every teacher must warn the learners to avoid learning and developing the following native Filipino *negative* character traits, e.g.:

1. *Propensity for Gambling.*   Filipinos will bet for almost anything—whether or not it will rain the following day, whether or not a certain political candidate would win in the election, or whether the first child of a newlywed couple would be a boy or a girl. The favorite expression amongst Filipinos—i.e. *pustahan tayo*—confirms the Filipino propensity for gambling. Their favorite forms of gambling are cockfighting, horse racing, jai-alai, jueteng, black-jack, poker, tong-its, mahjong, monte, etc.

2. *Fatalistic or "Bahala Na" Attitude.*   Filipinos generally believe that whatever happens is due to fate (*tadhana* or *kapalaran*). They accept whatever happens to them, good or bad, with a resignation and the famous expression, i.e. *Bahala na!*

3. *Sensitive.*   A Filipino would not tolerate anyone to berate himself especially by a foreigner. In work setting, it takes diplomacy, tact, more sophisticated language, or a great deal of public relations to talk to an employee—for a good-intentioned rebuke by a superior might be taken as a slight on his character or integrity.

4. *Extravagant.*   Filipinos love colorful fiestas, expensive clothes, jewelry and gay parties. Every baptism of a child, wedding, birthday, debut and graduation of a member of the family is celebrated with lavish party. They will spend their last peso or go to a "Bombay" for a "5:6 loan," just to make the celebration a success.

5. *Lack of Discipline.*   The Filipinos lack discipline in time management and in keeping appointments. In school and in work, they tend to ignore scheduled times and just come as they wish. When making appointments, they also do not follow and disregard the agreed time; in some cases, they even do not come for the appointment.

6. *Lack of Perseverance/Ningas-Cogon.* In many undertakings, Filipinos normally begin their work with great enthusiasm. Such enthusiasm however is only temporary.
Later, they divert their attention to something else and leave their initial venture for next day or for some other times. The *mañana habit* cools off the enthusiasm. Like a cogon fire, the enthusiasm burns brightly for a brief time and eventually flickers out; hence, the famous description of Filipinos as *ningas-cogon*.

7. *Lack of Initiative.* The experience of many college and university professors reveal the miserable fact that an average Filipino student has to be hammered normally and whipped into line in order to make him work harder.

8. *Jealousy/Crab Mentality.* Filipinos do not look with favor on a woman who flirts with several men. For a Filipino, a wife signifies a partner solely for himself. He does not like someone to stare at her even just to appreciate her beauty. Filipinos killed or get killed because of petty jealousy. Jealousy also results to *crab mentality*, i.e. pulling down somebody from top of the ladder, which is common to many Filipinos.

"Hospitality and Friendliness are Negative Traits"

Conceptual Basis. Many local educators are teaching students that *hospitality* and *friendliness* are foremost of the native Filipino positive traits. Yet if one is to think harder, hospitality and friendliness are *not* positive traits at all—they are undoubtedly negative character traits. Philippine historians wrote afterthoughts on the easy conquest of the Philippines by the Spaniards. They viewed the easy conquest as, due to eloquent teachings and sacrificial labors of the missionaries and the divisive traits of the Filipinos. In contrast, this writer has a different concept on the issue: The easy conquest of Filipinos was *due to native hospitality and friendliness.*

Filipinos are known worldwide for the native traits of hospitality and friendliness, which foreigners immediately notice and commend. And we are very proud for this trademark. Unfortunately, we do not understand that hospitality and friendliness are the *roots* of all corruptions in economic, social and political systems of life. Readers may find this concept as eccentric because many Filipinos believed that corruption was a legacy from the Spaniards. But this was not so. Corruption was already alive amongst Filipinos long before the Spaniards came—due to hospitality and friendliness.

Hospitality is "a friendly reception; a generous treatment of guests and strangers."[20] By nature, Filipinos are very hospitable, generous and friendly even to strange visitors during unholy hours. Visitors are normally given best reception, comfort, respect and delicious food—even a homeowner may miss succeeding meals. These acts are simple and indirect bribery on the visitors. Corruption starts from here—for a good deed done to a Filipino is not easily forgotten. The recipient would remain grateful and loyal to the host. This is the *utang-na-loob* or gratefulness aspect of hospitality. When time comes to return favor, the recipient would go-out-of way just to satisfy the benefactor.

---

[20] Op. Cit. Barnhart & Barnhart

"Ilabas ang Pulutan."   About the year 2001, a local company ran an advertisement on the national TV for its product i.e. "Veterano Brandy," showing a group of Spanish explorers who came from their ship, waded ashore and were met by a band of Filipino natives. This commercial may be considered by few intellectuals as a *direct insult* to the integrity of the Filipino people. The ad showed that—when the group of Filipino natives was about to attack the foreigners, the Spanish Captain so suddenly whisked up a bottle of brandy. This action influenced the Filipino Chieftain to order abruptly to hold the attack and to welcome and feast the foreigners instead. And this was clearly an offshoot of the *bribe* that the Spanish Captain offered—i.e. the bottle of brandy.

The advertiser was honest in depicting the hospitable and friendly traits known worldwide amongst Filipinos. Unwittingly, the ad exposed how *vulnerable* the Filipinos are—in terms of corruption. In consideration for a bottle of brandy raised on the right hand of the Spanish Captain, the Filipino Datu was corrupted totally, without any reservation. Seeing the brandy, the hospitable Datu shouted: ***"Ilabas ang pulutan!"*** (Bring out the savories!). This sign of weakness—indicating susceptibility to corruption—could be accounted to the Filipino brand of *hospitality* and *friendliness*.

A Supporting Historical Case of Corruption.   If a critic is to read between the lines on the pages of Philippine History, the Filipino native traits of hospitality and friendliness would appear as negative. When the Spanish Adelantado, Miguel Lopez de Legazpi, conquered Manila in May 1571, Legazpi gave *concessions* to Rajah Sulayman of Manila and Lakan Dula of Tondo—for not resisting the invasion. Legazpi allowed them to retain their patrimonial lands; exemption in paying taxes and in serving the *polo* or forced labor; and, some other benefits. Sulayman and Lakan Dula became good friends to Legazpi.

Unfortunately in the following year, Legazpi died due to heart attack on August 20, 1572.[21] A new Governor-General—Guido de Lavezaris—was sent to the Philippines by Spain. Immediately after arrival, Lavezaris confiscated all the lands and properties of Rajah Sulayman and Lakan Dula. This action led to the revolt of Sulayman and Lakan Dula in 1574—the first recorded Filipino uprising against Spanish oppressors.

Coincidentally, Lim-Ah-Hong—a notorious Chinese pirate—bombed Manila Bay during that period. The pirate would like to take Manila from the Spaniards to settle therein permanently because Lim-Ah-Hong was wanted in China. So, the Spaniards were left in a dilemma. They had two enemies attacking on both sides. Realizing the lop-sided situation in fighting two enemies, Lavezaris sent *Capt. Juan de Salcedo*—the grandson of the late Legazpi—and Fr. Geronimo Marin to the war-camp of Lakan Dula and Sulayman at Navotas to negotiate peace talks with the native rebels. Navotas was a suburban town about 30 kilometers away from Manila.

Salcedo did not take much effort in convincing the two Filipino leaders to go back to the Spanish fold. Firstly, Salcedo came from the family line of Legazpi. And secondly, the two Rajahs owed Legazpi some *utang-na-loob* or indebtedness. In Filipino culture, the friend's family line get same respect given to a friend—a practice of extended family.

---

[21] Zaide, S. M. The Philippines: A Unique Nation. Quezon City, Philippines. All-Nations Publishing Co., Inc. 1994.

Salcedo promised Lakan Dula and Sulayman to return back their lands and to reinstate their previously lost benefits. So as it could be expected, Lakan Dula and Sulayman acceded to the offers of Salcedo and Father Marin.

This writer could not help but imagine that probably, Lakan Dula and Sulayman could have shouted the same phrase as: *Ilabas ang pulutan!* And as such, they halted their revolt and sided back with the Spaniards. They helped their Spanish colonizers in fighting and driving away Lim-Ah-Hong. They chased Lim-Ah-Hong's fleet up to the shores of Lingayen, Pangasinan, until such a time when the pirates' ammunitions got depleted, thus forcing them to leave the Philippine shores.

In essence, this incident was similar to the "Ilabas ang Pulutan" TV advertisement. Because of offer by Lavezaris to return back the original concessions (of Legazpi to Sulayman and Lakan Dula), the two Rajahs stopped their uprising. Hence, the chance of Lakan Dula and Sulayman to free the Filipinos earlier from the claws of Spanish rule was lost. All was brought about by their hospitality, friendliness and the bribe. This act was indicative of weak moral values—particularly discipline, character and individuality.

Based on this historical fact, would the readers blame this writer in his concept that, *hospitality and friendliness breed corruption* on the social/economic/political systems of Filipino lives? And with all these negative traits that impede the total development and progress of the country, the National Education System should experiment in using this original **"Ethico-moral Theory,"** i.e. *applying an aggregate of enhanced ethico-moral values in teaching-and-learning process*. Indeed, enhancement of values, e.g. reverence for God, discipline, character and individuality is critical for ideal teaching-and-learning.

The "Ethico-moral Theory" in Learning

Rules in Teaching-and-Learning.   The short-route to productive teaching-and-learning requires *ethico-moral rules* to follow in order to achieve learning objectives or results. This writer has conceptualized five aggregates of significant ethico-moral protocols that teachers *must teach* the learners to *learn, develop* and *practice* (LDP)—from childhood to adulthood— in order to become successful career professionals. These five aggregates of ethico-moral rules in learning are going to be expounded in the succeeding sections. Below is an outline of the five *ethico-moral rules* that learners and teachers must learn, develop and practice to facilitate productive teaching-and-learning, i.e.:

- ✓ RULE-1. **Learn, develop** and **pratice (LDP)** the personal moral values of *reverence* (for God), *discipline, character* and *individuality* (RDCI). Note: RDCI are core moral values inherent to a person, enhanced by parents/teachers/elders of the learner.
- ✓ RULE-2. LDP the skill, method and social competencies (SMS) needed in your job.
- ✓ RULE-3. LDP the core ethico-moral values of *professionalism, dedication, responsibility* and *commitment* (PDRC) in doing your job. Note: PDRC are ethico-moral values learned by professionals, as ethical standard in a profession.
- ✓ RULE-4. LDP the ethico-moral values of *respect, love, empathy* and *compassion* (RLEC) to the people, clientele or community that you are serving.
- ✓ RULE-5. LDP the "PIA" rule: *"pokus,"/ "ingat,"/ "alerto."* (PIA) in any job you do.

RULE-1: LDP the Core Values of RDCI.   Presently, there is a marked degradation of native Filipino culture, especially the moral values of *reverence* for God, *discipline, character* and *individuality* (RDCI). This debilitation of RDCI values results to a serious condition of disobedience to Philippine System of Rules. Consequently, the deadly virus of *graft and corruption* has infected the overall private and public systems of Philippine life thus, resulting to incidence of many forms of crimes (e.g. bank robbery, hold-up, rape, salvaging, car-jacking, drug trafficking, illegal gambling, terrorism, smuggling, money laundering and many others). These crimes are pulling the country's economy down the drain—contributing to mass *poverty, hunger* and *disease*. And where there is poverty, hunger and disease, the peace and order condition is surely unstable. This is the situation in the country today.

RDCI is an aggregate of core moral values—constituting a *paragon* of human morality. RDCI values are the *keys* to effective teaching-and-learning. From kinder schools, the teachers must teach what is morally *right* only; and, the learners must learn what is morally *correct* exclusively. Below is a discussion of the four personal core moral values which children must learn, develop and practice from the early developmental period because they are the rules in productive learning.

a. *Reverence.*   *Reverence* is a feeling of deep *respect, love* and *fear* (RLF) for the Almighty. **"Reverence is knowledge."** The easiest way to learn is to form and develop *first* and foremost, the traits of deep reverence, love and fear for the Almighty. Reverence for God is an effective generator of productive learning. A learner with *reverence* for God, easily attains good *discipline, character* and *individuality* (DCI). And with the aggregate of RDCI, every learner is guaranteed to learn, develop and practice other valuable ethico-moral qualities that will usher productive learning (for future personal and professional career developments).

Reverence for God is the most important moral value that a learner *must learn*. A learner with moral ascendancy will never be tempted to travel along the winding road of graft and corruption—that leads to the world of the dead. For, a righteous learner knows that if he/she disobeys and sins: "God will snatch wicked men from the land and pull sinners out of it like plants from the ground (2:22)."[22]

In the Book of Proverbs (1:7 to 1:9), the wise King Solomon advises the young men by saying: "to have knowledge, you must have reverence for the LORD." He continues his advice, i.e.: "Son, pay attention to what your father and mother tell you. Their teaching will improve your character as a handsome turban or a necklace improves your appearance."[23]

The wise King Solomon also emphasizes on the attributes of good family and social relationships, with bias on the constant practice in everyday life of good ethico-moral qualities, e.g.: discipline; character; individuality; righteousness; justice; fairness; humility; honesty; integrity; responsibility; faithfullness; loyalty; deligence; industry; patience; respect; empathy; compassion; love, etc.

b. *Discipline.*   *Discipline* is a trained condition of order and obedience to a system of rules necessary for harmonious relationships of the people in a particular community. It is a formed moral value in a person relative to thinking, feeling and doing any thing. In general, good discipline is a by-product of the learner's deep reverence for the Almighty. With reverence for God, a child learns to distinguish right from wrong. He/she *thinks, feels and acts* according what is *right, just* and *fair* only. Discipline formation

---

[22] Archbishop Whealon, J., Imprimatur. <u>Good News Bible</u> (Catholic Edition). New York. Thomas Nelson, Publishers. 1979.

[23] Ibid.

is very critical in the process of childhood development. It structures and regulates total life of the learner. It maybe a fact that discipline comes inherently from within. It cannot be doubted however, that meaningful type of training—done with respect, love, empathy, compassion, care, religiosity, motivation and commendation—influences self-discipline in a learner.

c. *Character.* *Character* depicts the special ways in which a person thinks, feels and acts. A person can have good or bad character. Good character sums up the best ethico-moral qualities in a person, which is set according to standards and conforming to the principles of right and wrong. A person with good character posesses moral concepts about personal existence; follows God's commandments; and, refrains from doing bad things which are against the Devine Laws.

A learner with exemplary ethico-moral character—e.g. reverence for God, discipline, love for others, kindness, principles, diligence, industry, harmony, integrity, honesty, self-control and other moral qualities—will definitely excel in any youth development program. Generally, learners with exemplary character learn faster anything that is necessary to be learned—including science and technology. It is extremely important that teachers also exhibit excellent moral character throughout their functions. This will influence learners to emulate the best examples set by teachers. In a classroom where teachers and learners are of good moral characters, mutual communication will prevail resulting to solidarity in solving various teaching-and-learning problems.

d. *Individuality.* *Individuality* pertains to particular exemplary abilities that make a person himself—an individual—able to think, act and do productive things, which could *not* be done ordinarily by everybody. From the time a baby is born, the process of building his/her own individuality begins. A child with best discipline grows up as a person with exemplary moral character and thus, easily achieves individuality as a person. Individuality, in a person, is marked by the possession of extra-ordinary productive skill, method and social (SMS) competencies.

RULE-2: LDP the SMS Competencies. Generally, in the school setting, the teachers are the most important human developers that *touch the minds and hearts* of the youngsters. Therefore, they must be qualified, trained, loving and caring professionals to ensure success in their functions—i.e. the ideal transformation of psychological, emotional and sociological developments of the youth. The teachers must be able to hone the skill, method and social (SMS) competencies of the learners in order to achieve individuality. Competency pertains to the ability of a person to *think, act* or *do* extra-ordinary productive things with the highest possible quality.

The succeeding presentation highlights three significant competencies that teachers must teach the learners to achieve and possess individuality, i.e.:

a. *Skill Competency.* This is the ability of a professional teacher or learner that enables him/her to *teach/learn* the combined practical and theoretical lessons; *solve* simple to complicated tasks; *obtain* all related information available; *share* and *participate* actively in teaching-and-learning process; and, *solve* or *master* education problems in a more innovative way. The italicized verbs used in this definition (i.e. *teach, solve, obtain, share, participate* and *master*) all involves *doing*. In the case of a skilled tradesman, skill competency is the ability to operate or manipulate various machines for production, applying more of the hand skills than knowledge. It is more in doing the operations than knowing information.

b. *Method Competency.* This is the ability of a professional teacher/learner to *plan, organize, implement, monitor, control, evaluate* (POIMCE) teaching-and-learning programs and solve teaching/learning problems through the application of various methods/strategies. In this competency, the teacher/learner has more of the ability to *know* the different ways on how to solve problems or do things, although the manipulative ability is not the same standard, as compared to skill competency.

c. *Social Competency.* This is the ability of a professional teacher/learner to work with the group as a team member—participating actively in planning, executing and solving educational problems. Teachers and learners, who possess social competencies, integrate their inputs together towards successful solutions to particular problems in youth development and education programs.

RULE-3: LDP the ethico-moral values of PDRC. The ethico-moral standard or values of *professionalism, dedication, responsibility* and *commitment* (PDRC) in teaching must be practiced by teachers. In similar manner, PDRC must be taught to learners to learn, develop and practice. PDRC are ethico-moral values learned by the professionals, as *ethical standard* in a profession. In working for any organization, all members are expected to become professionals, dedicated, responsible and committed to their jobs. These ethico-moral standard must be a part of the rules in teaching-and-learning.

a. *Professionalism.* This pertains to the ethico-moral character of a professional embodied in his/her heart, mind and spirit. Profesionalism is manifested in the exemplary standard, practice or method of a person—in thinking, feeling and doing anything—that distinguishes him/her from the others.
b. *Dedication.* This is an ethico-moral quality of devotion, or state of giving up everything—wholly or earnestly—to the teaching-and-learning purposes. A teacher must be dedicated to teach; and, the learners must be dedicated to learn.
c. *Responsibility.* Another ethico-moral quality of a person shown in being reliable, trustworthy and dependable to *accept* and *do* assigned obligations to the best of abilities, e.g. responsibility of teacher to teach/responsibilty of learners to learn.
d. *Commitment.* It is an act of undertaking, a pledge or promise to *do* an obligation, e.g. commitment of teachers to teach/commitment of learners to learn.

RULE-4: LDP the ethico-moral values of RLEC. At this juncture, we assume a situation where a teacher possessed already the four core values of RDCI in teaching-and-learning. Moreover, the teacher had also developed the skill, method and social (SMS) competencies in teaching. In total, this teacher is now an *individual*—who can teach any particular assigned subject much better than other professional teachers. But, this condition is *not* a full guarantee for a teacher to become 100% productive in teaching services and youth development. There is more to consider in productive teaching. To become totally productive, the teacher must apply the four ethico-moral values in *human services*, i.e. *respect, love, empathy* and *compassion* (RLEC) to learners in daily teaching-learning activities. A teacher who teaches with RLEC gets the learners' *contact, interest* and *attention* (CIA)—and the learners easily learn.

RLEC to clientele are core values that must be practiced by *service-providers* in any field of human services. In Medical-Nursing Care, for example, the speedy recovery of an ill client can be expected, if the doctors and nurses are performing services with RLEC to clients. This principle is true to all branches of professional services. Below is a brief discussion of the four significant *core values in human services*, as applied to teaching-and-learning.

a. *Respect.* Respect, in teaching, is the teacher's feeling and showing of high *regard, honor* and *esteem* for every learner—regardless of the learner's physical, emotional, mental and social status. Respect implies both recognition and esteem of the learner's worth—*with* or *without* liking. It must be extended to every learner in the manner of *right, just* and *fair* considerations. A teacher must *not* get angry to a learner, who often answers wrongly to questions in daily recitations. If he/she does, the teacher has *no* respect to the learner. The teacher does not deserve to teach. What the teacher must do in this particular case is to find time in order to assist the learner in grasping and adjusting to everyday lesson. Verily, learners are *learners*; and, teachers are inside the classroom *to teach* the learners productively to the best of their abilities.

b. *Love.* Love, in teaching, is the teacher's expression of strong and passionate feeling of *fondness, affection, attachment* and *concern* (FAAC) to learners—*with* or *without* liking. Regardless of worth, every learner must be loved tenderly by teacher—similar to very own sons and daughters. Teacher's love can greatly pave learning hindrances and can influence learners to learn faster and better.

c. *Empathy.* Empathy, in teaching, is the teacher's capacity to *enter fully* into the learner's personal feelings or motives by using keen imagination. In other words, the teacher has the ability to understand and feel the learner's feeling completely, e.g. when a learner is physically hungry, emotionally sad, or mentally wanting.

d. *Compassion.* Compassion, in teaching, is the teacher's awareness for learners' total difficulties—e.g. physical, emotional, mental, social or economical—that moves the teacher to feel *pity* or *sympathy*. This feeling of compassion for the learners forces the teacher to do everything possible to *help* alleviate or solve the learners' dilemma, as though the problems were truly his/her own.

RULE-5: LDP the "PIA Rule" in everything you do. In anything or any job that one does—whether it be in the home, organizational setting or anywhere—this writer has conceptualized the "PIA Rule" (in Filipino words), which everybody must learn, develop and practice. These are the rules of: *"pokus," "ingat,"* and *"alerto"* (with the acronym, PIA). In English, these words mean *focus, care* and *alert* (FCA). The acronym, PIA is easier to remember than FCA, so this writer is using the PIA concept for retention and permanency in learning. PIA is an original concept of this writer in teaching-and-learning that could apply to all kinds of public/private services. To understand the PIA Rule better, below is a supporting discussion:

a. *P-okus/Focus.* Focus (or *pokus* in Filipino) means to concentrate or direct the fullest attention of the teacher/learners to all classroom theoretical and practical activities. When the teacher and learners are in complete *focus* during delivery and discussion of the daily lesson, there is a higher possibility to retain the desired competencies in the permanent or long-term memories of the learners.

b. **I**-*ngat/Care.*   Care (or *ingat*) means watchful keeping—with feelings of interest and concern to the learners. It also calls for application of four ethico-moral standard in professional teaching, i.e. *respect, love, empathy* and *compassion* (RLEC) to learners. A teacher that applies respect, love, empathy and compassion in teaching duties gets back the same values from the learners.

c. **A**-*lerto/Alertness.*   Alertness (or *alerto*) implies readiness at all instances to the results of instruction given to the learners. It involves a wide-awake, keen and watchful observation on the behavior of learners during and after instructions. A teacher who is alert while teaching can spot negative result in time and can take necessary correction to maintain or usher the process of permanent learning.

The Value Enhancement Levels

The *"Tuwid-na-Daan"* Concept.   The newly-introduced policies of "No Wang-Wang" and "No Littering" by P'Noy Government are simple strategies in enhancing the RDCI values amongst Filipinos. The intention of P'Noy Leadership is to *stop totally* the evils of graft and corruption in public services through right, just, fair and strict implementation of existing constitutional laws. Because of the *strong* political will being shown by the P'Noy Leadership, many Filipinos now are beginning to toe the line. Corrupt officials are now thinking twice before entering into illegal deals or corrupt practices—which is the normal trend in private and public services for many years before. If P'Noy continues leading with *stronger* political will, the end-product would be Filipinos with exemplary moral values that would usher total economic development progress. Majority Filipinos are hoping, P'Noy will apply strongest political will and will not be just a *ningas-cogon.* In essence, the total economic development and progress of any nation depends upon the good moral values formation of the nationals residing therein. Singapore is a very rich country in Asia. Although very small in land area and with limited resources, Singapore excels in total economy due to RDCI of the people. Japan is another Asian country, where the nationals have a high standard of formed RDCI values, too.

Value Enhancement Levels.   Enhancement of RDCI among Filipinos must *not* be the sole responsibility of the present government. The government can succeed up to a certain point only in this vision. Moreover, whatever success of P'Noy Government in terms of Filipino value enhancement could be temporary only. After the six years term, P'Noy will be replaced by another President. What would happen, if another "corrupt" is elected by the people into the presidency? And this is very possible because of the susceptibility of Filipinos to corruption. Filipinos must ensure that succeeding Presidents and leaders of the country will have exemplary ethico-moral values—similar to P'Noy.

Quality value enhancement among Filipinos is the only hope! It must be continued by all future government leaders until such time when quality moral values become totally *permanent* within. This noble mission must be supported with utmost cooperation and active participation of various sectors/levels in the society, i.e.:

1. *Home Level.*   The formation/enhancement of core RDCI values in children must begin at home—facilitated by godly parents, grandparents and other family elders. While still young, the children must learn discipline, i.e.: "to do only what is right, just and fair only." When a person grows older, learning discipline becomes a bit difficult. As the native

Filipino saying goes: "*Ang kahoy na liko at baluktot—hutukin habang malambot. Pag lumaki at tumayog, mahirap na ang paghutok.*"

2. *School Level.* Value enhancement must continue its emphasis at school level. It must form a part in every subject of the curriculum. Every teacher must stress to the learners that RDCI are critical core values that every learners must possess in order to succeed in life. RDCI is the key to total development and success.

3. *Barangay/Community Level.* At Barangay/Community Level, implementation of local government laws must be right, just and fair. Barangay/Community leaders themselves must possess RDCI to set good examples for the community people.

4. *National Level.* Value enhancement of RDCI must be observed by all government leaders—applying the existing laws accordingly. Strong political will must be done in public services with emphasis on doing what is right, just and fair *only*.

Conceptual Summary: RDCI Formation. A child originally learns *reverence* for God from God-fearing, disciplined parents with exemplary moral character and individuality. A child with reverence (R) easily learns good *discipline* (D). A child with "RD" easily develops excellent *character* (C). A learner with "RDC" easily achieves *individuality* (I) and easily gains SMS competencies. RDCI values enable a person to be competitive and productive. The enhancement of these core values must be supported by schoolteachers, community and the national leaders, who must possess RDCI within themselves also.

Again, a Filipino people with enhanced RDCI will not engage in graft and corruption; bank robbery; hold-up; rape; salvaging; car-jacking; illegal drug trafficking; illegal gambling; terrorism; smuggling; money laundering and many other crimes.

In line with this concept, the psychological and sociological enhancement of RDCI values is a must for all Filipinos to eradicate mass poverty, hunger and disease; thus, ultimately promoting a permanent condition of political stability and economic progress.

The figure below is an original conceptual representation of the "Rules in Productive Teaching-and-Learning" that teachers and learners must *learn*, *develop* and *practice* to guarantee total success in the teaching-and-learning processes.

INPUT: (By: Teachers and Learners)

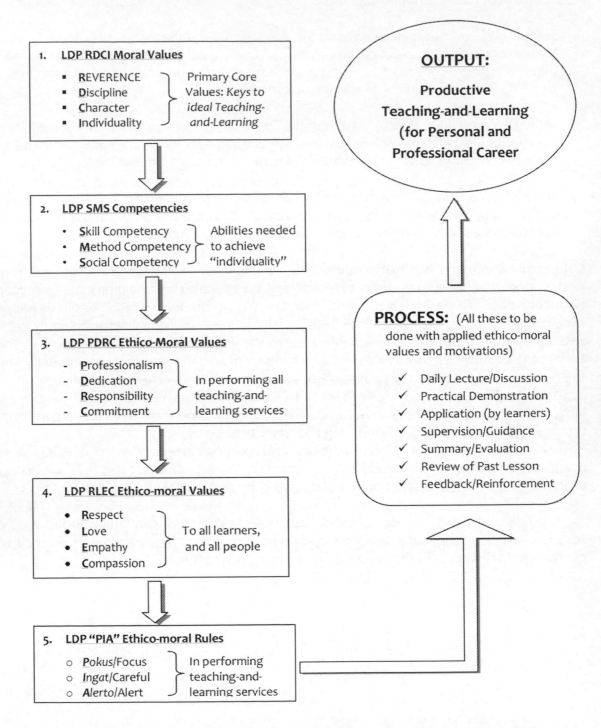

1. **LDP RDCI Moral Values**

   - REVERENCE
   - Discipline
   - Character
   - Individuality

   Primary Core Values: *Keys to ideal Teaching-and-Learning*

2. **LDP SMS Competencies**

   - Skill Competency
   - Method Competency
   - Social Competency

   Abilities needed to achieve "individuality"

3. **LDP PDRC Ethico-Moral Values**

   - Professionalism
   - Dedication
   - Responsibility
   - Commitment

   In performing all teaching-and-learning services

4. **LDP RLEC Ethico-moral Values**

   - Respect
   - Love
   - Empathy
   - Compassion

   To all learners, and all people

5. **LDP "PIA" Ethico-moral Rules**

   - *Pokus*/Focus
   - *Ingat*/Careful
   - *Alerto*/Alert

   In performing teaching-and-learning services

OUTPUT:

Productive Teaching-and-Learning (for Personal and Professional Career

PROCESS: (All these to be done with applied ethico-moral values and motivations)

- ✓ Daily Lecture/Discussion
- ✓ Practical Demonstration
- ✓ Application (by learners)
- ✓ Supervision/Guidance
- ✓ Summary/Evaluation
- ✓ Review of Past Lesson
- ✓ Feedback/Reinforcement

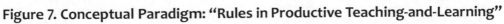

Figure 7. Conceptual Paradigm: "Rules in Productive Teaching-and-Learning"

TEACHING METHODS, TECHNIQUES AND STRATEGIES

> My goal is to find a method, by which a teacher teaches less; and, the learners learn more.
>
> . . . John Amos Comenius
> (1592-1670)

Teaching Methods

Characteristics of Good Teaching Method. A good teaching method refers to the *systematic order* of procedures—based on a carefully predetermined plan—that a teacher employs to accomplish the objectives of a specific learning module within a subject of a particular degree course. It is a series of interrelated classroom and laboratory activities, performed by the teacher and learners, to achieve predetermined outcomes.

Good teaching method involves meticulous planning and high performance standards of the instructor. It requires the teacher's competency—i.e. the ability to do everything possible—to teach and develop the learners. A good teaching method uses patience and understanding and makes learning enjoyable even for the slowest learners. As such, the teacher's job is generally tedious and methodical. The teacher has to prepare the daily lesson; guide or facilitate the learning of students; evaluate the learners' progress; and, set ideal examples for the students to emulate. In carrying out these functions, the teachers need to apply good teaching method that will identify and respond to the needs of learners. A good teaching method has the following *characteristics*, i.e.:

1. It adheres to the concept that: *Reverence is Knowledge*.
2. It stresses formation of the four primary core values for effective learning, i.e. *reverence, discipline, character* and *individuality* (RDCI).
3. It motivates and gets the full *contact, interest* and *attention* (CIA) of the learners.
4. It treats the learners with *respect, love, empathy* and *compassion* (RLEC).
5. It practices *professionalism, dedication, responsibility* and *commitment* (PDRC) in teaching-and learning process.
6. It guarantees students to learn *skill, method* and *social* (SMS) competencies.
7. It is based on valid educational *theories, principles, ideas* and *concepts* (TPIC).
8. It utilizes the theory of self-activity and the principles of *learning by doing*.
9. It provides adequate *related learning experiences* (RLE) or practical activities.
10. It follows "PIA Rule," i.e. "*Pokus*"/ "*Ingat*"/ "*Alerto*" in teaching-and-learning.
11. It encourages students to master activities involving the process of differentiation, discovery and integration.
12. It makes the teaching procedures suitable to every individual's need and interest; and, considers the learner's *physical, mental* and *emotional* (PEM) maturity.
13. It considers individual differences among students and liberates them completely.

14. It stimulates critical thinking and logical reasoning powers on the learners.
15. It provides continuous motivation during the teaching-and-learning process.
16. It feedbacks the learners and clarifies vague issues for reinforcements.
17. It is open and can be supplemented by other suitable teaching methods.
18. It guides the students to define own desirable intentions/ambitions and ensures their total personal growth and development.

Classifications of Teaching Method. There are two general classifications of teaching method—the *Traditional Method* (TM) and *Progressive Method* (PM). The two methods vary considerably in many aspects of considerations, as follows:

VARIABLES	TRADITIONAL METHOD (TM)	PROGRESSIVE METHOD (PM)
1. **Objectives**	The main objective is to make the students master the skills in the subject matter—in preparation for adult life. It is also considered as *subject-centered.*	The teaching-and-learning is *child-centered.* It principally aims for total growth and development of the child in terms of social, mental and emotional aspects.
2. **The Teacher**	The teacher *dominates* the activities of the lesson. He/she is the subject matter expert and sees to it that the desired results in the children are achieved.	The roles of the teacher varies, but with emphasis on the functions of a *guidance counselor.* The teacher allows more students' participation under this method.
3. **Curriculum**	The method follows very rigid or *fixed curriculum* activities—usually formulated by a number of appointed expert educators—and are characterized by the formal educational procedures and set standards.	The method adopts a *flexible curriculum.* Its primary goal is for personality development through proper stimulation, direction and guidance. Guidance and counseling go hand in hand with the regular techniques of teaching.
4. **Discipline**	*Strict discipline* is imposed in the classroom by the teacher. He/she expects the class to measure up to the established norms or expected standards. The teacher, most of the time, injects fears and tensions through formal process of elimination, rigid control and mental coercion.	Disciplinary approach mostly is *preventive.* Classroom activities are more democratic in ideals and principles. They are planned and carried out by the students—free from rigid regulation and control of authority. In classroom situations, friendly relation between teacher and students is normal.
5. **Techniques**	The method uses traditionally *time-tested techniques,* influenced by main objectives, teacher's role, curriculum and discipline.	The method adopts varied teaching techniques—mostly the *new* and *modern* ones—and are generally flexible in delivery.

Table 3. Traditional vs. Progressive Method of Teaching

Thin Line between Methods and Techniques. The following illustration shows the slight difference or the thin line between teaching method and teaching technique. In this example, the *goal* or end to be achieved is "population control." The *methods* that can be used are "natural" and "family planning." Under each method are the *techniques* that can be applied to achieve the goal of controlling population.

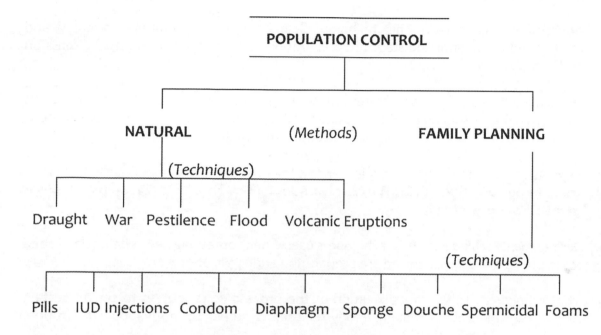

Figure 8. The Thin Line between Methods and Techniques

Teaching Techniques

Types of Teaching Techniques. Teaching technique is an effective *way* or *manner of teaching* under a particular method (TM or PM) in order to accomplish the desired goals. It requires combination of teacher's personality and acquired expertise in aspects of the course, pedagogical theory and technology. Teaching methods, teaching techniques and teaching strategies are three interrelated terms. They are often considered and used as synonymous by many teachers. There is a marked difference among the three terms though. The two general types of teaching techniques are:

1. *TM Teaching Techniques.* These are techniques that have stood the test of time and are still being used today under the Traditional Method (TM) of teaching. Some of the most common teaching techniques used under the TM classification are *Inductive, Deductive, Study Type Project, Laboratory* and *Demonstration.*

2. *PM Teaching Techniques.* Progressive Method Teaching Techniques are the newest, more improved and more informal ways of teaching. They are considered as innovation in modern teaching/learning practices, which have replaced undesirable features of the so-called "telling-and-hearing" lesson procedure.

Kinds of TM Teaching Techniques. The following presentation enumerates various kinds of TM teaching techniques used in the teaching-and-learning process.

1. *Application Technique.* This teaching technique gives the students a chance to apply or express what they previously learned. The steps are motivation; statement of a problem or task; and, application of information.

1. *Appreciation Technique.* This technique leads the class members to enjoy and understand the lesson. The steps are preparation, aesthetic and intellectual discussion and reproduction.

2. *Deductive Technique.* This is the reverse of the inductive method. This method begins with a rule that is applied to specific cases for the purpose of testing the rule. The steps are statements of the problem, generalization, inference and verification.

3. *Demonstration or Showing Technique.* In this technique, the teacher or a select group of students perform the activity. The class learns by merely observing. The steps are similar to the laboratory methods.

4. *Development Technique.* This technique is used when something new is being developed for learning. The steps involved are preparation and application.

5. *Drill Technique.* This is an application of the process of repetition to set off certain response or mental associations ready for use. Its steps are motivation, focalization, repetition and application.

6. *Expository Technique.* This technique is used a great deal in the lower grades as a means of exposition coupled with telling and explaining the lesson. The steps are establishing the proper mind set, presentation/explanation and application in the form of test or creative work.

7. *Inductive Technique.* This technique helps students to discover important rules or truth for themselves through careful observation of specific cases/examples, leading to generalizations.

8. *Laboratory Technique.* This technique uses experimentation with apparatus and materials to discover or study scientific relationships and verify facts. This technique deals with firsthand experiences regarding facts obtained from investigation and experimentation. The steps are orientation, motivation and practical activities.

9. *Lecture.* This teaching technique can be considered as telling technique as well, although they are not entirely identical. The lecture technique is more of exposition, while telling is more of narration. The dictionary defines lecture as "a planned talk on a chosen subject" for clarifying or explaining a major concept, theory or idea. This technique is effective when the lecturer has the information and materials which the students cannot avail of. The steps are introduction, presentation, demonstration, application, evaluation and summary or completion. This is considered as the most *authoritative* technique of teaching.

10. *Morrison Technique.* This is the forerunner of the Integrative Technique. This technique is often used when teaching Social Studies subjects particularly Geography, History, Government and Economics. Its various steps are exploration, presentation, assimilation, organization and recitation.

11. *Problem-Solving Technique.* This technique applies the John Dewey's "reflective thinking theory." It makes use of a problem as the nucleus, which the students work towards a solution. The steps are recognition and statement of the problem, critical evaluation or suggested solutions, verification of accepted solutions.

12. *Project Technique.* This is a technique where a problematic activity is carried on in a purposeful and constructive way. The involved procedural steps consist of purposing, planning, executing and evaluating.

13. *Review Technique.* In the case of a previous lesson, the term *review* means "to study again."[24] This means that the previous lesson must be presented into view again in order to clarify concepts, theories, ideas and procedures for learning reinforcement. Review of past lesson is done mostly before discussing a new lesson and when preparing the students for long test or periodical examination.

14. *Type Study Technique.* This is almost identical to the inductive technique, with the exception that only one case is studied. The steps are selection of topic; appreciation and motivation; statement of the typical model that will serve as basis for comparison; study and comparison of details with the model; and, generalization.

Kinds of PM Teaching Techniques. The discussion below enumerates the various kinds of PM teaching techniques used in teaching-and-learning process, i.e.:

1. *Conceptual Technique.* In this technique, the subject matter is taught to enable students to develop concepts. A concept is one's mental picture of anything—an idea, an object of procedure. The steps are initiation, recognizing, identifying and defining major and minor problems; hypothesizing, grouping, gathering data, organizing and summarizing, reporting, testing, accepting or rejecting hypothesis, conceptualizing, generalizing and evaluating.

2. *Discovery Technique.* This is similar to inductive technique in guiding students, i.e. discussing, organizing ideas and processes amongst themselves. It allows learners to use ideas already acquired as a means to discover other new ideas. The steps are preparation, identification and exploration, statement of hypothesis, experimentation, gathering data, solution to tentative hypothesis, verification and generalization.

3. *Individually Prescribed Instruction.* This is a highly structured instructional technique, where the students demonstrates mastery, with high level of performance on carefully sequenced learning tasks within a prescribed module or unit, based on criterion referenced test.

---

[24] Op. Cit. Barnhart & Barnhart.

4. *Integrative Technique.* This technique aims to integrate—what educators call—the "new learning" into an individual. This is concerned with the development of a well-rounded personality, one that can adjust and respond to situations in meaningful ways. The steps are initiation, culmination of activity and evaluation.

5. *Mastery Learning Technique.* This technique is optimizing the learning process, considering individual capacity and learning needs. The learner is treated as a unique being. Instruction is given in individualized form, supported by feedback.

6. *Process Technique.* This is a technique used in science instruction. The amount of emphasis is placed on the processes such as measurement, inference, hypotheses, prediction, variables control, experimentation and communication. The steps are motivation, preparing materials on the table, involvement in activities and evaluation.

7. *Programmed Instruction.* This technique is based on the principle of classical conditioning. Programmed instruction is a form of self-instruction. There are two types of programmed instructional materials, i.e. teaching machine and programmed textbook. The teaching machine is a mechanical device, which presents learning material to the student; tests him on his/her mastery; and, provides for the immediate feedback on responses.

8. *Team-Teaching.* As an innovative technique, team teaching is relatively new. In team teaching, there are two or more teachers involved who work cooperatively with the same group of students for some period of time. At best, three or more teachers are involved in planning the actual work and in the evaluation of learners. It is a way of developing the social competency or teamwork among the teaching staff.

Teaching Strategies

Teaching Strategy Defined. In instructional parlance, *strategy* normally refers to the *skillful use of outstanding practices* during presentation of the lesson. Strategy involves meticulous planning of the general design on *how* the teacher would present the lesson effectively and productively. For example, a lesson may be taught adopting *progressive method* of teaching and may utilize *conceptual technique*, while applying *case study strategy*. The succeeding presentation outlines various strategies used in classroom and small group instructions which can fall under one particular teaching method, or the combination of traditional and progressive teaching.

1. *Brainstorming.* It is a strategy for generating ideas and stimulating meaningful discussion on problem-solving activity. This is a "no holds barred" or anything goes discussion.

2. *British Style Debate.* A modification of the debate forum in which the class is divided into two groups or parties where party members—other than the presenters—may ask questions and make comments, as in a parliamentary debate.

3. *Buzz Session.* This strategy gives an opportunity to students to meet together briefly in small group of four to seven to share with their opinions, viewpoints and reactions. The buzz session can be held successfully with familiar topics that need group opinions, evaluation, planning or interaction.

4. *Case Study.*   Another group-centered procedure in which a situation or illustration relating to a topic is sketched out and the class is asked, "What would you do in a case like that?" This is a group study procedure using particular cases as the subjects for discussion.

5. *Debate.*   It is a very formal approach consisting of sets of speeches by participants of two opposing teams and rebuttal by each participant in front of the audience.

6. *Field Trip.*   It is one of the best ways to make instruction real. The students go out of the classroom and gather information from other places such as theater, museum, garden, swamps, rivers and other sceneries.

7. *Fishbowl Strategy.*   It is a means of decision-making or conflict resolution by groups, aimed at developing skills in group participation.

8. *Forum.*   This is a type of panel approach, in which a designated panel gives and talks on a particular subject with the audience.

9. *Jury Trial.*   It combines the elements of group work, research study and panel presentation. It uses simulated courtroom procedure to discuss an issue or problem.

10. *Panel.*   It is a fairly informal setting in which four to six participants with a chairman discuss a topic among themselves, followed by give-and-take with the class. Each participant makes an opening statement with speeches related to the topic.

11. *Problem-Solving Discussion.*   This is conducting a discussion that is aimed at solving a problem. Well-conducted discussions are excellent for solving problems, because students bring out so many ideas.

12. *Resource Person.*   This involves inviting a resource person to talk on a particular subject or topic inside the classroom during a regular session.

13. *Role-Playing.*   It is dramatic strategy in which the learners attempt to portray the situations through impromptu of unrehearsed drama, putting themselves in the role of participants and guided by the teacher.

14. *Round Table.*   This is a quiet formal group, usually with five or fewer participants who sit around a table, converse among themselves first; and then, conduct discussion with the audience later.

15. *Symposium.*   Like the panel, this strategy is used to give the audience pertinent information about a topic. The setting is more formal, where participants present speeches representing varied positions and then answer questions from the floor.

The "Salt" of Teaching-and-Learning. In the skillful presentation and management of the day's lesson, motivation is considered as the "salt" that adds taste to every teaching-and-learning process. Whatever technique or strategy that a teacher employs, motivation is an essential requirement to induce students to learn the target competencies.

Motivation is the practice of providing incentives to learners in order to establish *contact* and get their *interest* and *attention*. It is a critical part of teacher's preparation for the learners to learn. Through effective motivation, the learning behavior is *aroused, intensified, sustained, directed* and *reinforced*. Recalling and considering the almost forty years of teaching experience, this writer thinks that productive learning performances are primarily the results of effective motivation among the learners.

In his initial technical teaching assignment at Port Moresby (Papua New Guinea) in September 1976, this writer did a casual survey among students as to *why* they requested the administration of Plant & Transport Authority (PTA) Training Center to replace their former British Instructor (in his favor). The students cited the following, i.e.:

1. Our assignments were too long and too difficult to understand.
2. There were too many concepts and competencies to master within a subject matter tabled for a short one-hour period.
3. We began answering assignment in the classroom and at home; we did not know what to do next to complete the assignment.
4. Our instructor was *not* always accommodating to answer questions relative to a given assignment.
5. Our instructor was *not* even checking—if we did the assignment correct or wrong.
6. Our instructor was *not* always giving due credit to individual achievements.
7. Our grades were *not* determined properly or computed fairly.
8. Our instructors seemed racially discriminating us.

From the above-listed complaints of the PTA Training Center students, this writer is suggesting the following teacher's motivational strategies, i.e.:

1. Assignments should neither be too long nor too difficult, to motivate students' intrinsic satisfaction in creative and constructive activities.
2. The number of concepts/competencies to master in a subject matter per training period should satisfy learners' pursuit of skill, method and social competencies.
3. What are learned in the classroom should be competencies in progress—in other words, they could be applied at home when doing related learning activities.
4. Instructor's professionalism, dedication, responsibility and commitment (PDRC) to teaching duties must be shown to learners at all times.
5. Instructor's checking, evaluating, reinforcement and feedback on every assigned activity must be done religiously to achieve mastery of targeted competencies.
6. There should be reward, praise or approval by teacher, as due recognition or credit for meritorious learners' efforts or achievements.
7. Grades determined properly—computed fairly by the teacher—give a feeling of satisfaction and security among the learners.
8. The teacher's RCDI and RLEC to learners will remove all racial prejudices.

MODULE 4
CHARACTERISTICS OF A GOOD TEACHER

> Many teachers know *what, where, when* and *who* to teach. However, they find it difficult—***how*** to teach the learners, in terms of productive competencies.

Roles of Teacher

Harmonious Interaction.   A more critical requirement in teaching-and-learning is the *harmonious interaction* between the teacher and students. The effectiveness of learning depends largely on the teacher's behavior and the learners' reaction to that behavior. The teacher therefore must manifest genuine interest to teach—to muster full readiness and cooperation of the students to learn. Interest and cooperation between the teacher and learners should be mutual. This condition is generally dependent on the capacity of the teacher to lay the foundations of an ideal teaching-and-learning atmosphere, where learners are all *motivated* to participate actively in daily classroom activities. Again, the significance of learners' motivation is critical at this point. Preparing the learners to learn is the primary responsibility of the teacher. In so doing, the teacher needs to apply outstanding methods, techniques and strategies in teaching. The following are the various roles that a teacher performs in his/her daily teaching duties to ensure a high level of maturity, security and preparedness among the learners, i.e.:

1. *Facilitator.*   The learners are unique individuals needing security within an ideal learning environment that is full of *respect, love, empathy* and *compassion* (RLEC) to fully mature and develop physiologically, mentally and emotionally. A conducive learning atmosphere is realized when a teacher acts as an effective facilitator—guiding the learners' natural curiosity towards learning activities and encouraging the promotion of mutual respects amongst members inside and outside the confines of the classroom. The teacher is inside the classroom to guide and facilitate students' access to information and *not* to act as mere primary source of information. Generally, the learners' retention of knowledge is more lasting when they find the answers to the questions themselves. Mostly, the students seek the opportunity to discover and practice skills themselves, through repeated practical applications. Providing the learners access to hands-on activities and allowing them adequate time, space and materials for practical applications create an opportunity for individual discovery, resulting to learning and the retention of skill, method and social competencies.

   Guiding the learners to develop self-concept—with RLEC to others and the environment—is facilitated through participatory sharing of ideas and a judicious guidance to discipline. A harmonious teaching-and-learning environ exists when the voice of every student is expressed freely and is properly heard. The learners develop greater respect for the teacher and peers, when they are feeling safe and sure of what are expected of them from the daily lesson. The teacher therefore, must set consistent rules that are righteous, just and fair, stating clearly the importance of every activity, while showing marked appreciation for learners' participation and time. This strategy guides and motivates learners to develop self-respect.

2. *Counselor.* The teacher assumes the role of a *counselor.* The teacher assesses the physiological status and emotional feelings of the learners and provides constructive measures on how to deal with standing problems—personal or related to learning. To some extent, a good teacher may also gain access into the personal family problems affecting performances of students thus, giving advice on how to solve such problems to avoid stressful effects. As the situation allows, the teacher may even approach the learners' stressors—whether they be the parents, siblings, relatives and friends—and discuss the problems affecting the learners. In doing so, the teacher should show a genuine concern and RLEC for the students, in a way that the stressors would feel and recognize the teacher's honest desire for the learners' general welfare.

3. *Coordinator.* The teacher also performs the functions of a *coordinator* involving coordination of various services needed by the students. In many instances, the needs of the students, while at school, are varied. For example, a learner may develop fever with complications in other parts of the body. In such a case, the services of the school physician and other health practitioners may be required. In this particular case, the teacher must come in immediately to coordinate the urgent health services needed by the student, while giving information to the responsible members of the learner's family at the same time.

4. *Advocate.* A teacher is considered a learners' *advocate* because he/she intercedes for, or works on behalf of the students. For example in an emergency case, a teacher may request for the services of a private agency or of other residents towards speedy transportation of a sick learner to the nearest hospital in town. In other cases, a teacher may defend the rights of his/her student by interpreting and solving learner's problems. An advocate-teacher can also campaign for scholarships for indigent but deserving students—i.e. seeking financial and material supports from local residents, as well as advocating for supports from private and public sectors.

5. *Leader.* The usual teaching role of a teacher is expanded nowadays. Today, a teacher may be called to assume the responsibility of a *leader* for the implementation of a community development program. Community people generally regard a teacher as an authority in total learning and development. The teacher sometimes takes the responsibility to lead, direct, monitor and evaluate the implementation of specific community development programs in the place of assignment.

6. *Administrator.* The teacher may also perform the functions of an *administrator* in matters of administering and coordinating related learning activities/experiences for the students. This happens when working together in *team-teaching,* as in the case of an educational field trip. Somebody in the team should administer teaching-and-learning requirements during the activity for the total benefit of the learners.

7. *Role-Model.*   Most importantly, the community people consider the teacher as a *role model* in ethico-moral standard, learning achievements, clean habits and healthful living. As a model, the teacher should maintain exemplary professional qualities, good health habits and follow various health restrictions—e.g. don't smoke, don't drink and many others.

Teaching Philosophy

Conceptual Qualities.   A good teaching philosophy is a system for guiding learners that emphasizes on exemplary ethico-moral values, embracing and applying the concept of "Reverence is Knowledge" in the manner of thinking, feeling and doing productive teaching activities. Below are some *conceptual qualities* of a good teaching philosophy:

1. It pertains to the teacher's sublime obligation to develop and produce competitive professionals—with *reverence, discipline, character* and *individuality* (RDCI).

2. It embraces a genuine philosophical belief on the inherent goodness of the children— accepting learners *as they are* at their original footing—and making the best of them in the process.

3. It is the actual application of honed and tested *skills, methods* and *social* (SMS) competencies by the teachers in order to effect a meaningful psychological, mental, emotional and sociological development changes in the youth.

4. It embraces the philosophical attitudes of *respect, love, empathy* and *compassion* (RLEC) to learners—that shields the teacher from getting seriously upset when dealing with problem students.

5. It manifests optimum *professionalism, dedication, responsibility* and *commitment* (PDRC) to teaching—taking pride in the profession as a human developer.

6. It indicates the teacher's willingness and love for work—measuring remuneration *not* by the monthly earnings, but by the ultimate success in molding the youth.

Selected Philosophical Concepts in Teaching.   This writer believes that children are born with *inherent goodness* and that teacher and parents must be always beside the learners to guide them and facilitate moral awareness primarily on the reverence for God and including the reasons for self-existence (e.g. *what they have, who they are* and *who they want to be*). The following discussion presents four selected philosophical concepts in teaching, based on this writer's personal teaching-learning experiences (i.e. as a learner and as an educator) for so many years.

1. *"Reverence is Knowledge."*   Every child must learn reverence for God *first* to hasten development of exemplary personal moral values particularly discipline, character and individuality. Children with reverence for God always think, feel, speak and do things right, just and fair. If all learners have deep respect, love and fear for the Lord, there will be *no* corrupt. And, as Pres. Benigno Simeon C. Aquino III puts it in the vernacular: *"Kung walang korap, walang mahirap."* This concept is very applicable to the Philippine

conditions today. This writer therefore is advocating a genuine veneration for God in order to realize a new vision where righteous, just and fair Filipinos are walking through the *Tuwid-na-Landas.*

2. *"Godly Parents are Productive Teachers."* The parents are the *first* teachers that guide the children to develop deep *respect, love* and *fear* (RLF) for the Almighty. Godly parents easily lead their children along the path of *Tuwid-na-Landas.* In the Philippine setting, the mother mostly assumes the role as the first teacher because the father is always *overseas*—looking for family resources. The mother must examine closely *how* she teaches. Emphasis on value formation particularly reverence for God, must be the first lesson in teaching the children. The mother should be godly herself to succeed in teaching RDCI values—key requirements for total human development.

3. *"Enhanced RDCI is the Short Route to Tuwid-na-Landas."* Originally, a child learns *reverence* (R) for God from the God-fearing parents and schoolteachers. A child with 'R' easily learns best *discipline* (D) in thinking, feeling and doing things. A learner with 'RD' develops excellent moral *character* (C). A learner with 'RDC' achieves *individuality* (I) very easily. A Filipino people with reverence, discipline, character and individuality (RDCI) will not engage in graft and corruption; bank robbery; hold-up; rape; salvaging; car-jacking; illegal drug trafficking; illegal gambling; terrorism; smuggling; money laundering; and, many other forms of crimes. Enhanced RDCI is the only short route to *Tuwid-na-Landas.*

4. *"Hospitality and Friendliness are Negative Traits."* Hospitality and *friendliness* are *not* positive character traits at all—they are undoubtedly *negative* traits. Filipinos are known worldwide for being hospitable and friendly, as immediately noticed and commended by foreigners. Unfortunately, Filipinos do not understand that hospitality and friendliness are the *roots* of all corruptions in economic, social and political systems of life. It works on the principle of: "Help me and I will help you." This is equivalent to the Filipino saying, i.e.: *"Kamutan mo ako at kakamutan din kita."* Filipinos must observe limits and draw the exact border lines especially in business dealings and *not* to cross over the negative side of friendliness and hospitality.

Attributes of a Good Teacher

Seven Habits of a Good Teacher. In addition to reverence, discipline, character and individuality (RDCI), a good teacher should possess exemplary attributes for use in actual teaching intervention for effective and productive youth training and development. Teaching habits are part of professional attributes of a good teacher, developed through the years of good teaching experiences. This writer is recommending adoption of "Seven Habits of Highly Effective People,"[25] as conceptualized by Stephen R. Covey.

These *seven habits,* as applied to teaching-and-learning process, will surely enhance the instructor's SMS competencies and will ensure success in the expected teaching-and-learning outcomes. They are presented below, as follows:

---

[25] Covey, S. R. Principle-Centered Leadership. New York, USA. Simon & Schuster. 1992.

1. *"Be Proactive."* A teacher who is proactive possesses the endowment or capability of *self-knowledge* or *self-awareness*; he/she has the ability to choose the right, just and fair response to a particular situation. As such, he/she assumes responsibility for any act done—not transferring the blame to other people, events, or the environment when negative outcome happens as a result of his/her action. To become proactive in guiding the learners, the instructor must possess adequate skill, method and social competencies in the subject being taught. He/she should have general awareness on the significant social supports to be extended to the learners.

2. *"Begin with the End in Mind."* This is the capability of *imagination* and *conscience*. A teacher with imagination and conscience will be able to write learning programs intelligently with consideration to value of time, learning competencies and teaching aids to work with. This habit will enable teacher to imagine the realization of target goals, purposes and innovative efforts for productive learning activities in hindsight. With imagination and conscience, a teacher is guided accordingly all the time.

3. *"Put First Things First."* *Willpower* is the endowment in this habit. In the field of education services, a professional teacher with willpower possess a highly disciplined life that concentrates heavily *first* on most important activities relative to teaching-and-learning. Willpower is leverage for success in teaching.

4. *"Think Win/Win."* This is the capability of *abundance mentality*. It pertains to doing activities, applying principles with feelings of self-worth and noble desire to share power and recognition with the learners for the mutual benefit. Abundance mentality is an important attribute of a professional teacher enabling him/her to maintain an ideal harmonious relationship with the students.

5. *"Seek First to Understand, Then to Be Understood."* The endowment of this habit is *courage, balanced with consideration*. This principle is critical especially in dealing with the learners and their family members. The teacher should maintain an effective two-way communication with students and family members, balancing courage with consideration in order to be understood.

6. *"Synergize."* The endowment in this habit is *creativity*—the capability that enables two conflicting parties to agree on productive things. This pertains to an agreement for a common ground or solution—understood by the teacher and students—as in case of personal differences between them. Synergizing is applicable also to family relationships, i.e. talking about differences and agreeing on a win/win solution. A teacher must emphasize family solidarity as most important always.

7. *"Sharpen the Saw."* The unique endowment of this habit is *continuous improvement* or *self-renewal* for further professional development. A teacher with this capability will surely overcome unexpected breakdown of communication with the students and other community people. With continuous improvement, innovation and refinement of the teaching functions, an instructor will never have problems in dealing with the students and their families, as well as the other members of the community.

Basic Job-Related Attributes. Aside from the ethico-moral values forming as part of teacher's characteristics (e.g. RDCI, PDRC, RLEC and the acquired SMS competencies), the teacher should also possess additional attributes that will make him/her outstanding in performing daily teaching functions. Some of the job-related attributes that a good teacher must possess are explained accordingly in the succeeding discussion.

1. *Knowledge of the Subject.* The instructor must be well-versed—both in theory and practical—in all the subjects that he/she teaches. Theoretical competency is not sufficient to become effective in teaching. Practical application of skills is needed to support the theories contained in the subject for realistic impacts to the learners. For productive teaching, theoretical instructions must always be supported by effective practical demonstrations, followed by doing or application of the skills.

2. *Knowledge of Teaching Techniques.* A teacher should know by heart the sequential stages in effective instruction, i.e. the lesson selection, preparation, motivation, presentation, practical demonstration/application, summary, review, evaluation and reinforcement. He/she must also be able to apply the ideal methods, techniques and strategies of instruction.

3. *Positive Personality.* An instructor with positive personality gets respect and favorable response from his/her students, colleagues, superiors and other community people. Positive personality can be developed by concentrating upon and improving the aspects of good personality, e.g. enthusiasm, sincerity, honesty, integrity, righteousness, fairness and justice. A good teacher should avoid showing negative characteristics that interfere with effective teaching, e.g. the feelings of superiority, impatience, irritability and indifference.

4. *Professional Attitudes.* Whatever the teacher thinks, feels and speaks; and, however he/she does things during classes—reflects teacher's attitude towards learners; the subject being taught; and, the teaching profession as a whole. An instructor with exemplary attitudes thinks, fells, speaks and acts according to professional standards. He/she continuously enhances SMS competencies in teaching and makes every effort to raise the standard of the teaching profession. In essence, the general attitudes of the teacher have a great influence upon the value and moral formation of the students, as well as in total productive learning developments of the learners.

5. *Leadership Ability.* The teacher's good leadership ability facilitates developments of proper moral attitudes and character traits amongst students—which are significant attributes to achieve individuality in learning. With leadership ability, an instructor can ensure that discipline is maintained inside the classroom; can influence and guide the students to behave properly at all times; and, can establish control of classroom activities to secure the smooth procedures of teaching-and-learning situations.

6. *Desire for Professional Growth.* Education is a life-long process and everyone is a life-long learner. Professional growth or enhancement therefore, must be regarded as a continuous effort on the part of the instructor. The fact that a teacher had taught for some years does not warrant to have achieved excellent SMS competencies in the art of teaching. An instructor may be rated in the last Annual Performance Review as "Very Satisfactory," but it does not mean that he/she will get the same rating for next year. It

is therefore a must for an instructor to exert constant efforts to ensure a continuous professional growth and development. Generally, teacher's professional improvement can be hastened by:

a. Analyzing own personal characteristics, e.g. identifying his/her weaknesses and applying effective solutions to improve them;
b. Determining good instructions through continuous studies/learning;
c. Concentrating on specific teaching-and-learning elements;
d. Seeking help and learning from colleagues;
e. Maintaining good relations with students; and,
f. Making constant efforts to improve.

7. *Effective Communication.* An instructor must establish effective communication to earn the respect of students, colleagues and superiors. Respect is being earned and is *not* being demanded. Teacher's respect can only be gained by practicing correct attitudes and showing sincere or genuine interests towards people in the surroundings. A good instructor must recognize the personality of everybody regardless of racial, social and intellectual groupings. RLEC must be applied in dealing with the students, colleagues and community members; and, must be righteous, just and fair at all times.

A good teacher however, should maintain and observe a proper demarcation line with the students—guarding against over-familiarity. Like the responsible parent, a good instructor can consider learners as own beloved sons and daughters. He/she can live with the learners; work with them; learn with them; play and enjoy with them; and, help them in their total development needs toward progress. In all these concerns, the learners will maintain deep respect on the teacher—if there is a marking boundary against over-familiarity.

Ethico-moral Qualities of a Good Teacher. A good teacher can be defined simply as a *humane motivator* and a *model follower.* The ethico-moral qualities of a good teacher are the combination of acquired *professional* (i.e. *ethico*) qualities; and, the native *personal* (i.e. *moral*) attributes inherent to the teacher. The ethico-moral values/standard practiced by a teacher in teaching, determines the exemplary value formation among the learners.

Veritably, it is not that easy to find all these traits in a teacher. However, since the objective of this manual is to enhance capacity-building among teachers—for the holistic training and development of learners—this writer considers all applicable qualities to describe what a genuine good teacher really is. By so doing, the target instructors may be motivated to pick up from the list some attributes, which they can adopt to form as part of their life-long personal characteristics. The ethical characterization describing the total qualities of a good teacher is being presented in the following discussions for perusal and understanding of the readers. Take note that the writer purposely uses the word *competent* under each description level, to emphasize that—skill, method and social competencies are primary requirements in productive teaching.

1. *Humane* (Adjective). A *humane* teacher is a facilitator of productive teaching-and-learning, done through the application of RLEC to learners in the daily performance of classroom duties. Some related adjectives describing a humane teacher are: *competent*; respectful, loving, empathetic, compassionate, benevolent; well-disposed; understanding; sympathetic; kind-hearted; merciful; unselfish; generous; liberal; obliging;

charitable; philanthropic; altruistic; friendly; righteous; just; fair; lively; warm; helpful; flexible; enthusiastic; modest, diligent and broadminded.

2. *Motivator* (Noun).   A good teacher-*motivator* is someone who is effective and productive in touching the minds and hearts of learners towards a meaningful psychological, mental and emotional development and change. A good teacher-motivator can be described as *competent*; intelligent; logical; active; persuasive; persistent; punctual; industrious; ambitious; attractive and entertaining. He/she can also be considered synonymously as innovator; communicator; planner; self-starter; delegator; leader; enhancer; producer, builder and developer.

3. *Model* (Adjective).   A *model* teacher is someone with a moral ascendancy beyond reproach. He/she must possess a paragon of ethico-moral values in thoughts, in words and in deeds. His/her ethical and moral behaviors must be *competent*; exemplary; strong; perfect; faultless; immaculate; spotless; unblemished; impeccable; exquisite; serious; dedicated; responsible; honest; religious; committed; disciplined; self-confident, incorruptible and clean.

4. *Follower* (Noun).   A good teacher-*follower* is one that follows the vision-mission of his/her educational institution actively and loyally—maintaining personal devotion to youth training and development and adhering to the highest teaching standards. A good teacher-follower emphasizes the beliefs of the educational institution and reflects such devotion into daily teaching performances. He/she is known as a *competent*, cooperative organizer; implementer; coordinator; supervisor; monitor; controller, evaluator and a reverent disciple of teaching profession.

Basic Rules of Conduct.   To earn genuine respect from the students, a good teacher must observe basic rules of conduct in his/her daily performance of duties, e.g.:

1. *Do not bluff to cover lack of knowledge and skill.* If you don't know the answer, say so; just tell students that you will give the correct answer next meeting.
2. *Do not use profanity or obscenity* in order not to lose dignity and respect.
3. *Do not use sarcasm or ridicule.* If you do this, the students become resentful and their minds automatically close to learning.
4. *Do not "talk down" to the students.* Make the students feel a sense of belonging and that you are sincere and serious to share your competencies with them.
5. *Do not lose patience.* When students are slow in learning, use effective strategies.

MODULE 5
PREPARING A DAILY LESSON

> Lesson Plan is *indispensable* in teaching. Your daily skill Lesson Plan however, does not have to be sophisticated. Keep it short and simple (KISS)!

Lesson Preparation Protocols

Introduction. To ensure success in the teaching-and-learning process, the teacher has the primary obligation to perform two significant tasks, i.e. preparing the learners to learn and preparing himself/herself to teach. Preparing the learners to learn normally involves giving advance home assignment questions to the students, with corresponding effective motivations on the importance of the next lesson. Students' motivation should be done before and during lesson delivery. The teacher's self-preparation to teach requires careful planning of adequate/logical coverage of subject matter to be tabled in a given time. To achieve maximum productivity in instruction, the teacher should spend ample time in planning and preparing the daily lesson.

The Lesson Plan. Lesson Plan is an absolute necessity in any form of teaching-and-learning activity. Generally, the key to success in teaching delivery is the efficient lesson planning and the *coherent, simple, clear* and *effective* (CSCE) presentation of the subject matter. Before facing the class, it is important that a teacher carefully plans in advance the skills that are to be taught; the teaching methods/techniques/strategies to be used and preparation of needed training aids. The daily Lesson Plan does not necessarily have to be very sophisticated. Make it short and simple. The succeeding presentation outlines the basic steps to consider in preparing and planning a daily lesson.

1. *Follow the Subject Syllabus.* Every educational institution has a standard subject syllabus or outline to be followed by the teacher when teaching competencies to the learners. The subject *syllabus/outline* summarizes the logical coverage of the main concepts in various modules; the significant subject matter/topics to be taught by the teacher; the intermediate competencies to be learned by students; the classroom and related learning activities; the number of hours needed to cover the contents of the subject matter/topic in classroom and in related learning activities; and, the evaluation system to be used after the lesson. To avoid confusion among the readers, the terms *course, curriculum, subject* and *subject matter* are operationally defined in separate sub-headings below, i.e.:

   a. Course. The term *course* implies a series of formal studies in a school, college or university institution that leads to a particular degree or title. For example, Bachelor of Science in Nursing (BSN) and Bachelor of Science in Education (BSE) are classified as *undergraduate* degree courses.

b. Curriculum.   The *curriculum* is a program of study—consisting of a number of selected interrelated subjects—designed as requirements for the completion of a particular course (e.g. for BSN) that leads to a specific title or certificate.

c. Subject.   *Subject* implies a branch of knowledge and competencies being taught and learned within a particular course. Each degree or certificate course is designed with a number of minor and major subjects to comply with the standards as determined by education experts. Example: English, History, Social Science and Mathematics are compulsory subjects in many certificate/degree courses.

d. Subject Matter.   As used in teaching, subject matter means the main concept in the daily lesson that a teacher discusses with the learners to facilitate learning the targeted skill, method and social competencies.

2. *Determine the Subject Matter.*   The subject syllabus outlines the logical coverage of the main points or concepts in every module. These main points highlighted in every module can be taken as the *subject matter* for successive daily lesson presentation. In determining the subject matter, all the teacher needs to do is to stick to the logical arrangement of the subject matters or concepts as prescribed in the subject syllabus. It is important for the teacher to follow the *sequence* of subject matters—as listed in the implementing syllabus—to facilitate learning the order of targeted knowledge and competencies and to achieve the total learning objectives.

The daily subject matter—or concepts to be taught by the instructor—must be allotted with ample training hours to ensure learning of the targeted competencies by the students. The teacher must assign adequate time for classroom discussion and for practical applications in related learning activities. Enough time should be assigned also in summarizing the lesson and in evaluating expected learning outcomes. In some cases, a teacher may rearrange, adjust or modify the order of subject matters and the time allotments for lesson discussion, practical application, summary and feedback—based on long/valid experience in teaching the subject.

3. *Select Performance Objectives.*   Once the subject matter for the day's lesson is determined, the instructor can now itemized the *skill, method* and *social* (SMS) competencies that a learner should be able to perform/do as a result of the instruction. These learning outcomes expected from the students are technically termed as the *performance objectives.*

As a rule, the teacher must be able to do personally—with effectiveness and proficiency—whatever performance objectives are tabled for the day's lesson. The teacher must be keen in observing the quality of learners' performances and evaluate those performances according to defined measurement standard. Such a condition will qualify the teacher to influence learners to learn the targeted SMS competencies for future productive endeavors.

The type of learners' performances when doing the practical application of skill, method and social competencies can be used as evidence by the teacher—if the students are learning the lesson's performance objectives or *not*. In situations where students' performances are seen as logging behind, the teacher should give enough practical demonstration, review and follow-ups to reinforce targeted competencies.

The number of performance objectives set for a particular day's lesson, must be attainable within the time allotment for specific topic instruction. An extremely broad performance objective may *not* be realized within a short period of lesson delivery. The teacher must therefore ensure that the targeted performance objectives are accordingly limited—based on the time allotment period for the topic.

4. *Determine Lesson Organization.* The efficient organization and development of the subject matter and the sequential presentation using effective teaching methods, techniques and strategies are significant considerations to enable the students to attain the lesson objectives. Below are some procedural strategies that can be adopted when organizing a daily lesson, i.e.:

   a. Chronological. This procedure is applied when the teacher arranges the teaching steps in logical order due to limited allotted time.
   b. Procedural. In this strategy, the teacher has a ready-written sequence of instruction for teaching the subject matter (e.g. a ready-made Lesson Plan).
   c. Whole-part-whole. Psychologists advance that this is the best strategy in lesson organizing. Here, the overall picture is presented; then the details and followed lastly by the summary of the complete picture.
   d. Simple-to-complex. In this strategy, the teacher starts with the basic points of the lesson and builds up slowly step-by-step to more difficult details of the subject matter.
   e. Orderly. This is used when explaining the compositions or operations of a technical equipment or device, e.g. proceed from left to right; right to left; top to bottom; bottom to top; center to outside; outside to center; etc.—whichever is the most logical and easiest order.

5. *Write an Effective Lesson Plan.* The Lesson Plan is a form of written outline to guide the instructor in effective presentation of subject matter. It does not contain every word that a teacher is going to say during lesson delivery. The main parts of a simple Lesson Plan are (Note: See a typical example of Lesson Plan on next page):

   a. Subject Matter. This is the title/topic of the day's lesson. The subject matter should contain exact concepts or competencies that can be studied, discussed and learned within a particular period. It should neither be short nor too long.
   b. Performance Objectives. These are the competencies that the learners should be able to do after the discussion of the lesson.
   c. Presentation. This part contains the steps in presenting the lesson i.e. theory, demonstration, application, evaluation, reinforcement and including teaching aids/materials and teaching techniques to be used.
   d. Assignment. This is the learners' homework consisting of a number of questions to be answered as advance preparation for the next lesson. The set of questions should pertain exclusively to the next lesson or subject matter.
   e. Reference. This is the list of book/s to be used for students' advance study and preparation. The year of publication is significant in selecting reference books as well as the concepts contained therein.

WANG-WANG UNIVERSITY (WWU)
0210 San Miguel, Manila

LESSON PLAN (Sample)

Subject   : NCM-101   Date   : Feb. 14, 2013
Time   : 7:00 – 8:00 P.M.   Term/Yr. : T2; SY 2012-13
Professor   : Celina C. Serrano, RN, MAN Room No   : D-402

1. SUBJECT MATTER: "Treating Wounds"

2. PERFORMANCE OBJECTIVES: At the end of the lesson, the students should be able to:
    a. Explain the causes and types of wounds.
    b. Identify cases of abrasion, incision, puncture and avulsion.
    c. Perform basic First Aid for open wounds.

3. PRESENTATION:
    a. Theory/Lecture:
        1) Review of past lesson. Definition, causes and types of wounds, i.e.: abrasions, incisions, lacerations, punctures and avulsions.
        2) Open wound conditions requiring first aid treatment.
        3) First Aid for severely bleeding open wounds; precautions to observe.
        4) Elevation, direct pressure on open wounds to prevent blood loss.
        5) Pressure point technique to compress main artery blood supply.
    b. Demonstration:
        1) Direct pressure technique to stop blood loss; compressed technique.
        2) Tying of bandage over a pad on open wounds.
        3) Applying tourniquet.
    c. Application: e. Teaching Aids/Materials:
        1) Teamwork: Wound dressing   1) OHP
        2) Group Discussion   2) White/blackboard
        3) Film viewing   3) Multimedia PowerPoint
        4) Reporting   4) First-Aid kit
    d. Evaluation: f. Learning Reinforcement:
        1) Graded Oral Recitation   1) Question and Answer
        2) Written Test   2) Summary/Feedback

4. ASSIGNMENT:
    a. How do you prevent wound contamination and infections? Discuss.
    b. How do you remove foreign objects from open wounds? Explain.
    c. What interim emergency care is necessary for administration to open wounds?
    d. How do you handle treatment to animal and human bites? Discuss.

5. REFERENCE: American National Red Cross. Advanced First Aid and Emergency Care. New York, USA. Doubleday & Company, Inc. 1973.

Figure 9. A Typical Lesson Plan

6. *Rehearse the Lesson.* A rehearsal of the new lesson is very necessary before its final presentation, especially for a *new* teacher, or for an instructor who is assigned to teach a particular subject, the first time. This will ensure preparedness and readiness of the teacher to perform actual teaching effectively and productively. The rehearsal should be complete in all aspects, following the order of presentation, as designed in the Lesson Plan. The designated teaching aids should be used effectively during the instructional process. There should be practical demonstrations and applications, with related questions-and-answers, to test the learners' comprehension of the lesson. Ideally, review and reinforcement of the lesson should be conducted first, before giving any practical or written test on the subject matter.

   Similarly, the physical environment conducive to learning should be maintained. In addition, the teacher's assistant (if there be any) should be present during the rehearsal and should perform his/her duties—the way they should be done during the actual lesson presentation. A teaching colleague should be invited to observe during the rehearsal, to give valuable constructive criticisms about the lesson presentation. The rehearsal should result to mastery of subject matter and procedural presentation, to ensure productive teaching-and-learning.

7. *Final Check before Presentation.* As final preparation—on designated date for lesson delivery—the teacher should check the following items before the students begin entering the classroom, i.e.:

   a. Needed training aids/devices, e.g. computer, Liquefied Crystal Display projector (LCD), overhead projector, screen and flipchart are available;
   b. Instructional materials/handouts are on hand for distribution to learners;
   c. Seating, lighting and ventilation are properly arranged and adjusted;
   d. Training assistants (if there be any) should be prompt to perform their duties;
   e. Lesson Plan, class records and other checklists are ready for use and are arranged on the teacher's table; and,
   f. The teacher is completely awake—properly dressed and groomed, physically and psychologically comfortable—ready to teach.

8. *Actual Lesson Presentation.* During actual lesson presentation, the teacher must first establish full *contact* with the students, arouse their *interest* and maintain their *attention* (CIA). To achieve the CIA level, below are logical pointers for the teachers to follow when delivering or presenting a lesson:

   a. Begin with opening praises of thanks to Almighty (Reverence is Knowledge);
   b. Continue with an effective introductory statement related to the day's lesson;
   c. Specify title, scope and objectives of the lesson;
   d. Emphasize importance of the lesson to the personal lives of the students;
   e. Refer to previous subject matter—review and reinforce previously learned skill, method and social competencies;
   f. Connect previous lesson to new lesson; present new lesson logically effective;
   g. Ask rhetorical questions to influence learning among students; and,
   h. Use and maintain good speech techniques during the entire lesson delivery.

Integrative Conclusion. Similar to an organizational manager, the classroom teacher *plans, organizes, implements, monitors, controls* and *evaluates* (POIMCE) the daily lesson proceedings to achieve success and productivity in instruction. The teacher at every level must prepare a daily Lesson Plan that helps in actual and effective delivery of lessons. To become effective in classroom instruction, the teacher must develop a plan to provide direction toward attainment of lesson objectives. Normally, an organized teacher is more effective in teaching-and-learning. Writing a daily Lesson Plan is a critical aspect of the classroom teacher's management functions.

Writing a daily Lesson Plan is always a boring part of preparation that most teachers abhor. However, it provides a sure guide for enhancing a perfect learning environment and is an essential tool, especially for the new or substitute teacher. Lesson planning involves much more than making an arbitrary decision on what a teacher is going to teach for the day. A number of activities have to be considered in the process of designing and implementing a daily Lesson Plan. In addition, the job of systematic lesson planning is not complete unless the teacher has assessed learners' attainment of anticipated outcomes and the effectiveness of the lesson in making the learners to learn.

The Lesson Plan varies widely in format, design, style and content. Some teachers construct elaborate and detailed typewritten lesson outlines. Others prefer brief and simple notes, handwritten on the lined pages of notebooks or bond papers. Regardless of the format, all teachers need to make wise decisions concerning methods, techniques and strategies they will employ to bring learners systematically toward achieving educational goals. To become more professional however, this writer is recommending to all teachers to use a separate, clean and special notebook that will contain all the daily Lesson Plans for the subject within the semester or for the whole year round.

A teacher may prepare a good Lesson Plan, but should stick to it fairly close only. Usually, the need for presentation innovations arises only when the teacher is actually discussing the lesson with the students. The fundamental elements of lesson planning can remain unchanged, but the basic steps can always be modified to suit lesson presentation according to learners' needs. Even teachers who develop highly structured and detailed lesson plans rarely adhere to them in rigid manner. Such rigidity may hinder—rather than help—the teaching-and-learning process. Lesson preparation should allow flexibility during delivery, to enable instructor to make artistic adaptations to classroom instruction.

The time factor is another problem in daily lesson preparation. Classroom teachers normally are running against time; teachers have so much of it only, which is always limited and insufficient. Many effective teachers succeed in guiding and facilitating the total physiological and mental developments of the learners—but, they fail in providing the significant supports to their families and members. At most, family bonding is being affected tremendously because teachers are always busy in their classroom duties. But effective teachers will certainly manage and control the way how time is used. Time management is a competency that every teacher must learn, to gain ample time for productive classroom instructions and close family bonding. Finally, the teachers must also develop and practice the skill, method and social competencies required in the profession. They must be proficient in the skills and knowledge of particular discipline they are teaching to realize the objectives and goals of General Education.

MODULE 6
SEQUENCE OF INSTRUCTION

> Consider the classroom as your **own** home: the learners
> are your sons and daughters; you are living and learning
> with them; you are playing and enjoying with them; you
> are respecting and loving them; hence, you definitely know
> their developmental needs. Then, go ahead . . . **teach them!**

Stages in Instructional Process

Introduction.   The instructional process is the standard procedure in teaching-and-learning a single lesson or the entire content of a subject matter. It involves six critical stages, i.e. *lesson selection, preparation, presentation, application, evaluation* and *summary/feedback* of the lesson. During the presentation, application, evaluation and summary/feedback, the teacher applies various effective teaching methods, techniques and strategies to achieve utmost productivity in teaching-and-learning delivery. These six stages in instructional process are practically the same sequence of procedure when designing a daily Lesson Plan (meant for daily classroom instruction). These stages are presented accordingly in the succeeding discussions.

1. *Lesson Selection.*   The everyday lesson should be selected properly according to the sequential importance, based on the implementing course syllabus. It should contain learning competencies sufficient to cover for one session only. Moreover, it should specify abilities that learners should be able to do at the end of the lesson.

2. *Preparation.*   Preparation includes writing an effective daily Lesson Plan. Lesson planning is indispensable in teaching. A key to success in teaching-and-learning process is efficient daily lesson planning, coupled with effective delivery during the presentation of the subject matter. It is important that teachers plan in advance all competencies to teach and the training aids to be used, before facing the class. A key element of this stage is, *preparing the learners to learn.* Teaching-and-learning takes place productively if the teacher and learners are well-conditioned. This involves motivating the learners—both intrinsically and extrinsically. There is no standard motivational technique applicable to all students. Each learner is unique with own individual traits and specific learning needs. The teacher should therefore be flexible in using suitable motivation strategies.

3. *Presentation.*   This is the stage where the students learn the concepts in the lesson. Before touching the new lesson for the day, it is a must to review the learners first on the past lesson, to assess if they had retained previously learned SMS competencies. As necessary, make a clear follow-up discussion for possible reinforcements. Provide the learners with enough feedback on their learning progress and encourage them to do

better. Presentation may be done through various strategies, e.g. interactive discussion, demonstration, practical exercise and others.

4. *Application.* In this stage, the learners are usually given opportunities to apply practically the new concepts gained from the presentation period. This is the most important stage in the process where active participation of the learners is required to learn the competencies. What makes the students learn the knowledge and skill is *not* what the teacher teaches, but what the learners *do* during practical application.

5. *Evaluation.* The teacher checks here the learners' responses through formal written or oral examinations. The result of the evaluation enables the teacher to determine the progress of learning and to do follow-up reinforcement as needed.

6. *Learning Reinforcement.* Summarizing the outcome of previous instruction is very vital especially if the evaluation shows a low level of success. Even if the evaluation result is highly satisfactory, there is always an advantage in spending a few minutes reviewing the highlights of past lesson while giving feedbacks to learners for lasting learning reinforcement.

Sequential Lesson Presentation. At the start of the lesson, the instructor should practice and apply effective strategies to establish full *contact* with the students, arouse their *interest* and maintain their *attention* (CIA). Different teachers have different strategies in presenting instruction. To achieve the CIA level in instruction however, a teacher should follow logical procedures in presenting classroom instruction, e.g.:

1. *Start with opening praises of thanks to the Almighty.* Impress upon learners the awesome power of God, which will guide them to become individuals with good moral reverence, character, discipline and individuality (RDCI). Emphasize the concept, i.e. "Reverence is Knowledge" and that the only way to learn productively is to develop and practice reverence for Him *first*.

2. *Do an effective introduction of the subject matter.* For example, in sample lesson, "Treating Wounds" (Page 62), a teacher may introduce the lesson, saying: "Class, *Treating Wounds* is a critical competency that everyone should learn. A person who knows how to treat physical wounds can treat emotional wounds, as well."

3. *Specify title, scope and objectives of the lesson.* Here, the instructor can state the title of the lesson and outline its scope and objectives, i.e. telling exactly what concepts they are going to *learn* and what competencies they will be able to *do* after the completion of the lesson.

4. *Emphasize importance of the lesson.* Continue emphasizing importance of the lesson on the personal lives of students, e.g. "if every learner knows how to treat physical wound, he/she will be able to save money meant for professional service fees." Moreover, he/she can use and apply the acquired competencies to members of the family, peers, friends and to the members of the community as necessary.

5. *Review previous subject matter.* Before introducing the new lesson, a brief review of what had been discussed before is necessary. The review serves to recall and reinforce previously learned skill, method and social competencies.

6. *Present new lesson logically effective.* Connect the previous lesson to new lesson logically and effectively. The connection must be so organized that the learners can follow the sequence of instruction without difficulty. The number of concepts to be covered in the lesson should be limited. Generally, students will remember one-to-two concepts with little effort. Three-to-five concepts per lesson may also be learned comfortably. But, six-to-eight concepts may *not* be retained easily by everybody. And, nine-to-ten tabled concepts may already bring confusion to the students. During the lesson presentation, the teacher must apply the following techniques:

   a. Show genuine *respect, love, empathy* and *compassion* (RLEC) to the students and help the learners in their learning difficulties.
   b. Use effective speech, while outlining details of the lesson clearly for the learners to appreciate its significance.
   c. Maintain *contact, interest* and *attention* (CIA) of the students. A way to do this is by asking rhetorical questions that will require deep thinking and logical answers. For example: "To stop bleeding, why do the First-Aid nurses prefer the use of pressure points technique over the tourniquet?"
   d. Explain practical job operations in *coherent, simple, clear* and *effective* (CSCE) manner. The standard procedures; job specifications; and, the use of special tools, measuring devices, equipment and materials should be taught with the corresponding practical demonstration.
   e. Emphasize safety precautions during practical demonstration. The teacher must ensure that all learners can view the step-by-step procedures clearly and that they understand well the steps in performing the job.
   f. Repeat the demonstration procedure slowly until all the learners feel very confident in their practice.
   g. Allow the trainees to practice the job *doing* procedures under instructor's close supervision. At this stage, the instructor must be keen in identifying learner's mistakes; and, must correct such errors through a more detailed re-explanation and re-demonstration of the correct steps.
   h. Require the trainees to explain the steps while doing actual job; highlight key points for permanent learning. The practice must go on until the students have reached a satisfactory level of learning.
   i. Appoint Training Assistants from advanced learners to assist in practical supervision, especially in learning situation where learners are left in groups doing their jobs at the same time. The Training Assistants must be available to help slow learners while the instructor ensures that all learners are doing the correct procedures according to performance standards.
   j. Encourage learners—during supervision and follow-up—by showing interest on their practical performances, recognizing or giving credits to exemplary jobs done by individual student to reinforce learning.

"Ten Commandments in Teaching." As a professional teacher, this writer believes that—given the opportunity for correct training and development—every learner has the potential to contribute something unique, special and productive to this beautiful world. To provide this opportunity to learners, the teacher must be fully competent in the total performance of his/her daily functions.

Generally, learners develop fullest potential in conditions where environment is safe, conducive to learning and allowing the sharing of ideas through harmonious interactions. Such ideal condition is generated by the teacher, who primarily assumes the role of a good learning facilitator. The teacher therefore must practice *respect, love, empathy* and *compassion* (RLEC) to learners—to influence productive learning activities.

Productive youth development and training is truly a sublime responsibility of the teacher. Because of this noble obligation, this writer—who is a teacher all his life—has developed a philosophical guide to follow in preparing and performing actual sequence of classroom instruction. This *conduct* for teaching had been tested and proven already and had achieved a high level of efficiency and productivity in various teaching-and-learning situations locally herein and abroad. In the local scene, this writer had been a high school and college instructor in Manila for more than 15 years. Abroad, his 19 years experience in human resource development and training includes teachers' training consultancy or assignments in Papua New Guinea, Somalia, Malawi, Namibia and Mozambique.

This teaching guide is a product of the long years dedicated to teaching services by this writer. He had conceptualized it in the form of "Ten Commandments in Teaching." Following these commandments will guarantee total effectiveness and productiveness of the teacher's performances in daily sequential instruction.

1. *Master your competencies.*   Your previously acquired skill, method and social (SMS) competencies—and your teaching methods, techniques and strategies (MTS) applied in the classroom/laboratory—will surely indicate your total productiveness as a teacher. The technical theories and practical demonstrations that you give every day will definitely influence the learners to learn. Hence, it is important that you *master* your SMS competencies and improve your MTS on how to teach productively. A productive teacher possesses high-level SMS competencies with effective MTS.

    Expertise in teaching-and-learning is more of an acquired special competency. It is never inherent to any particular instructor. It develops progressively through the years of correct practice and experience. Many instructors know *what, where, when* and *who* to teach. However, they find it difficult—*how* to teach the students, in terms of productive competencies. To know how to teach productively is not at all difficult for a professional teacher, like you. Through the years, you have acquired the needed competencies expected of a teacher. You have developed the ability to perform the step-by-step procedures in lesson delivery. Just master your SMS competencies and teaching MTS a little bit more. Follow these commandments strictly and you will discover it a lot easier for you to teach.

2. *Organize your skills logically.*   An expert instructor can be an extra-ordinary skilled teacher, yet he/she still needs an organized guideline when teaching certain modules. In your case as a licensed educator, you will also need to plan and organize the skills that you are going to teach, to achieve a productive learning-transfer. You will need to sit down and devise a *subject syllabus* or *outline* to be able to teach the various concepts within the subjects according to the logical order of importance.

Designing a subject syllabus is not exactly the job of your College Dean or the Area Coordinator in your department. It is actually *your job*, as the subject-teacher. You can do your syllabus better than anybody else can, because you know well the exact teachable competencies, time allotment, training needs, teaching techniques and strategies. Therefore, you are the best syllabus developer in your department.

3. *Plan your daily lesson.*   Lesson Plan is indispensable in teaching. Generally, the key to success in teaching-and-learning delivery is the effective planning of the lesson toward a coherent, simple, clear and effective (CSCE) presentation of subject matter. It is important that you carefully plan the skills that you are going to teach, including the needed training aids, before facing the class. Your daily Lesson Plan does not necessarily have to be very sophisticated. Keep it short and simple (KISS).

4. *Prepare yourself to teach.*   You have the mastery of competencies in the subject. You have a logically programmed syllabus or course outline. You have a ready daily Lesson Plan with suitable training aids. Now, *prepare yourself to teach*, i.e.:

   a. <u>Appear neat and respectable in front of students</u>.   Your students will respect you best and adopt you as a model—if you conduct yourself as a respectable professional instructor. Be neat and smart in your looks.
   b. <u>Set classroom conducive to teaching-and-learning</u>.   The classroom should always be kept clean every day. The teacher's table and the students' chairs should also be cleaned and arranged. Training aids and devices should be strategically accessible. The room light and ventilation should be adequate. The classroom should be free from unnecessary noises and interruptions. Your Lesson Plan and class record should be ready on top of your table.
   c. <u>Leave your worries and personal problems outside the classroom</u>.   Meet the students with a happy or genial face. Show RLEC to your learners. Generally, the students will feel comfortable when they see you with a smile in your lips. Inversely, they will feel nervous when you show them an ugly face.
   d. <u>Always take pride in your job as a teacher</u>.   Exert utmost *professionalism, dedication, responsibility* and *commitment* (PDRC) to your work. Love your work. Your remuneration is *not* solely measured by your monthly earnings, but by your ultimate success in training and developing the youth.
   e. <u>Be inside the classroom always at the starting time</u>.   At any instance, avoid coming late considering the scheduled period. You are a humane motivator and a model follower. Students will imitate you in your ways of behavior.

5. *Prepare the learners to learn.*   Teaching-and-learning takes place productively when teacher and learners are well-conditioned. As you are set to teach, your target now is to *prepare the learners to learn*. Motivation is widely accepted as a key concept in learning. You must be able to motivate the students first—both intrinsically and extrinsically. Your efficiency in motivating the learners will largely depend on native capabilities and the resourcefulness as a teacher. There is no standard motivational technique applicable to all students. Each individual is unique, with his/her own inherent traits, characteristics and specific learning needs.

   Students have different ways and rate of speed in learning. Their abilities to understand vary considerably according to personality, background and inherent talents. These differences influence learning creativity and the development of new competencies. In all these variations, learners can develop faster because of *respect, love, empathy* and *compassion* (RLEC) they receive from you—as a *humanistic* teacher. Your assistance must be based on correct insights of the backgrounds, e.g. what the learners are aiming for and the nature of difficulties they encounter. It is therefore a must that you be extra-flexible and versatile in your motivation techniques and strategies. Below are suggested hints in motivating students, i.e.:

a. Be a constant good role model.   As a good role model, you are expected to think, feel, talk and act with righteousness, justice and fairness. Your good model behavior will influence respect and willingness of learners to learn.

b. Maintain your daily preparedness as a teacher.   Your daily preparedness will get favorable reactions from the learners. In general, when you show serious preparedness to teach, the learners will (in return) manifest their cooperation and willingness to learn also.

c. Be inside the classroom well ahead of the students.   The students are matured people. They will be ashamed to come late whenever they see—that you are always at your post well ahead of time.

d. Place yourself standing in front of your table as the bell rings.   Wait for their coming. Be the first to greet them for the day. Show your RLEC to learners. Your mouth will not run dry by uttering "Hello, good morning," or "How do you do?" with a friendly smile.

e. Allow the students to sit down first, before conducting roll-call.   Keeping a class record is very important. It shows the students that you are serious in your job and that you are formally recording the class progress.

f. Assess the conditions of the students before presenting your lesson.   Some of the students may be sluggish yet. If so, crack a clean funny joke to enliven their spirit. This is an effective form of motivation strategy.

6. *Present your lesson skillfully.*   Don't forget to make a list *first* of the skills that the students should learn after the completion of the day's lesson. Start your lesson with an *invocation* to the Lord. Before touching on the new subject for the day, it is essential to review the class of the previous lesson. Assess the students if they are able to retain the skill, method and social competencies you taught them the other day. Do frequent follow-ups. Give a lot of feedback and encourage learners to do better—to become productive. You may do the review exercise by using effective question-and-answer technique that will stimulate active class participation. Give open questions that require long answers—making the student to think deeper and conceptualize logically. Allow the students to speak more than you do. Do not allow one or two students only to dominate the discussion or demonstration. Encourage the timid students to share their own ideas, as well. Ensure that the discussion does not wander too far off the subject. Know the timing when to come in and to cut-off irrelevant discussions. Be tactful in leading the discourse back to the right track. Wind-up review with a summary of important skills and link it to the new lesson.

   Always give the *title* and *performance objectives* of the *new* lesson. Since you gave them home assignment questions (pertaining to the new lesson) during previous meeting, continue your instruction with question and answer.

Just act as facilitator most of the time. Allow the students to contribute actively during discussions or demonstrations. This strategy is called the "liberating approach" in teaching-and-learning.

When summarizing subject highlights, teach the points in a coherent, simple, clear and effective (CSCE) manner. Avoid wasting your time writing long lectures in the blackboard. Just outline the basic steps or operations in doing the skills. If you need a long explanation of the subject, prepare printed handouts for distribution. Make your lecture from 30-45 minutes only. Remember that you are teaching competencies and students learn the abilities faster *by doing* the actual operations themselves. If it is necessary for you to demonstrate on how to do a particular skill, show it actually to the learners. Then, allow learners to do the same practical demonstration repeatedly for reinforcement and the final retention of skill.

7. *Make demonstration for every skill.* Demonstration is an effective technique in teaching-and-learning skills. The students learn better when they are shown actually the logical steps in performing a particular skill. After each demonstration, the student must be allowed to master the skills under the teacher's supervision. This is called "teaching-by-doing," which is the actual application with teacher's supervision. The following are useful hints when giving demonstration with supervision:

   a. Make sure you have the training aids needed for the demonstration.
   b. Explain *what* you are doing and *why*? Discuss the safety precautions clearly.
   c. Demonstrate the procedures in doing the skills very clearly.
   d. Pause once in a while to ask questions. Encourage students to ask questions.
   e. Repeat difficult steps very slowly and clearly.
   f. Repeat the entire demonstration procedures.
   g. Ask student to outline steps of the skill, before allowing doing it his/her own.
   h. Allow every student to practice the skill. Supervise the practice and encourage group members to ask questions.
   i. Evaluate individual performance. Correct student's error tactfully. Commend good performance accordingly.
   j. Give feedback to individual student on his/her performances. Follow-up weak points for reinforcement. Summarize important points.

8. *Evaluate your daily efficiency.* Evaluation is a requirement in any formal teaching program. It is a measurement of the SMS competencies that students have learned after the lesson. Similarly, it is an instrument to evaluate the teacher's effectiveness in teaching SMS abilities to learners—a measure of success in teaching-and-learning.

   If the students did not learn, the instructor *did not teach*. If one student did not learn, the instructor is *not effective*. If all the students learn the skills for the day, the teacher is undoubtedly *efficient and productive!*

   When you teach skill competency, the best way to measure output is through *performance test*. Require each student to perform the actual procedure in doing the skill. Make the student explain while performing the job. Ask questions on particular operation and why? Do not help learners during the test. Remember that you are testing the student and you would like to find out the extent of his/her learning. Make a record of performance. As necessary, make follow-up demonstrations after the test and do not forget to give feedback for learning reinforcement.

If the evaluation result is unsatisfactory, set another assessment date to allow the student to repeat and master the skill. Bear in mind that your objective in evaluation is not merely to determine how fast the learner learns—but how effective and lasting he/she will keep and apply the skill. Be patient and give each student enough time to develop. Your efficiency as a teacher is measured based on the ability of the students to perform and apply the actual competencies later.

9. *Give home assignment daily.*   As a teacher, you need to maximize the students' potentials to hasten professional developments. Do not allow the students to have plenty of idle periods where their minds can be diverted to unproductive activities outside the study program. Give learners enough activities to do inside the classroom, laboratory and at home. This will prevent them from temptation to wander aimlessly at the City Malls and other nightspots. Before the end of the daily training session, you should give home assignments to the students in the form of open questions that would require reference reading and/or surfing the Internet for answers.

A type of assignment that would require longer research is the graded oral reporting. You can divide the students into groups and assign them related subjects to be reported on scheduled particular dates.

Another assignment that you may give the students is a set of questions to answer for every learning module or chapter. They will answer those questions in a separate assignment notebook. You can allot 10 percent mark for this assignment—grading it accordingly to its *contents, format, grammar* and *neatness* (CFGN).

10. *Record students' progress.*   Design a "Skill Checklist" where you can list down all skills that you will teach the students for a particular grading period and record their performances in doing the skills. In addition to this, you must keep a "Daily Training Record," containing class attendance, quizzes, recitation, class participation, reports, attitudes, major examinations and related learning experiences.

At some point and time during the scheduled school semester, a student may approach you and inquire *why* his /her grade in your subject is failing or so low. With a Class Record maintained and kept safely, you can promptly show the right, just and fair computation of grades. Thereafter, give concerned advice to the learner to study harder for better competition and to help and satisfy his/her parents.

As a competent teacher, it is a must and a primary obligation for you to keep updated records of all events relative to your teaching practices the whole year round.

SELECTION AND USE OF TEACHING AIDS

> In some ways, teaching aids are similar to vitamin supplements. Veritably, they *hasten* learning and development growths!

Selection of Teaching Aids

Introduction. Teaching aids are extremely vital for effective instruction. They are very important tools for an instructor to hasten total learning and development growths of learners. They help the learners to improve reading skills, reinforce such skill, fact, or idea. Teaching aids also relieve anxiety, fears and boredom as they are made like games.

As previously discussed under Chapter 2, there are five significant human senses which are stimulated during instruction, thus sending information to the brain resulting to learning. These senses are: hearing, sight, smell, touch and taste. Example: a musician learns tuning the piano by hearing; students learn faster by seeing; a mother learns if the meat she buys is double-dead by smelling; manual skill is best learned by touching; and, delicious food is normally determined by tasting. In general, it is better if more senses are stimulated at the same time. This will ensure productive learning to take place. A teacher must be adept in selecting, preparing, producing and using the proper teaching aids.

The main reason for the use of teaching aids in instruction is for the learners to learn easily. Good training aids add emphasis to the subject discussion. They help to simplify and clarify difficult parts of the subject matter. Teaching aids stimulate learners' senses; develop interests; hasten learning process and save precious time.

New Technological Demand. With the advent of modern technology, a wider range of teaching aids for use in instruction also becomes available. The trend of using computer PowerPoint presentation in instruction is now a requirement in most high school, college and university institutions. This condition brings advantages and disadvantages (in some cases) on the part of the teachers.

The fresh graduate newly-hired teachers enjoy the advantage of using PowerPoint program, simply because they had previous college training on *how* to use it. Before being hired, most of them are already adept in the use of PowerPoint. But, to those senior instructors who have grown older in the profession—this is a new challenge for them. They have to adjust to the new demand in order to survive. Consequently, they have to study the various computer applications to evolve with the modern time. For some older members of the teaching profession, this is an additional stress. Generally, at age 40 to 50 years, learning a new kind of technology is not that easy. Moreover, the additional time and expenses involve in learning the new trend are subsidiary factors that bring resistance to the required adjustments. Some older teachers are able to adjust easily. But, a number of senior teachers find it hard to keep abreast with the new technology. As a result, a few of them are forced retire earlier—a better choice than to remain ineffective in teaching.

Types of Teaching Aids.   Lesson objectives should carefully be determined to specify exactly the type of teaching aids to be used during instruction. Lessons must not be designed to conform to available teaching aids. Instead, teaching aids must be used conforming to the daily lesson. The use of too many aids can create confusion and may hinder the smooth flow of learning process. It is important that a teacher uses enough and suitable instruction aids that will heighten learners' interest for learning. The teaching aids are generally divided into three main groups, i.e.:

1. *Audio Teaching Aids.*   These are teaching aids using sound or audio frequencies to hasten learning through hearing. Some of the aids/devices under this group are tape recorders, tape recordings or records and radios.

2. *Audio-Visual Teaching Aids.*   These are teaching devices or equipment involving both hearing and sight. They overcome reading limitations and improve retention of information for permanent learning. Films, slides, television, video recorders, computer (PowerPoint) and LCD projector are considered as audio-visual teaching aids. As possible, the teacher and learners should not rely mainly in purchasing or renting professionally-made video films. They should venture to make their own film/ photographs/slides about the lessons for more impression and impact. When doing this, care must be taken to ensure that produced teaching aids are kept safely and well-maintained in a drawer or cabinet.

3. *Visual Teaching Aids.*   This group has the widest range—ranging from the actual object to a model. They include almost anything that a good teacher can imagine, conceptualize, plan and produce to serve as effective teaching aids. The most commonly used are overhead projector, wall chart, flip chart, chalkboard, flannel board, picture, textbook, handouts and many more.

Characteristics of Good Teaching Aids.   Good teaching aids enhance the process of productive teaching-and-learning. Good teaching aids possess basic characteristics that make them effective tools in hastening learning and development growth. The basic characteristics of good teaching aids are:

1. *Attractive, meaningful and appropriate* (AMA).   Attractive teaching aids are always meaningful to the learners and appropriate to the subject matter being discussed. AMA aids must be selected with good judgment/taste considering the level of learners' intelligence. When planning what teaching aids are to be used for a particular session, the teacher must consider the size of class and venue of instruction. Moreover, the instructor must ensure that the teaching aids are large enough to be seen by everyone—including those sitting at the rear of the class.

2. *Simple and understandable.*   Good teaching aids must be simple and easy to understand and tailored to the average level of the class. When teaching aids are complicated, they can require detailed explanation that may deflect attention of

learners. The learners may focus more on the complexity of the aids rather than on learning the concepts in the subject being discussed.

3. *Accurate and factual.* Good teaching aids must be absolutely up-to-date and correct in facts and figures contained therein. Facts and figures must be based from recently organized studies on standing public/private policies and practices, where the findings are generally accepted as accurate and factual.

4. *Neat and attractive.* Neatness and attractiveness are regarded as basic attributes of good teaching aids. As in the case of PowerPoint presentation—the *concise, simple, clear* and *effective* contents; proper labels; effective highlights; and, correct spacing in the slides enable the most important points to stand out, thus attracting the learners' attention. The use of long discussion in the slide renders it as ineffective and confusing. The application of color should be done carefully. Use of too much color is often distracting and is reducing emphasis on the main points or concepts to be learned.

5. *Lightweight but durable.* As possible, training aids should be constructed lighter made of durable materials. When using models, they should be capable of being broken down into component parts, following standard procedures. This will enable the learners to practice the disassembling and assembling processes.

6. *Realistic, as in actual object.* Generally, in teaching technical skills, the most logical training aid to use is the actual object. In the case of teaching the repair of starting motor for example, the actual starting motor is ideal because it is capable of being dismantled down into main component parts. During dismantling the parts, the learners can observe and learn the correct procedures—which they will use as basis when assembling the main parts back together after doing the needed repair. The use of actual object is best for learning manipulative skills.

7. *Easy to operate and manipulate.* Teaching aids should be made easy to operate and manipulate. Operating complicated devices can disrupt the flow of training instruction and may dampen the focus and interest of learners. As possible, aids should be simple, practical and easy to use.

8. *Economical and a necessity.* The expenses and efforts in the construction of teaching aids should be justified in the value of skills to be learned. If available, the use of actual object is recommended—for it brings more productive results. However, if it will entail higher expenses in procurement, it is logical for the teacher just to construct or improvised cheaper but effective and meaningful models for reason of economy.

9. *Suitable to mental level of learners.* Teaching aids must always be suitable to the mental capacity of learners. Complicated aids may be used when teaching a class with higher grade level, e.g. college students. For elementary and high school learners, the use of simple and meaningful aids will serve the purpose.

10. *Useful learning supplements.* Similar to vitamin supplements, good teaching aids enhance the teaching-and-learning process. They help in achieving the target learning goals. *However, no teaching aid will ever replace a good teacher!*

Purpose of Good Teaching Aids. In any type of teaching-and-learning activity, the use of good teaching aids is always an advantage. Learning becomes easier, effective and productive when *attractive, meaningful* and *appropriate* (AMA) teaching aids are used. The use of AMA aids is a must in daily classroom instruction, to:

1. *Supplement verbal instructions.* In general, verbal instruction becomes clear, simple and understandable when supplemented with AMA teaching aids.

2. *Attract contact, interest and attention of learners.* Application of good teaching aids during lesson delivery gets the *contact, interest* and *attention* (CIA) of the students because they can understand the instruction easier and better.

3. *Provide variety in lesson presentation.* A teacher using the proper teaching aids during lesson discussion enjoys a variety of teaching presentation strategies.

4. *Save time and energy.* The use of good teaching aids makes the lesson easier to learn, thus enabling the teacher to save time and energy.

5. *Encourage healthy classroom interaction.* The use of attractive, meaningful and appropriate teaching aids encourages healthy classroom discussions/interactions.

6. *Facilitate learning among beginners.* AMA teaching aids facilitate effective instruction, even for beginning learners. Because of AMA aids, teacher presents the lesson clearer; and, learners follow the discussion attentively.

7. *Influence discipline among students.* Discipline is one of the end-results in any classroom setting where learners learn better, because of using AMA aids.

8. *Unify individual differences.* Individual differences in learning (e.g. ideas and concepts) become more unified and solid through the use of AMA teaching aids.

9. *Improve speaking ability of learners.* The classroom discussion with AMA aids is lively and participative, helping the learners to improve as good speakers.

10. *Enhance language skills of learners.* Lively classroom participation of learners, brought forth by AMA aids, enable them to enhance their language skills.

11. *Make abstract ideas concrete.* The use of AMA aids in lesson presentation make abstract ideas concrete and thus help in making learning more effective.

12. *Substitute for the real objects.* AMA aids are good substitute for the real objects and makes learning more meaningful and faster.

13. *Develop related skills.* AMA teaching aids develop related skills among learners, e.g. drawing a diagram or illustration about the lesson.

14. *Make learning vivid and permanent.* In general, classroom instructions using the AMA aids result to vivid and permanent learning.

The Use of Teaching Aids

Tips in the Use of Teaching Aids. There are certain protocols to observe when using teaching aids, especially the conventional ones. A teacher should therefore know how to use teaching aids properly and should always be ready to answer questions from the learners pertaining to their uses. For the useful application of teaching aids in lesson presentation, a good teacher should observe the following tips, i.e.:

1. *Know/prepare teaching aids thoroughly.* A good teacher should know what specific aids are needed for a particular lesson and should prepare them thoroughly ahead of time, including the rehearsal of lesson using such aids. He/she should make notes in the lesson plan the time and type of aid to be used. Teaching aids, e.g. book page, graphs, slides, models and samples should be marked accordingly to ensure that the prescribed aid is used at the correct time.

2. *Cover the teaching aids when not in use.* It is a good practice to cover the visual aids when not actually in use to control possible distraction from learners during the lesson presentation.

3. *Explain the use of complicated teaching aids.* Complicated teaching aids used in more technical lesson should be explained, as to their functions. Such introduction is necessary to avoid confusion from the learners who may concentrate thinking about the use of the aids—rather than the concepts being discussed.

4. *Expose the teaching aids to all class members.* Aids should be displayed in a manner that all students—including those seating at the rear of the class—would see them clearly. As needed, the teacher may modify the seating arrangement or enlarge the size of the teaching aids. A teaching aid is effective only when everyone sees and recognizes it very clearly.

5. *Talk to the class—not to teaching aids.* An instructor may become so involved with the teaching aids that he/she forgets maintaining eye contact with the class. Aids should be positioned properly along instructor's side during the presentation to eliminate the impression of talking to the aids rather than to the class.

6. *Adjust teaching aids properly.* Teaching aids, e.g. projectors should be focused properly when being used. The video films should also be adjusted properly considering its clear image and volume. When using aids, e.g. posters, pictures and other illustrations, they should be larger in size—enough to be seen clearly by the whole class. They should not be too big in size or too expensive to buy (on the part of the teacher).

7. *Assign an assistant, as needed.* In cases of using complicated or the large-size teaching aids, an instructor may appoint a student-assistant. The assistant should be selected from the cream of the class and should be rehearsed before the lesson presentation so that he/she knows exactly what to do. The use of training-assistant is a good way of building the capacity further on deserving students.

The Chalkboard Strategy. Despite the advent of modern technology, the chalkboard teaching strategy is still being widely used in the modern-day teaching-and-learning. The chalkboard strategy depicts, to a large extent, the personality and teaching style of an instructor. The productiveness of learning does not solely depend on the use of modern teaching aids. Conventional aids, like the chalkboard, can be very effective depending on the subject matter to be taught and the teacher's general competencies. For powerful use of the chalkboard, a good teacher should:

1. Ensure legible and visible handwriting;
2. Print main headings or titles in capital letters;
3. Summarize concepts in concise, simple, clear and effective manner;
4. Avoid writing irrelevant, long and boring explanations; limit writing explanation to very important items only and avoid the use of unnecessary details;
5. Maintain proper spacing, layout or format;
6. Use the chalkboard section accordingly; if the chalkboard part is too wide, divide it into two sections with chalk marks;
7. Use colored chalks selectively for emphasis—use of too many colors may create confusion among learners;
8. Prepare the templates or cutouts for drawing irregular and repetitive shapes to save precious time; and,
9. Avoid writing or drawing for a long period, disrupting valuable class contacts.

Modern Teaching Aids. The use of modern teaching aids has become the order in the teaching practice today. Since modern equipment and devices are very expensive, the teacher should be keen in deciding whether the day's lesson truly demands using them or not. Where modern equipment and devices are supplied and are available in the school laboratory, the teacher can use them all the time. However, if teacher is the one who is to shoulder the expenses for the purchase of those expensive aids, the teacher should be flexible and smart enough to find or construct other suitable models. Doing this, the teacher should give time to experiment and learn how to use the model effectively. As needed, the aid should be revised to suit the purpose before the actual use.

The use of *computer* device in teaching should not involve complicated presentation, e.g. animated games. A teacher should focus mainly in providing information and in learning word-processing that will help the learners to become competitive in the future. Students should be taught on how to find and evaluate the usefulness of information properly. Good and bad information are widely available in the Internet—and the learner should be advised strongly to pick up only the good ones.

Today, a teacher must be well-versed in the use of *word processing*. This skill is a very significant tool in modern teaching practices nowadays. The students' assignments, individual/group reports, stories, projects, including research writings require application of word processing. Some teachers recommend that students use a software program that teaches proper finger placement when typing. Others simply advise students to practice as often as possible to develop proficiency. Whichever option is preferred, the students should be taught in the effective use of computer keyboard, as well as in saving, storing, retrieving files, adding color, downloading images, changing font size and others.

Some technologically-advanced teachers use computer email in communicating with students. Teacher-student email communication is a good means of following-up learning of students with special needs. The teachers can provide guidance to particular students considering the level of competency and interests. In similar way, the teacher should be willing to learn from the students, too. There is always the case that a couple of computer wizards are included in his/her class.

PowerPoint Presentations. In modern classroom teaching, the use of PowerPoint during lesson presentations has become an absolute necessity in providing logical information pertaining to various concepts and competencies being learned. Richard Stowell (2008) writes that, "there are two ways a digital presentation can be made more interactive: through its production and its delivery."[26] Below is a brief summary on how to make an "engaging and interactive" PowerPoint presentation, based on the 10 tips that Stowell had originally conceived, i.e.:

1. Give your viewers scenarios and pose questions to your audience. Questioning and predicting will help students stay involved. Slides that ask audience members to predict content will get them more engaged with the material.

2. Include charts and graphics to support content. Tables and columns can help student organize and make sense of information.

3. As possible, add video clips and colorful pictures to make it more interesting to the viewers' memory.

4. Use transitions between slides to give your slideshow a professional look and ease students from slide to slide. The smooth transitions help connect content from one slide to the next in your audience members' minds.

5. Use custom animations on paragraphs, bulleted lists and photos to ease the viewer into your content.

6. Paraphrase slides and elaborate on bullet points. The slideshow ought to be more of an outline, with details provided in the notes section below the slide.

7. Make use of the notes printout options in PowerPoint. They are in the Print menu. Choose from several different format options.

8. Get Students involved in the presentation. Check for understanding often by periodically asking students questions about previous slides.

9. Involve learners in activities during your slideshow. Certain activities can break up the monotony of a long presentation.

---

[26] http://www.suite101.com/content/ten. . . Dec. 7, 2008.

10. If students are using computers connected to Internet, they can perform relevant web searches or research. Plan group tasks to be done during a presentation.

PowerPoint—A Collaboration Tool. The PowerPoint presentation has some other uses Tammy Andrew states that, PowerPoint presentations "can be used as a collaboration tool within a group."[27] For this purpose, Andrew suggests that:

The original file should contain the essential guiding questions or steps for the collaboration activity, one question or step per slide. Students put their names or group name on the title slide and make sure to save initially in the way directed by the teacher, so that any future saves or auto saves go to the correct version of the presentation file.

At this point, students would answer questions or record their research on the appropriate slides. If the computers are on a network, they also could use the Internet to do any research that might be necessary. Once finished, their work is ready to present to the class.

PowerPoint in Brainstorming Strategy. In a computer-equipped class, PowerPoint software can also be used to initiate a brainstorming session among students. The teacher can make several slides containing thought-provoking questions that the learners would contemplate to answer. Each slide with provocative question should be assigned to a group of students to answer within an allotted a time limit and with specific instructions as needed. This exercise enables learners—individually or within the group—to quickly come up with their own interesting ideas and concepts.

When the students finish answering their assigned question in the slide, the teacher may continue with the option to allow each student or group to do an actual reporting presentation of the ideas and concepts contained in their slides. Students can engage further in intelligent discussions depending on the interesting answers that they have encoded into their slides. After the session, all the slides can be saved by the teacher to create a class document for future use in brainstorming exercise.

PowerPoint—Useful but a Dilemma? The PowerPoint is very useful in modern day classroom instructions. A teacher with computer never forgets to make PowerPoint lectures despite the long period of time spent during preparation. Sad to say, the poor teacher has to sit with his/her computer down to early morning hours, just to finish the preparation of PowerPoint lesson in slides. This is one of the sacrifices in teaching profession. The time meant for family bonding is limited because of the teacher's desire to have a successful lesson presentation for the following day.

For a teacher *without* computer, the dilemma becomes weightier. The teacher stays in school after classes to avail of free use of the school computer, to get ready for next day lesson. Where school computers are all occupied, the teacher goes to a "Computer Café" to prepare the PowerPoint. Aside from spending teacher's own money, the time for family bonding is lost. The teacher arrives home at 11:00 P.M., when the children and partner are already asleep. And to make matter worst, the poor teacher again has to wake up early morning to prepare and report for school duties. At the time he/she leaves home for school, the children and partner are still in bed—snoring.

---

[27] http://www.suite.101.com/content/teach-students. . . Mar. 25, 2009

MODULE 8
SPEECH TECHNIQUES

> A lesson delivered with *no* speech techniques is like a lullaby song that puts the students to sleep.

Attracting the Learners

Introduction.   In classroom settings, lesson delivery calls for functional communication with the learners to accomplish desired learning goals. The use of effective speech techniques during lesson presentation is very significant. It attracts learners to maintain *contact, interest* and *attention* (CIA) for maximum learning. A lesson delivered with *no* speech technique results to boredom; confuses the learners; blocks their nerve cells or receptors for learning; and, thus making them bored and sleepy.

The primary objective in using speech techniques during lesson delivery is to allure, charm, fascinate or attract the learners to respond seriously and attentively to the ongoing lesson. Getting the full CIA of learners cannot be obtained through power and coercion. CIA cannot be demanded from the students—especially in today's generation. However, CIA can be *earned* through attraction. The teacher must develop the ability to charm and fascinate learners to gain their respect. One way to do this is the use effective speech.

Unless oral instruction is presented with attractive speech technique, the students' interest will wane; attention will be marred by confusion; and, the desire to understand and learn the lesson will be considerably discouraged. To attract learners, an instructor must be effective in speaking and presenting the subjects thoroughly. Effective speech in lesson presentation, supported by a high level of SMS competencies, triggers learners' respect and holds their CIA—resulting to more productive learning.

Developing an Attractive Speaking Style.   Adequate lesson planning and preparation contribute immensely to smooth lesson presentation. There is more to smooth teaching delivery however, i.e. the use of attractive speaking style during discussion. Speaking style in lesson presentation varies in qualities, depending on the acquired ethico-moral values and teaching competencies of the teacher/speaker. As a professional teacher, you can develop an attractive speaking style that will entice the CIA of learners by observing the following pointers, i.e.:

1. *Coherent, simple, clear and effective* (CSCE) *opening.*   You should get the full attention of the class first before beginning the session. A simple: "Class, we offer first our thanks to the Lord . . ." will usually get the attention of the class. Begin with a prayer and explain to the learners *why* they must listen and learn the important competencies in every subject, for their future applications in daily life. When the

students are ready, you may begin by stating the *title* of the subject and explain the expected competencies that learners will learn and do after the lesson.

2. *Follow the logical presentation outline.* Follow your Lesson Plan logically during presentation. As needed, motivate your students by telling funny stories about the subject, which they can relate to. Present your ideas step-by-step. Make the learners follow "where you are," and "where else you are going to."

3. *Inject humor, as necessary.* The use of clean jokes closely related to the lesson is often an effective way of calling the CIA of the class. Humor must *not* be used just to make the learners laugh. There must be a message to learn from the joke. You may inject clean and appropriate humor when class focus is wandering or waning only. Do not use abusive or disgusting humor that will offend anyone in the class. Clean humor is indicative of your personal values and outlooks in life. As a teacher, you should know what clean and appropriate humor is.

4. *Maintain eye-to-eye contact with learners.* Maintain an eye-to-eye contact with your students. Look at, and talk with the class directly—and *not* to the visual aids or to some other visible objects inside the classroom.

5. *Speak in a conversational tone.* Do not talk with a voice reflecting a seemingly indifferent and an impersonal tone. Address learners using the pronoun, "you." Identify yourself with the students by using the pronouns "I" and "we." Impress upon the learners that you have something in common with them.

6. *Be constantly alert.* While speaking, observe the learners' responses closely. Be alert always. Spot the inattentive members of the class quickly. Where one is not focusing closely to the lesson, be smart to call his/her attention. In doing so, ask a question related to the lesson diplomatically. If the answer is not satisfactory, advise the learner to pay close attention to understand the ongoing discussion.

7. *Be genuinely enthusiastic.* Enthusiasm is always contagious. Enthusiastic lesson delivery secures the students' CIA. When the learners see that you are adept in the subject matter—and that you are very serious in conveying ideas and concepts to them—they will always be interested to listen and learn.

8. *Use documental references.* Always make available the copies of recognized documental references from where you quoted, to support your ideas during the lesson presentation. This will be handy and useful to you, in case a class member asks: "Sir, where did you get your facts?"

9. *Quote from known authorities.* Always quote from recognized authorities in the subject. This will prove to the learners that you are doing extra effort to give them the best ideas and concepts.

10. *Refer back to productive teaching experiences.* As a teacher, you are regarded as an authority in the subject. You can prove this status to your students by referring humbly to your previous productive teaching experiences. Avoid being boisterous in

your statements. Humble narration of your experiences gives more credibility to your story—generating genuine belief and respect from learners.

11. *Close with a CSCE statement.* After presenting the important highlights of the subject matter, you need to summarize the vital ideas and concepts to reinforce learning among learners. You may give your conclusion by, e.g.: "Now that you know the importance of the skills, I am counting on you to practice/master the correct procedures and apply the skills for your total development and progress."

Promoting Self-Confidence

Tips in Controlling Nervousness. Nervousness is a common feeling for a newly-hired teacher (or even for some senior teachers) during initial presentation/appearance before a class. This is a typical indicator that the teacher is very much aware of the class; and, is concerned about the students' reaction to his/her instruction. This can also be a sign of low-level personal confidence in teaching. A teacher must control nervousness to achieve smooth and powerful lesson delivery. Below are helpful tips to control nervousness during lesson presentation, thus promoting self-confidence in a teacher, i.e.:

1. *Prepare your lesson thoroughly.* Prepare a CSCE Lesson Plan considering the size of the class; abilities of learners; teaching aids to use; time and location of lesson presentation; and, possible learning distractions. Remember, the better your preparation is—the lesser nervous you will become.

2. *Master the required lesson competencies.* Full mastery of SMS competencies within the lesson enables you to teach the subject authoritatively. If you have the mastery of SMS competencies in the lesson, you are not going to feel nervousness during lesson delivery. Instead, you will develop complete personal confidence that will help you in the meaningful and successful lesson presentation.

3. *Rehearse your lesson.* Rehearse the lesson before actual presentation, following the established standards. Practicing the presentation out loud several times before the real thing will make you feel more confident, especially if you practice under condition that is close to actual situation, as possible. For new and inexperienced teacher, do at least one dry-run in front of an audience, even with a friend only. After presentation, you may ask for comments and improve on them accordingly.

4. *Know your audience very well.* Before the initial meeting with the class, you should know well the general attitudes and characteristics of the members; their school-year level; their learning needs and varied expectations. This will guide you in planning what type of presentation is best suitable for the group.

5. *Assume confident mental attitude.* Assuming confident mental attitude to control nervousness is another asset of a teacher. To be in the proper frame of mind, you should not allow fear to overcome you. Do not fear of what the learners will think about your presentation. Be confident always. As you go on, be consistent in making rational analysis of the classroom situation and make intelligent decisions as needed—to ensure productive teaching-and-learning.

6. *Prepare your teaching aids.* Test all of your teaching aids/equipment in advance and set them ready. Arrange the classroom ideal for teaching-and-learning. This will help you visualize your presentation and control unnecessary worries about equipment failure. Have a backup plan in case the projector fails to work. Be prepared to present without your visual aids. Have chalks and markers readily available and use them properly, as situation demands.

7. *Overcome your fears.* If you are nervous, list down particular problems causing you to fear and consider workable solution that you could do to overcome those fears. Some health professionals recommend the use of relaxation exercises, e.g. stretching; deep breathing, etc. to help in maintaining the normal heart rate. They even advise to eat bananas, which are high in potassium that calms fear caused by the stomach. Remember also to drink lots of water before and during lesson presentation. Irregular breathing and sweating will dehydrate your body quickly hence, you need to drink more water.

8. *Start the lesson from known to unknown.* Start your presentation with reference to previous lesson. Doing this, you will attract the learners to focus attention on something familiar, enabling you to meet them on common ground.

9. *Apply a bit of humor.* Injecting a bit of clean humor by using funny stories or jokes during presentation charms the students to give you their full CIA. It also releases your tension very quickly, enabling you to maintain the self-confidence needed for a more powerful lesson delivery. In making jokes however, avoid directing it to a particular class member. No matter how witty and sensible your joke is—such will register as a grave insult to the learner. It is even better and human to use self-directed jokes or personal story relative to the lesson. Telling personal story enables the audience identify with you, resulting to a warmer classroom atmosphere. If the students laugh on you, laugh with them and enjoy the *minutes to win* them completely.

10. *Talk and move with purpose.* Talk clearly and slowly during your presentation. Be deliberate in your movements and do not talk and move too fast, as if you were an "Andrew-E." Remember that you are not a *rapper*. A rapper is more effective in sending a particular message by quick talks and movements. You are a teacher—a facilitator of productive learning. You will be more effective when you send messages in a slow CSCE manner.

11. *Focus your attention.* Focus complete attention on your audience and the topic and *not* on yourself. Concentrate on the competencies you want to teach and control your nervousness. Focus on the learning needs of the students and apply possible methods, techniques and strategies to teach them effectively.

12. *Avoid over-consciousness in delivery.* Avoid over-consciousness that distracts your focus during subject delivery. As possible, video-tape your presentation so you can restudy it closely during breaks for needed adjustments.

Proper Voice in Teaching

Voice Factor in Teaching-and-Learning.   In teaching, the use of pleasant voice is a significant asset. Teachers are expected to possess agreeable voices for the magnetic attraction of the learners. A pleasant voice is easy to get along with—critical for a strong and successful lesson delivery. The teacher's voice must be clear, expressive, ideal in resonance and agreeable in pitch. It must be louder when needed and softer as required.

The process of learning is immensely affected by the disagreeable voice of a teacher during lesson presentation. A teacher may have some kinds of birth defect affecting his/her voice, but with the use of special strategies in speaking, the speech will be received interestingly by the listeners. It will not bore the students and will not affect the desire to pay close CIA and participate actively in ongoing discussions. Monotonous speech normally originates from the teacher's failure to vary the speed, volume and pitch of the voice during delivery. The use of proper voice in teaching is very significant to maintain continuous CIA of the learners.

Valuable Pointers in the Use of Voice.   One of the most effective tools you have as a good teacher is your competency to speak using a powerful voice. As a teacher, you have the ability to create an ideal learning atmosphere in the classroom with your voice. By using your voice agreeably, you can touch the hearts and minds of your students. For all you know, you may be remembered by your students as their favorite teacher for years to come, because of your teaching abilities heightened by your pleasant voice.

At this juncture, try to recall your high school days and think of your favorite subject teachers. What were their qualities that won your heart and mind? Chances are—your chosen favorite teachers possessed the abilities to speak and teach with good voices. They used pleasant voices in effective delivery of lessons. They touched your heart and mind and inspired you to learn because they succeeded in getting your full CIA through the application of their potent voices.

The following presentation suggests a list of useful hints that will help develop your speech techniques, using the appropriate voice—considering the pitch, volume, use of whisper, rate of speech, choice of words, pronunciation and expression.

1. *Talk with your students using a natural pitched voice.*   The pitch of your voice, i.e. the degree of lowness and highness in tone, should be natural and variable as used in actual conversation. You should know when to use the low pitch or high pitch level of voice to achieve needed emphasis. The pitch of your voice should vary accordingly while presenting the lesson to add attraction to the delivery. This strategy will make you more effective in getting the CIA of learners.

2. *Set your voice volume accordingly.*   The rise and fall of volume helps maintain the CIA of learners. Example in History, you may enumerate past Presidents of the country with different voice volumes to emphasize notable accomplishments. In making announcements, giving assignments and posing questions to the class, use a bit louder voice volume to enable everyone to hear you clearly. Never use a loud yelling voice—showing your impatience and hatred to the learners.

3. *Intrigue your students once in a while.*   A whisper is sometimes more effective in calling the CIA of learners. It signals intrigue, *blind items*, secret or classified

information. You may use the whispering strategy by putting a finger across your lips to signal for quietude and then speak in a whisper to introduce the intriguing story. Example: *"I have got a new juicy story to tell you. Listen carefully and enjoy the Shalala."*[28] Then, proceed with your story, which must be related to the lesson always. Whisper strategy must be used occasionally only. If you use it every time you tell a story, it will soon lose its appeal to intrigue.

4. *Maintain an ideal rate of speech.* Your rate of speech should be based on the concept, idea or emotion that is being communicated to the learners. Complicated subject matter must be presented slowly and deliberately. It is important that you consider the learning ability of your learners, to determine the ideal rate of speech delivery. In general, changes in the rate of speech create pleasing vibrations and produce the needed emphasis for effective learning.

5. *Choose your words carefully.* The right words in the right place are the keynote in effective speech. You must choose your words carefully and develop your sentences clearly and logically. Do not use high-flown terms that are not familiar with the learners. Consider the educational level of the students and use terms that are common to their vocabularies. Your job is to teach clearly and *not* to confuse. If it is a must to use complex terms during discussion—use them, but be sure to simplify the terms later. Always use CSCE sentences, when explaining and avoid unnecessary words and phrases.

6. *Pronounce your words distinctly clear.* A teacher must always strive for clarity of expression by speaking distinctively. Words and syllables must be enunciated or pronounced clearly, especially when teaching a large group. New terms used in the lesson must be enunciated properly and must be explained simply to learners. Avoid slurring, mumbling or swallowing of the words.

7. *Be sincere with your expressions.* In classroom setting, *what* and *how* you say a word is significant. Use sincere and expressive voice to entice the learners to struggle in learning new concepts. Show emotional RLEC to learners, especially those who seemed to have very little encouragement at home. Use calm, sincere and steady voice when the students become over-excited—to control the situation.

    Show pride and appreciation to the learners as they proved cooperative and helpful. On scheduled special events, share your enthusiasm through the tone of your voice. As you speak, manifest a compassionate facial expression, supported by the appropriate tone and pitch of your voice. Show your genuine concern as you teach and never hesitate to inject emotional feelings into your voice. All these motivate the students to learn and to become expressive, too.

---

[28] Note: "Shalala" is one of the TV hosts/comedians in the current Channel-5 program entitled, "Juicy." He is famous for his intriguing blind items and flashbacks about top movie personalities. His round face, big eyes and thick lips are enough assets to make many viewers laugh.

MODULE 9
QUESTIONING TECHNIQUES

> In teaching, questioning technique is an *art*. It is an effective tool to reach out the hidden level of the learners' inherent competencies.

Gauging Learners' Competencies

Introduction.   The art of good questioning is one of the required skills in any teaching-and-learning process. It is the teacher's effective tool in reaching out and measuring the hidden levels of students' inherent abilities. It can also serve as a preliminary basis for planning, organizing, implementing, managing, controlling and evaluating whatever learning enhancement efforts are required for learners' holistic development growths.

Basically, a certain level of skill, method and social (SMS) competencies are intrinsic among learners. It is therefore the function of a competent teacher to analyze and gauge the hidden level of learners' abilities—to hone them further to the highest degree of productive learning competencies.

The instructor's daily exposures to students during lesson presentation/demonstration exercises offer very little guarantee for productive learning; the learners can assume receptiveness—as if understanding the lesson. In many cases, this can only be a passive absorption and *not* a positive indicator for active learning. Active learning is often manifested by serious, active and dominant students' participation in the ongoing classroom discussions and in the performance of related learning activities. This is the main reason why a teacher should ask thought-provoking questions to the learners during classroom sessions. The teacher must find the exact level of students' learning—to guide them to the highest degree of SMS competencies.

Objectives of Effective Questioning Technique.   A good teacher normally gathers factual information about the learners' existing competency level through the art of effective and evaluative questioning technique. The factual information gathered enables the teacher to explore the deeper level of learners' ability in thinking, feeling and doing things productively. As necessary, the teacher should guide the learners to develop more abilities; formulate concepts; make right, just and fair inferences; enhance creativity with imaginative thoughts and strengthen their critical thinking processes.

In general, a good teacher musters the serious, active and dominant participation of students in all class activities and related undertakings through the use of effective questioning technique. Effective questioning technique aims to:

1. *Improve class interest*. Thought-provoking questions awaken the native prides among learners. The learners are dared to stand up and assert their rights to do *what* they

are doing; and, to be in the position *where* they are. Such feelings of self-worth and self-respect challenges learners to concentrate deepest on concepts and ideas being discussed, thus generating class' CIA—resulting to serious, active and dominant students' participation. In general, learners are more interested to listen to a class member, rather than to the lengthy lesson discussion of the teacher. They feel proud when permitted to ask questions and to respond to questions raised by the teacher and peers.

2. *Stimulate learners' thinking.* The "question-and-answer" technique in teaching, otherwise known as *recitation*, makes the learners directly responsible for their learning. During graded recitation, the learners pay closer attention and interest on the subject being discussed. The learners are stimulated to think more about the lesson, knowing that they could be questioned anytime. Questions however should not come solely from the instructor. The students should be allowed to ask provocative questions to peers—a way of sustaining CIA among learners.

3. *Adjust instructions accordingly.* The learners' answers to provocative questions enable the teacher to measure the rate of learning on the students. In cases where the class consistently fails to respond correctly, the teacher must re-explain the concepts/ideas in CSCE manner. The teacher must ensure that every lesson is learned fully by the students.

4. *Reveal students' attitudes.* The learners' responses to questions often indicate their true interest and attitudes towards the subject and the entire degree program. If a teacher discovers a learner with low interest and negative attitudes towards learning, he/she must talk to the learner personally. The teacher must delve deeper into the problem—touch the learner's heart and mind—to motivate and guide him/her to go on and strive hardest for a successful future.

5. *Allow learners to contribute.* Provocative questions often produce relevant and valuable ideas coming from learners, based on their own experiences, e.g. in work, through reading or surfing Internet. The teacher must adopt good ideas contributed by the learners that are applicable and relevant to modern education. Such contributions are valuable in adding variety to lesson materials. For each contribution however, the teacher must give due credit and recognition to the contributor—a way to maintain the learner's support and cooperation.

6. *Provide reinforcement of main points.* Retention of important ideas/concepts is made easier by frequent recalls through question-and-answer. A teacher purposely asks questions pertaining to a particular idea/concept to emphasize its importance and to store such in the permanent memory storage. Responses to questions during oral evaluations reinforce learning of ideas/concepts among learners.

7. *Evaluate effectiveness of instruction.* The best strategy in checking the learning of ideas/concepts is by direct questioning *during* and *after* the lesson. A question during the lesson enables the teacher to know if the learners are following the discussion. Questions after the lesson tell the teacher as to what degree of abilities the students have learned—allowing teaching adjustments, if necessary.

The Art of Questioning

Characteristics of an Effective Question.   In general, effective questions influence the structure and direction of the lesson. Spontaneous questions that come out so suddenly during the actual lesson discussion are acceptable but for more effective results, the questions should be constructed purposely and accordingly to the target objectives of the lesson. The succeeding discussion outlines basic characteristics that are common to good and effective questions, which can maximize teaching-and-learning outcomes. For a holistic teaching-and-learning process, effective questions should:

1. *Serve a specific purpose.*   A question should be planned and designed for specific or definite purpose. For example, a question may be asked to emphasize a major concept, while another may be used to stimulate active interest and attention of learners. Another question may be raised to measure learners' level of understanding on the ongoing discussion, while later question may be asked for the purpose of recall and learning reinforcement.

2. *Be easy to understand.*   Questions should be constructed using simple terms and plain language for easy understanding of learners. Avoid lengthy questions that may confuse students. Direct and simply-worded questions are understood easily and are the best ones to use in the teaching-and-learning process.

3. *Emphasize a single point.*   An effective question emphasizes a single point only. Avoid asking complicated question that requires several responses from a single student. If the question calls for several answers, allow other learners to give their shares with the answers. It is always unfair to require a student to give lengthy and detailed answers to a question. This can be misconstrued as a discrimination practice by some short-tempered students.

4. *Require a definite answer.*   An effective question requires a definite answer. To obtain a definite answer, the question must be given in CSCE manner. A vague or unclear question equally gets a vague answer.

5. *Discourage guessing.*   As possible, avoid asking closed-ended question that can be answered by "yes" or "no," unless the answer is followed by explanation of the reasons behind it. Mostly, this style of questioning encourages guessing.

6. *Suit the level of students' abilities.*   The questions should vary in the degree of difficulties and should be asked according to the level of learners' abilities. More difficult questions can be asked to students with higher level of intelligence. Easy to answer questions should be directed to less intelligent learners. A slow-learner who answers an easy question correctly reinforces self-confidence. He/she is also motivated to study harder to be able to answer questions every time when asked. In contrast, a learner who fails to answer a difficult question experiences shame which can result to de-motivation. This is the reason why a teacher should adjust questions according to the level of learners' abilities.

7. *Be logical and sequential.* Effective question is logical or reasonable. It can be answered with correct reasoning. It should also be sequential in arrangement, i.e. according to the flow of ideas/concepts that are being studied during the lesson.

8. *Be directed uniformly to all levels.* Some teachers ask questions directed to the intelligent members of the class only. The intention is good—i.e. to get the correct answers which can be shared by the entire class. But, this is not an ideal practice. It may condition other members of the class to become passive listeners only. Questions should be asked uniformly to various levels of the class to motivate and challenge everyone to strengthen imaginative thinking and critical creativity.

9. *Follow up on students' responses.* Effective questions can generate positive and negative responses from the learners. Positive responses should be reinforced for permanent learning. Accordingly, negative responses should be corrected tactfully and promptly right there on the spot.

10. *Allow students reasonable time to think.* The teacher should give reasonable time for the learners to think after they are questioned. He should not goad the student to answer the question right away. In case where a student takes a longer period before beginning to answer, the teacher can facilitate the exercise by indirectly guiding the learner towards the proper answer.

Common Types of Question. The most common types of question applied in formal classroom instructions fall under the following classifications, i.e.:

1. *Factual Question.* This type of question requires a reasonably straight-forward or simple answer, based on actual facts or awareness. It is usually at the lowest level of cognitive or affective process and falls under the *close-ended* type of question. A close-ended question gets quick response from the student. It can be answered often by a word, a brief phrase, or by plain "yes" or "no." Examples:

   a. "According to President P'Noy, who is his *real boss*?"
   b. "Is President P'Noy serious in saying: *Filipino people are my real boss*?"

2. *Conceptual Question.* This question requires a different level of comprehension, application and analysis wherein learners make inferences or conjectures (that can predict different outcomes) based on personal awareness or on the various materials read. It is an open-ended style, leaving the person answering the question to elicit more thinking/information. Example:

   • "Reflecting over the 'Tuwid-na-Landas' concept of President P'Noy, what happens if 'his straight road' eventually leads to farther corruptions?"

   Note: This is not the true vision in P'Noy's slogan. Here, the learners make their own inferences as to what can happen—if P'Noy fails to stop corruption during his six-year term as President of the Philippines.

3. *Evaluative Question.* This type of question usually requires a higher level of cognitive and emotional judgments. In answering evaluative questions, students may apply combination of logical and affective thinking process, or may use the comparative analysis during evaluation. The answer to the question is often analyzed at multiple levels and from different perspectives, before arriving at a synthesized conclusion. It is categorized as falling under the *open-ended* question or probing style, requiring comprehensive answers. Examples:

   a. "In your opinion, what are the marked similarities and differences between the administrations of P'Noy and that of GMA?"
   a. "Why and how can the August 23, 2010 Luneta hostage-taking incident affect the political relationships between the Philippines and China? Who could have possibly leaked the Incident Investigation Review Committee (IIRC) report to Hong Kong authorities, even before the official review of P'Noy? What do you think are the hidden motives behind this treacherous (leaking) act?"

Strategies in Handling Questions Effectively. During classroom discussions, it is a normal thing when a student will suddenly raise hands to ask you various types of questions. A student may purposely ask you a difficult question to test your competency as a teacher. You will easily recognize such intention based on his/her general behavior while shooting the question. Assuming that the student's intention is just to test your abilities, ignoring the student and *not* answering the question can generate a feeling of disrespect. Any difficult question raised by learner should be addressed tactfully to maintain your respectable and authoritative status inside and outside classroom. There is no reason for teaching—when students do not believe in your professional competencies. Below are some *strategies* on how to handle students' questions effectively, i.e.:

1. *Rephrase vague questions.* You may rephrase vague questions for purpose of clarity and to insure that all class members will hear and understand the query. Rephrasing unclear question—in CSCE manner—also sends a strong message to the inquiring student that you understand the question perfectly. This will erase doubt that you do not know the answer and will contribute more to the learners' respect being enjoyed by your status.

2. *Answer questions directly.* For a factual question which is reasonably easy, you may redirect it to the other learners to encourage active class participation, critical thinking and problem-solving skill. If the question is conceptual and *no* class member can answer it appropriately (and you have the answer), you may answer it right away to save time. Answering questions directly takes less time than engaging class members to come up with correct answers. When answering the question, be sure to go directly to the point—i.e. in CSCE manner. After responding, check if you have answered the question correctly by asking the inquiring student, e.g.: "Did I answer your question correctly?" "Did I give you the right answer?" "Did I satisfy your query?"

3. *Discourage irrelevant questions.* There are times when a student asks irrelevant question to get class attention or possibly to embarrass the teacher. Handling such a question presents a slight dilemma. If you allow and consider it, just like an ordinary appropriate question, you may encourage the questioning student to ask more of

this irrelevant query. On the other hand, if you answer roughly or turn him/her down abruptly, you may discourage that student from asking any other kinds of question further. The same can hold true also to other members of the class. In handling such a situation, you need to be tactful in explaining *what part* of the question is inappropriate or irrelevant to the subject being discussed.

4.   *Touch the heart and mind of antagonistic students.*   It is not unusual in a class situation to find a student who seems antagonistic toward the teacher or possibly hostile to the subject matter. Such student usually asks question with expressed disagreements with much different ideas from the rest of the class. This kind of behavior usually stems from emotional gripes rather than intellectual concerns. As a teacher, you must be tactful in answering question from such learner. It is best for you to meet the student outside your class. Show him/her genuine RLEC to help. Ask exactly what seems to be the problem. Explain that you are inside the classroom exactly like a parent, who has the obligation to love and serve every student. Touch the heart and mind of the learner and assure understanding. A heart-to-heart talk is often effective in making the student reflects on bad behavior in the class, thus instituting positive moral reforms.

5.   *Postpone answering particular questions.*   A question, when asked and answered correctly, hastens students' learning. You must communicate to all students clearly, indicating willingness to answer their questions. In general, you should answer questions right away to encourage students to ask more questions. Avoid postponing answers as much as possible. On certain occasions however, you may decide to postpone answering particular questions, e.g.:

   a.   The question needs a longer time to explain complex concepts.   You may say: "Alright class, this question needs a longer period to explain complex concepts. We don't have much time now, so we are postponing this for next discussion. Don't forget to remind me about it in our next meeting."
   b.   The question is of interest only to a few class members.   You may tell them: "The question concerns a few members of the class only. Those who are interested can meet me after the class for the answer, okay?"
   c.   The question is going to be covered in upcoming sessions.   You may say: "This question is going to be covered at length in our upcoming sessions. We are postponing discussion of this question for our subject next week."

6.   *Redirect questions to other learners.*   Redirecting some easy questions to other members of the class for further elaboration of an issue is a good practice, if there is ample time. You can ask other students—especially the silent type—to respond to the questions and share views on the issue. This brings student participation, while asserting students of their roles as positive contributors to learning process.

7.   *Answer difficult questions tactfully.*   A teacher is always considered an expert information source. There are instances though when you will get conceptual or evaluative questions that are too difficult-to-answer. Admitting to the students that you *do not know* the answer will lessen your credibility. If you are not ready to answer the question, postpone it for the next session tactfully. You may explain

to them, e.g.: "Class, this is truly a very significant question. However, we need a longer period to elucidate the various complicated concepts within. We are going to discuss it comprehensively during our next meeting. Thank you, Mr. . . . for raising the question." Note: Giving credit to the student-questioner cools off the intention to make further objections. Make sure however to do needed research and prepare to answer the question clearly during the next session.

If you decide to fake an answer just to assert your status, there is a possibility that your students may find it out. For instance, if the student-inquirer had already done an advance research on the subject, he/she may argue and insist on the correct answer. This situation can seriously damage your credibility. It is a must that you are always prepared to answer every question correctly to maintain the students' confidence in you. Always remember, even a close-ended question—answerable by *yes* or *no*—must be answered clearly and correctly.

8. *Involve majority in class discussions.* It is a good practice to involve majority of the students to answer questions during classroom discussions. Usually, students have considerable differences of opinions about the answer to particular issues. Allowing majority class members to share their opinions or suggestions is more ideal than the traditional classroom setting, where the instructor and a few students monopolize the discussion, with the rest of the class assuming as passive listeners only. In many classroom situations, it is very common to have one or more students monopolizing the discussion process. Do not allow this old practice in teaching-and-learning. You should accord equal preference to everybody, most especially to those who are not participating actively. You can give equal chance to others by saying: "Alright class, let us hear comments from others who have not given their inputs yet. Now, we will hear from Mr./Miss. . . .."

9. *Encourage students to ask questions.* During discussion of subject highlights, you should give opportunities for the students to ask questions, to evaluate if they are following your presentation. After explaining an important concept or idea on the topic, pause for a while and ask the whole class by saying: "Alright class, any questions? Are you with me? Did you get my explanations?" This strategy will allow you to know if there is a need to repeat explanation of difficult concepts. It will also give time to organize your thoughts before going further to the next concept or idea. Give the students time to ask relevant questions before you move on. Call on students with raised hands and make sure you do not miss any one. Be clever in reading the behavior of each student. When you see members of the class with wrinkled foreheads, shaking or scratching their heads—it is evident that they are confused with your presentation. You therefore need to repeat and improve your discussion using the CSCE style.

10. *Answer students' questions adequately.* In responding to a student's question, you must satisfy the questioner as best as you can. Your must answer in CSCE manner and very much direct to the point. After your answer, evaluate for clarity and correctness by asking the student, e.g. "Did I give you the correct and clear answer?" This strategy allows you to know if your answer satisfies the learner fully. Moreover, this practice enhances more accurate communication between you and the students.

11. *Focus attentively to students' comments.* Focus your attention attentively to the student who is questioning or commenting. Listening attentively to a question or comment communicates a message to your class about the kind of ethico-moral attitude that you have as a person. A good teacher looks directly to the students who is talking or discussing issues. You must show that you are following his/her discussions by nodding your head or by reinforcing statements made during the explanation. Little sign of approval like this means a lot to the learners. They are assured of their importance and are feeling more identified with you.

12. *Avoid being misunderstood.* There are times a teacher may unconsciously do something that can communicate negative impact in the minds of learners. For example, you may accidentally look at your wrist watch while a student is asking you a question. In some cases, this may be misunderstood by the learner, thinking that the question he/she is raising is irrelevant and a waste of precious time. This misinterpretation can embarrass the learner, resulting to a communication gap (between you and the learner). But in reality, you simply want to check the exact time to find out if there is still a chance to hold related practical demonstrations on the subject. To avoid being misunderstood, your movements or gestures inside the classroom must be acceptable to the learners at all times.

13. *Never embarrass anyone of your students.* As a good teacher, you must avoid embarrassing any student in your class. A student may ask silly question, but this is not a ground to put him/her down. Instead of responding roughly—knowing that the student's question is lacking on standard ethico-moral values—you may ask a probing question. You may redirect the question back to the student by saying: "Your question is pretty difficult. If you were in my shoes, what would be your correct answer?" Then, make the needed follow-ups.

14. *Allow students reasonable time to think.* When asking questions, allow students reasonable time to think about the possible correct answers. For conceptual or evaluative question, it deserves a considerable waiting time. Questions at higher level require a longer waiting time for the learner to think before he/she can adequately answer. After waiting for a minute or two and the learner has not responded, you can ask another student who may know the answer. Also, you may assign the question in groups of two or three students to work on viable solutions to solve the problem. Such strategy will make all of the students to participate actively working on the correct answers—and not just the brighter ones dominating the classroom activities.

MODULE 10
LEARNING DISTRACTIONS

> The awkward *mannerism* in speaking, writing or behaving during the daily lesson delivery *distracts* the contact, interest and attention (CIA) of learners; and, eventually *impedes* the learning process.

Occasional Learning Distractions

Introduction.   *Learning distraction* is anything that draws away the mind or attention of the learners from ongoing lesson discussion due to confusion or disturbance of thoughts. Learning distraction can be classified into two categories, i.e. *occasional* and *repetitive*. Occasional learning distractions happen only once in a while during classroom sessions, while repetitive learning distractions occur very often during every day meeting. In general, learning distractions—whether occasional or repetitive in nature—distract the *contact*, *interest* and *attention* (CIA) of the learners, thus eventually impeding the smooth flow of learning process. As a rule, a teacher must avoid or control any form of learning distractions during sessions to ensure effectiveness of instructions.

In ordinary classroom setting, the eyes and ears of learners are crucial channels for stimulation of changes in the mental activities of their bodies. Occasionally, when a teacher improperly speaks—the learners hear and see it immediately. When an instructor writes illegibly on the blackboard—the students notice it easily. And, when a teacher behaves negatively inside the classroom—the entire class recognizes it so suddenly. Learning distractions can result from ineffective speaking, writing, behaving; negative personal appearance, behavior, mannerism and other contributing factors.

Distraction from Speaking.   The teacher's language accent while discussing the lesson generally distracts CIA of learners. A new teacher for example, who hails from the Ilocos or Visayan Region, may have a strong native dialectal accent. This speech condition is natural to many persons who were born and raised from these regions—and not necessarily to all. Teachers who finish their degree in education within these regions and who get teaching assignments therein after graduation, will *not* generate distraction when speaking or discussing subjects inside the classrooms. Their dialectal accent in speaking and the unusual pronunciation of words will not be treated as peculiar by the students, because such is a natural and prevailing practice.

In contrast, a native Ilocano or Visayan and a regionally educated teacher, who is assigned to teach in the Tagalog Region, may be seen as funny by the students because of dialectal accent and unusual pronunciations of words during instructions. This does not mean that the students are with tribalistic attitudes. To them, this form of distraction is a natural thing because they are not used to hear instructions with strong dialectal accent. Anyway, this type of distraction is only temporary. It mainly happens during the first few days of class meetings with the new teacher. When the students realize that their teacher comes from a region with native dialectal accent, they accept him/her, for as long as the speech is understandable. Of course, it is always best for the teacher to improve in the overall speech techniques during lesson presentation.

Distraction from Writing.   During lesson presentation, a teacher who emphasizes highlights or important points of the subject on the blackboard must write legibly, i.e. in the CSCE manner. Writing on the blackboard using the "chicken-scratch" technique or the confusing "medical prescription" style will surely distract the CIA of learners. Non-legible notes written on the blackboard confuses the minds of learners because they cannot read and understand the information being introduced. In such a condition, learning distraction may result. In worst case scenario, it can even create a rift in the mutual teacher-students relationships. Some students may not be able to control themselves and make offensive remarks about the teacher's handwriting. Should this happen, a hot-headed instructor may find it degrading and thus, heated arguments between the questioner and the teacher can take place.

To avoid distraction and confusions brought about by illegible or impossible to read handwriting, a teacher must exert best efforts to improve on his/her writing style. If it is difficult to do this, the teacher must avoid using the chalkboard strategy. Instead, he/she may present the lesson with the use of actual objects, PowerPoint, OHP, films and other modern technology teaching aids and devices.

Distraction from Physical Appearance.   The sub-standard physical appearance of a teacher—e.g. improper dressing, unusual posture and gesture—distracts CIA of learners. Similarly, a teacher with inborn physical defect—e.g. one leg is shorter, or one hand is smaller than the other—may also distract the learners' CIA. Again, this particular type of distraction can be temporary only. The students will learn later to accept and respect the teacher's physical condition, for as long as they understand the lesson being taught. In general, the students are adept to know that they have very little or nothing to say about the unfortunate natural physical appearance of their instructor.

An instructor must meet certain standards in physical appearance and body control, i.e. posture and gesture, because the learners normally react to what they see. Physical appearance and body control are highly expressive. When attractive, they can stimulate learners' CIA toward an excellent and enthusiastic presentation. If sub-standard, it can make the lesson dull and uninteresting—with very little response from the learners.

As an instructor, your physical appearance must always be neat and respectable in front of students. The students consider you as their model. They will respect you when you are smart in looks and acting as a true professional. In addition, your posture and gesture must also be attractive and acceptable to all learners to avoid distractions. Below are suggested pointers on how you can maintain correct posture and gesture:

1. *Correct Posture.*   In literal meaning, *correct posture* in teaching is the right positioning of the body during lesson presentation. While discussing, you must assume a position where the entire class can see you and vice-versa. Be physically and mentally alert. You must stand erect, with weight evenly-balanced on your feet. Your arms and hands must hang freely at your sides until you need to use them. If you cannot do this, clasp your hands behind you or rest one hand temporarily on the lectern, if available. Do not twist or wring your hands nervously. Also, do not stand rigidly in attention glued to one spot only and avoid moving all the time also. If you keep moving and moving

all the time, you may be mistaken as a rapper. When you need to move, do it naturally and spontaneously with a purpose. Of course, with increased teaching experience, you will later refine your movements, making them attractive—and not distractive.

Figuratively, the term "correct posture" can also mean the right mental or spiritual attitude. A teacher with right mental and spiritual attitude possesses deep reverence for God, able to develop exemplary ethico-moral values—particularly discipline, character and individuality. Such correct posture makes the teacher think, feel, speak and do things right, just and fair. It is very critical for a teacher to possess the right mental and spiritual attitude to gain the respect of learners and secure their full CIA for meaningful learning and total developments.

2. *Correct Gesture.*   *Correct gesture* is the right movements used instead of words—of the hands, arms, or any parts of the body—to help express an idea or feeling. Your arms, hands and body are the principal tools in reinforcing oral expressions. When instructing, your gestures must be natural and spontaneous, arising from conviction, emotion and enthusiasm. Do not overemphasize every statement with gestures or else you can develop distracting mannerisms which will defeat the educational purpose. Rarely-used gestures can be emphatic, but gestures used very often during instructions can produce distractive results.

Other Occasional Learning Distractions.   Other occasional learning distractions do not necessarily originate from the classroom. They may come from different sources. Generally, schools are built in safe and quiet places to ensure achievement of educational goals. In cases where a school is situated in less ideal area, e.g. closed to main road or within a busy business district, it is the teacher's duty now to control the situation so that learners will focus attention on the lesson. Other occasional learning distractions are:

1. *A passing parade or demonstration.*   Any ongoing parade, civil or political demonstrations—as seen through the classroom windows—can trigger distraction. The kind of class-control that you will do depends on the duration of the exercise. If the event will take a long period, you must control the class and proceed with the lesson. If it will need a few minutes only, you may join the students in watching the passing activity, while giving positive comments on its relevance.

2. *Loud noises external to the classroom.*   If the noise will take a long period, control the class and proceed with the lesson. If noise is just temporary, e.g. from a passing ambulance or fire truck, wait until the noise subsides.

3. *A misbehaving student.*   As a general rule, every teacher is a guidance teacher. You must approach case of misbehaving student with RLEC. Find the causes of misbehavior tactfully and remedy or solve the problem right away.

4. *External smoke or foul smell getting inside.*   You must investigate and decide right away on how to remedy this form of distraction. This condition is a health-hazard and it demands your urgent or immediate action.

5. *Uncovered visual aids not in use.*   A good teacher always keeps the visual aids safe and covered after using, to avoid creating learning distractions.

6. *Overhead projector left switched on.* After using an overhead projector, you must not forget to unplug it from the electrical source and put it safely in an ideal place inside the classroom where it will not invite distraction. After the lesson, you must return it back to the laboratory section to free you from responsibility.

Repetitive Learning Distractions

Mannerism Defined. Mannerism implies the *repetitive* or "too much use of some manner in speaking, writing, or behaving"[29] that makes the act to look strange, peculiar, queer and distracting. Mannerism is like a sickness, which is most difficult to cure or treat. It is always distractive to learning. Certain mannerisms in speaking, writing, or behaving may be amusing to the eyes of the learners—if used very occasionally.

When a teacher *repeatedly* applies sub-standard acts during daily lesson discussions, the acts become awkward and disgusting. These awkward acts develop into mannerisms of queer habits that are difficult to rectify. In many instances, teachers may *not* be aware of the mannerisms developing as part of their habits. This is true to many individuals; they only realize certain shortcomings when a trusted someone reminds them purposely. It is therefore necessary for a teacher to invite a close colleague to sit down with the class; observe the instruction proceedings; and, make constructive criticisms on the entire performance delivery. The teacher must seriously do the needed innovations to improve weaknesses in teaching procedures, as recommended by the critiquing colleague.

Some Forms of Mannerism. The meaningful contents and good lesson preparation are *not* exact guarantees to effective lesson delivery, which can culminate to productive learning. Effective lesson presentation for productive learning is one that maintains the CIA of learners, thus generating active participation in the ongoing topic discussion that hastens total learning and developments. To maintain the CIA of learners, a teacher must avoid creating learning distractions emanating from speech, writing, personal appearance (e.g. posture and gesture) and from other sources.

The worst form of learning distraction is the strange, peculiar, queer and repetitive acts, called *mannerism* that an instructor unconsciously does *very often* during lesson delivery. As already stated, a teacher may *not* be completely aware of the distracting mannerism being shown to the students during the course of lesson discussion, unless a friend or close colleague has seen and has told about it. This is the reason why it is a must for a teacher to request a trusted friend or colleague to sit/observe in the class and critique during one or two sessions. Any constructive comments coming from a trusted associate will surely help the teacher to rectify and avoid distracting mannerisms during lesson delivery. The following presentation portrays some awkward mannerisms done unconsciously and repeatedly by few instructors, thus impeding the smooth flow of learning process among the students, i.e.:

1. *The Senior Citizen.* This is an instructor who leans or slumps heavily over the lectern or teaching table— and without movements, manifesting an air of total exhaustion— while discussing a topic. This posture can qualify the teacher to become a member of the Senior Citizen's Group.

---

[29] Op. Cit. Nault, W. H. et. al.

2. *The MERALCO Post.* It describes a teacher whose hands are kept clasped in front below the waist; with feet firmly anchored in the floor and with very limited movements during the entire lesson discussion.

3. *The Rapper.* This refers to a teacher, who never stands still, keeps pacing the classroom briskly while talking fast with continuous gestures of hands, arms and other parts of the body.

4. *The Chained Elephant.* This pertains to a teacher who stands with the weight first on one foot and later, on the other. Sometimes, the non-weight bearing leg is positioned crossing the other loaded leg.

5. *The Swordsman-Warrior.* It characterizes a teacher who uses a pointer or stick as if it were a sword; constantly performing dueling actions with the pointer, without putting it down during the entire lesson presentation.

6. *The Monkey-Scratcher.* It portrays a teacher who keeps scratching some kind real or imaginary itches. It also describes a teacher who frequently touches various parts of the face while teaching, e.g. nose, ears, cheeks and lips.

7. *The MRT-LRT Rider.* This pictures a teacher who keeps putting hands in and out of the pockets every now and then, as if counting the loose change to ensure paying a home-bound ticket with fare hikes on MRT-LRT services.

8. *The Juggler.* It represents a teacher presenting a lesson, who keeps fiddling with available teaching aids, e.g. chalk, marker, pointer, pen, pencil, etc. probably to practice certain skill or to control nervousness.

9. *The Handcuffed Preacher.* This is a teacher who always hides the hands clasped behind the back while presenting lesson. This position can be misinterpreted as similar to a military man standing in full attention. In worst case scenario, it can be misconstrued as a handcuffed snatcher or preacher.

10. *The Face-to-Face Accuser.* It depicts the mannerism of a teacher who uses the forefinger continuously, pointing to the class when emphasizing ideas or concepts. Pointing the forefinger repeatedly to the class can annoy students, who may feel that the teacher is accusing them "face-to-face" of some negative acts.

Beating Learning Distractions. Rectifying learning distractions is not a big problem for the teachers today. The use of modern equipment—e.g. computer, video camera, LCD projector, etc.—is now a common practice in teaching and learning. In most educational institutions, video equipment is now readily available. As a teacher, you must exert best efforts to discover your own shortcomings in presenting lesson and do the needed solutions to rectify them later. One way to see it yourself, the sub-standard teaching practices you are doing, is to video-tape one or two sessions of your actual lesson presentation. In doing this practice, you should observe the following pointers:

1. Prepare yourself to teach. For guidelines, review and follow the recommended "Ten Commandments in Teaching" (Page 68-72).
2. Hire a good cameraman to videotape the class proceedings properly.
3. During your relaxed moments at home, run the video film, sit down and watch it very closely on your own.
4. If you so decide, invite a close colleague to watch the film with you and ask him/her to spot and note for negative practices resulting to learning distractions.
5. Be sure to take down notes yourself of what strikes you as negative performances during the entire presentation. Ask your colleague to do the same also.
6. Rate yourself using the standard "Annual Performance Review Form" designed by your school administration. Make notes under the criterion or item, which you feel you need to improve and how. Ask your colleague to rate you also using the same standard performance review form.
7. Watch it for three to four times and identify teaching distractions that may result from your speech, writing, personal appearance and mannerisms.
8. If there are a few things needing changes, rectify specific items according to its importance. Do not try to change all shortcomings at the same time or you may end up being distracted yourself, thus losing your interest to improve.

Summary.   Learning distraction is anything that draws away the mind or attention of the learners from the ongoing lesson discussion due to confusion or disturbance of thoughts. *Occasional* learning distractions are manifested by the instructor once in a while—*not* repeatedly—originating from negative speech, writing, behavior and personal appearance (e.g. dressing, posture and gesture) and other external sources. This form of distraction can be rectified easily with serious efforts coming from the teacher.

Mannerism is a *repetitive* form of distraction done unconsciously by the teacher using some manner in speaking, writing, or behaving—making the act to look strange, peculiar, queer and annoying among the students. In essence, mannerism can be classified as a form of sickness, which is extra-difficult for the teacher to cure. The repeated practices of sub-standard manners during lesson discussions usually make the session annoying, thus distracting the CIA of learners. And where there are distractions standing on the way of teaching, the students' learning progress is considerably hindered and affected.

As a rule, the teacher must avoid and control mannerism that will distract the CIA of learners. Effective and productive teaching-and-learning takes place mostly when the students concentrate mainly on the valuable ideas and concepts being presented in the class, without getting distracted by the negative mannerisms of the instructor.

MODULE 11
EVALUATION TECHNIQUES

> A written test gets a *telling* answer only, while a performance test gets a *doing* answer. Now . . . which is your choice?

Evaluation Procedures

Introduction.   *Evaluation* is a significant phase in any formal teaching-and-learning program. It is a process of assessing the desirable changes in the mental, emotional and social behavior and development of the learners based upon standard criteria, e.g. formulated attainable objectives; organized curriculum contents; levels of learners' readiness and abilities; needs for targeted developmental changes; appropriate facilitation of learning process and periodic measurement of learning outcomes.

There are a variety of evaluation procedures used by the instructor to appraise the actual learning achievements, e.g. oral exams, performance test, check list, group report, achievement or objective test and many others. These evaluation procedures are being applied to measure the extent of desirable changes achieved, in order to:

1. Determine the appropriate placement of learners;
2. Diagnose the marked learning difficulties of students;
3. Establish needs for more effective guidance in learning;
4. Specify current productive learning needs;
5. Assess the effectiveness of teaching methods, techniques and strategies; and,
6. Adjust the specific curriculum contents, as needed.

This particular section will center mainly on the common types of achievement tests or objective tests commonly used to measure the skill, method and social competencies of the learners—as standard requirement for professional proficiency and productivity.

Achievement Testing Terminologies.   *Quiz, test* and *exam* are forms of achievement tests. These three "terms" are mostly used interchangeably in teaching. However, they have marked differences, considering the *scope* or content covered and the *weight* or value in calculating the final grade for a specific subject. In general, these tests are also considered as *objective tests* because they are oriented towards appraisal of significant, generalized and permanent learning objectives.

A *quiz* is very limited in scope, normally with 20-30 items only and is administered in 15 minutes or less. It is usually given after completing the discussion of two to three related topics (in a module) covered in one or two days period. A good teacher usually gives one to three "recorded" short quizzes weekly. When students know that a number of quizzes are lined up for every week, they are compelled to study harder and get ready for the quizzes. Such teaching strategy sustains students' motivation to study seriously in order to get high grades during quizzes. This motivational practice eventually becomes as part of the learners' quality that facilitates learning developments. As a rule, the more quizzes are administered per week, the harder the students study and prepare.

A *test* has a wider scope in the topics covered, e.g. a complete particular module. It is longer than a quiz—normally consists of 30-50 items—and is allotted a time of 20-30 minutes. There can be six to eight recorded tests within a subject per trimester/semester, depending on the teacher's discretion. As already mentioned, when more tests are given, the more study efforts the students put in.

An *exam* or examination is a more comprehensive form of testing. It is generally given at three scheduled periods within the term (trimester/semester). It covers several modules or chapters designated for the entire subject—with 100-150 items or more and are allotted one hour or more to complete. Elementary, secondary and tertiary school levels require a preliminary exam; a midterm exam; and, a final exam within a term.

When assigning percentage weight for calculating the periodic grades in a specific subject, 10-20% is normally given to tests/quizzes; 20-40% is allotted to long exams (i.e. prelim, midterm or final exams). The remaining percentages are reserved accordingly for class recitation, reporting, project, assignment, attendance, behavior and other criteria. The final grade is the average of the computed three periodic grades.

Functions of Achievement Tests. The achievement test serves important functions in teaching-and-learning. It helps the teacher assess students whether they are learning what are expected of them to learn or not. It enables the instructor to understand if the lesson presentation is successful or not. It provides indicators to students as to what topics or skills they have not learned yet and therefore must concentrate on. The test results motivate the students to structure their academic efforts, thus reinforcing learning. Basically, achievement test can be used as an aid in improving instruction; providing incentive for learning; criterion for the computation of grades and basis for selection and guidance. These are explained further in the succeeding presentation below, i.e.:

1. *Improving instruction.* The results from properly constructed achievement tests will reveal students' learning gaps or difficulties which can be corrected by teaching reinforcement. Where the test result is unsatisfactory, the teacher is guided as to the need for reviewing the students with all the materials already presented, ensuring that the learners retain the concepts and competencies more vividly and lasting. Such condition will enable the teacher to provide adequately for all the needs in effective learning—including innovations of various methods, techniques and strategies used during previous instructions.

2. *Incentive for learning.* The students learn better when they are held responsible for their learning. For example, the learners pay more attention in watching a training video-film when they know that a graded quiz or even an oral evaluation will be conducted after the show. Similarly, they listen attentively to the teacher's discussion if a quiz or an oral examination is scheduled to follow after the lesson. In general, an instructor who gives frequent tests makes the learners more alert, focused and serious to learn better because of the desire to get higher grades. Achievement testing is a basic motivation for learning—if done properly.

3. *Criterion for grading.* Achievement tests are administered by the teacher in order to determine if students have attained the prescribed standard in learning performances. In general, it is ideal to record the extent to which learners excel or fail during examination, based on the set marking criteria. This practice however should be explained clearly to the students to motivate them to study harder—and to prepare for all the achievement tests designed for the subject.

4. *Basis for selection and guidance.* Tests should *not* be given just for the purpose of selecting the best performing students in the class. The teacher should take special attention to identify the failing students and should give needed follow-up and guidance, so they can pass the prescribed standard performances along with the other class members. The test is not administered mainly to select the brightest among the students. Most importantly, it must identify those slow learners who need individualized remedial assistance.

Characteristics of a Good Test. School teachers and guidance counselors rely heavily on test results when making important decisions relative to many teaching and guidance functions. Because of this, the quality of examination is very significant in order to justify their test-guided decisions properly. For a more successful teaching-and-learning, good quality achievement test should possess the following *characteristics*, i.e.:

1. *Valid.* A *valid* test is one with appropriate results enabling the teacher to assess the level of students' achievement. Validity refers to the appropriateness of the interpretation of results; and, *not* of the test itself. A test is *valid* to the extent that it can measure the attainment of significant educational objectives. To ensure test validity, the teacher should follow a recognized procedure in constructing it. For example, the teacher may use lesson objectives as basis for test requirements so as to measure what has been taught. The selection of appropriate achievement test must also be considered. If the teacher wants to measure the skill competency of the learners, he/she must give a form of test that will require the learners to demonstrate the "doing" abilities. Achievement test must be designed in a CSCE manner for easy understanding. Information that is not directly related to the teaching points should be discarded from the test.

2. *Reliable.* A *reliable* test is trustworthy, accurate and free from error of the scores on it. The test items should represent significant objectives in the field for which it is intended. It must be constructed with consistency, appraising learners in the same way—considering identical time, conditions, materials, equipment, etc. Test standards applied to one learner must be applied to all. In addition, teaching points included in the test should not be repeatedly emphasized—as if the teacher is teaching mainly for purpose of examination. "Teaching for the test" is a spoon-feeding practice and must be avoided. The more responses required of the learners, the more reliable the test will be. All efforts must be taken to be more objective when marking the test. Tests should be constructed skillfully; be used discriminately; and, be scored carefully to become reliable.

3. *Objective.* An achievement test/examination is considered to be objective when it is constructed, administered and marked by the teacher free from bias and judgmental

opinion. Other forms of test, e.g. "essay" and "observation" may not likely cover an adequate and representative sample of objectives and are liable to become less objective. When giving essay form of test, there should be specific objective questions given to represent the explicit areas of *what is wanted* and the source of facts to use in answering the question. Also, in checking the essay, the use of well-defined and standard scoring key is needed to avoid subjectivity. A scoring key or rubric can be adopted when assigning marks, e.g. 50% *content*; 20% *grammar*, 15% *format*; and, 15% *neatness* (CGFN) of the answer.

4. *Discriminating.*   The test should be constructed in such a manner that it will detect or measure even the slight differences in the learners' achievements. This is very essential especially in giving the appropriate grades to the students.

5. *Comprehensive.*   The test should be comprehensive enough to include the major lesson objectives. It is true that it is impossible to cover every objective that is taught in the subject, but a sufficient number should be taken to provide a valid and reliable measure of learners' achievement within the subject.

6. *Simple.*   An achievement test should be easy to use (i.e. administer, mark and interpret). The time and effort utilized by the students in responding to the test questions should be justified in terms of expected learning achievements.

Achievement Test Construction.   Quiz, test and exam must be constructed skillfully to become effective. As a teacher, you should devote an adequate amount of time in developing a good periodic achievement test—i.e. carefully considering the format or layout of the test; desired learning outcomes to be measured; best suitable measuring item; range of items' difficulty; time allotment and the scoring criteria. Ideally, tests are designed to measure learners' achievement based on the standard educational objectives required in the course syllabus. Test items should assess the SMS competencies expected from the students. To keep abreast on how well the tests progressively reflect the course objectives, the teacher can maintain a student checklist, containing the specific SMS competencies targeted for the course. For every test administered, you can put a check mark under each competency learned. Below are some considerations you should take note when constructing a good achievement test, i.e.:

1. *Use various test formats.*   From this writer's experience, administering a variety of test formats helps in encouraging the students to do their level best during the evaluation process. Ordinarily, a teacher may administer short quizzes using the conventional *Fill-in the Blanks* or *True or False* types of test. For preliminary, midterm and final exams however, the combination of six types of test formats are normally used, e.g. *Identification; Fill-in the Blanks; True or False; Multiple-Choice; Matching-Type* and *Essay* tests. The *Identification, Fill-in the Blanks, True or False* and *Multiple-Choice* formats are recommended when assessing learners' mastery of specific abilities. *Essay* test questions assess comprehension or ability to synthesize, integrate and apply information to various situations. Be consistent in using standard test formats during midterm and final examinations. It is not logical if you change the combination of six types of test formats used during midterm into an *exclusive* Essay type in the final examination.

2. *Design the test layout professionally.* Give clear directions/instructions on how to answer the questions under each type of test. Proper margins and line spacing should be observed to make the test easy to read. Questions should be constructed based on the sequence of cumulative topics presented and covered inside the classroom, following the prescribed syllabus content. Cumulative tests enable the students to integrate acquired competencies, thus reinforcing what they have already learned. As already stated, the combination of six types of test formats are sequentially used in long examinations by many teachers, i.e. Identification; Fill-in the Blanks; True or False; Multiple-Choice; Matching-Type and Essay. You may seek the help of the Area Coordinator or a trusted colleague to read the test copy—to comment/validate effectiveness of your test construction and design.

3. *Begin your test with easy-to-answer questions.* If your examination is consists of 100 items, for example—you can make the first-10 test items very easy to answer by most of your students. When the learners are able to answer easier questions at the beginning of the test, they can overcome nervousness and develop self-confidence—which are vital factors that can help them succeed in passing the entire examination. This strategy will also help you to identify students with low academic competency—enabling you to plan on how to help them further in order to develop faster with the rest of the class.

4. *Give most difficult questions near the end of the test.* One way of identifying the brightest among your students is to include 5-10 very difficult items in the test. The questions should be based from the previous lessons and should not be tricky or insignificant. The questions should be placed at, or near the end of, the test. This practice challenges the interest of the best students in your class and inspires them to develop more in terms of competencies.

5. *Make a new set of examination each time you teach a subject.* The fact that constructing an examination is time-consuming, it is logical to develop a *new set* of test every time you teach a subject. An old exam may not reflect the changes you made in presenting the lesson material or the topics you have added emphasis in the subject. It is also possible that hard copies of the old exam are kept by your previous students, which can be passed on to new batch of learners. To avoid cheating or dishonesty, it is best that you construct a new examination.

6. *Keep or save test items throughout the term.* A way to ensure that examination reflects the topics highlighted in the course is to write test questions at the end of each class session and place them on index cards or computer files for later sorting. Software that allows you to create a test bank of items and generate exams from the pool, is now available.

Bloom's Taxonomy for Test Development. Author B. S. Bloom (1956) suggests that in constructing examination, the test questions should test the skills of the learners, other than the ability to recall information. Bloom emphasizes that it is very significant for tests to measure the higher level of learning related to *analysis, application, comprehension, evaluation,* *knowledge* and *synthesis*.[30] In order to do this, Bloom introduced the six-level taxonomy for test development. They are the recognized general laws and principles in classifying and developing test questions, namely:

1. *Analysis.* *Analysis* is the ability to recognize mere assumptions or logical errors in reasoning. It is the ability to distinguish between facts and mistaken beliefs. To measure analysis, the teacher should ask questions by using the following action words, e.g. diagram, differentiate, distinguish, illustrate, infer, point out, relate, select, separate, subdivide, etc. Example: "In P'Noy's inaugural address of June 30, 2010—relate corruption to *Tuwid-na-Daan.*"

2. *Application.* *Application* is the ability to solve problems by applying concepts and principles to new situations. To measure application, the teacher should ask questions by using the following action words, e.g. demonstrate, modify, operate, prepare, produce, show, solve, use, etc.. Example: "Demonstrate a short-cut passage towards the *Tuwid-na-Daan.*"

3. *Comprehension.* *Comprehension* is the ability to understand principles, facts and including interpretation of materials. To measure comprehension, the question should apply the following words, e.g. convert, defend, distinguish, estimate, explain, extend, generalize, infer, predict, summarize, etc.. Example: "Explain the basic principles of the *Plea-Bargain Agreement.*"

4. *Evaluation.* *Evaluation* is the ability to judge and assess concepts and principles according to standards. To measure evaluation, the test question should use the following verbs, e.g. appraise, compare, conclude, contrast, criticize, describe, discriminate, justify, interpret, support, etc.. Example: "Justify the individual's *right against self-incrimination,* as blatantly invoked by the two AFP Generals during the recent Senate Blue Ribbon Committee hearing."

5. *Knowledge.* *Knowledge* is the ability to understand the common terms, facts, principles, methods and procedures. To measure knowledge, the questions should use the following words, e.g. define, describe, identify, label, list, match, name, outline, reproduce, select, state, etc.. Example: "Describe the principles of *Pabaon* and *Pasalubong* for the AFP Generals."

6. *Synthesis.* *Synthesis* is the ability to integrate learning from different areas, or solve problems by creative thinking. To measure synthesis, the question should use the following verbs, e.g. categorize, combine, compile, devise, design, generate, organize, plan, rearrange, reconstruct, revise, etc.. Example: "Design a system that will *stop corruption* in all branches of Philippine Government."

Common Test Formats. There is no standard assessment package required by the Department of Education or the CHED for long examinations. In many local colleges and universities today, the assessment package used in giving long formal examinations (e.g.

---

[30] Bloom, B. S. (Ed.). Taxonomy of Educational Objectives. New York, USA. Longmans. 1956.

preliminary, midterm and final exams) is made up of six types of test formats, i.e. *Identification, Fill-in the Blanks, True or False, Multiple-Choice, Matching* and *Essay.*

Note. For short quizzes or phased-progress test (which is normally 20-30 items), the use of one of the six types of the above test formats is sufficient to measure the acquired knowledge and understanding of the students on certain topics covered. The combination of the six types of test formats is used mostly in long formal examinations. The succeeding discussions summarize the main descriptions of the six common types of test formats, with corresponding test examples.

1. *Identification.* The *Identification* test format uses structured questions pertaining to people, place, dates, events, etc. that require specific, definite and short response. This type of test is easier to write than the other five test formats. It gives opportunity for the teacher to see how well the students can recall important knowledge or information discussed during previous lessons. It is used mostly for short quizzes as a measuring tool. Below is an example of Identification test format, designed as Part I of the midterm examination in the college subject: *"Life/Works of Dr. Jose P. Rizal."*

I. IDENTIFICATION
Direction: Identify and write the correct answers. Observe *no erasure* policy.

1) Give the exact date when Dr. Jose P. Rizal left Manila for his *first* trip abroad.
2) What was the first foreign country that Rizal saw on his initial trip abroad?
3) On June 15, 1882, where did Rizal take the train for the last lap of his trip to Barcelona?
4) Who advised Jose Rizal to move to Madrid, Spain—to enroll and study there?
5) In November 3, 1882, Rizal enrolled in what particular university in Madrid?
6) Give the title of the poem, which Rizal wrote and declaimed in 1882 at the Filipino New Year's Eve celebration in Madrid.
7) Identify the name of the Masonic Lodge that Rizal joined in Madrid, in March 1883.
8) On June 21, 1884, what academic degree did Rizal obtain at Universidad Central de Madrid?
9) Specify the complete name of the expert ophthalmologist in Paris, France that Dr. Rizal worked with after his studies in Madrid.
10) In what German City did Rizal go after his three months of on-the-job training in Paris?
11) Who was the German ophthalmologist whom Jose Rizal worked with in Heidelberg?
12) What was the title of the poem, which Rizal wrote during his stay at Heidelberg?
13) In what specific village at Heidelberg did Rizal write the remaining chapters of his famous book, entitled: Noli Me Tangere?
14) Specify the name of the Protestant Pastor who accommodated Jose Rizal at Heidelberg.
15) Write down the title of the book of Rufino B. Hernandez, which Rizal sent to Dr. Ferdinand Blumentritt while in Heidelberg.
16) Where was the destination of Rizal after his stint at Heidelberg?
17) Who was the Director of Anthropological & Ethnological Museum that Rizal met in Dresden?
18) Where did Jose Rizal go after his stay in Dresden?
19) Who was the scientist-traveler who wrote the book, entitled: Travels in the Philippines?
20) Give the name of the ophthalmologist, whom Rizal worked with while he was in Berlin.

2. *Fill-in the Blanks.* The *Fill-in the Blanks* test uses structured questions designed to measure learners' knowledge and understanding on information relative to people, place, dates, events, things and others. The questions require definite and specific answers. Below is a

typical example of Fill-in the Blanks quiz, designed as Part II of the midterm examination in the college subject: "Philippine History."

II. FILL-IN THE BLANKS
Direction: Write the correct answer in the space provided for each number.

1)   The Philippines is an archipelago, consisting of _____ islands and islets that stretch almost a thousand miles from north to south.

2)   The total land area of the Philippines is _____ square statute miles with mountain ranges forming the circuit and watersheds of the Pacific basin.

3)   The largest and most important island in the Philippines is _____, famously known as the "Rice Granary of the Philippines."

4)   _____ is the second largest Philippine Island—locally referred to as the "Land of Promise."

5)   _____ is the local name given to the Muslim tribe Filipinos who live in Sulu, Mindanao.

6)   The Ifugao Rice Terraces—considered as one of the eight wonders of the world—are found in _____.

7)   _____ is the longest continuous range, beginning at Baler, Quezon and crossing Isabela, Nueva Vizcaya and Cagayan Valley.

8)   _____ is the largest river system in the Philippines, found in Mindanao.

9)   The largest lake in the Philippines is _____, covering 344 square miles or 891 square kilometers and is found in Central Luzon.

10)   _____ is considered as the lowest depth in the world (37,782 feet sea deep) and is situated off the eastern shores of Mindanao.

11)   Mt. Mayon—the most famous of Philippine volcanoes—erupted on February 1, 1814 and erased the town of_____ in Albay, killing more than 1,200 lives.

12)   Earthquake is another agent of death that visits the country often, because the Philippines is located near the _____ (or the seismic belt).

13)   _____ is considered as the staple crop in the Philippines and is produced largely in the Central Plains of Luzon.

14)   The largest eagle in the world is the _____ ; and, is found in the jungles of Luzon and Mindanao.

15)   _____ is a whale shark found in the Philippine seas and is considered as the largest fish in the world, with more or less 50 feet in length and weighs several tons.

1. *True or False.* The *True or False* test uses structured questions designed to measure learners' knowledge and understanding that requires specific and definite response. Some educators consider this test as less reliable than the other types of examination format because of the random guessing by learners. However, this format is adequate enough to measure the level of knowledge and understanding of the learners and is commonly used when giving occasional short quizzes. Below is a typical example of True or False quiz for the subject, "Philippine History."

III. TRUE OR FALSE

Direction: Write "T" if the statement is correct and write "F" if the statement is wrong.

1) _____ The revolt of Sulayman and Lakandula was made in the year 1574.

2) _____ The religious revolt in Bohol (1621-1622) was led by a Babaylan named Tamblot.

3) _____ The longest Philippine revolt (1744-1829, i.e. 85 years) was led by Dumagat.

4) _____ Manuel Vicos was the leader of the Ilocos revolt of 1762-1763.

5) _____ Apolinario dela Cruz led the first religious revolt in Tayabas.

6) _____ The early Filipino revolts failed—due to the divisive traits of the Filipinos.

7) _____ "La Liga" was the official organ of the Reform Movement in Spain.

8) _____ The main objective of the Reform Movement was independence.

9) _____ La Liga Filipina was founded by Marcelo H. del Pilar in Manila on July 3, 1892.

10) _____ The Katipunan was founded in Manila by Dr. Jose Rizal on July 7, 1892.

11) _____ Teodoro Patiño was the traitor who revealed the Katipunan to the Spaniards.

12) _____ The Tejeros Convention was held at Tejeros, Cavite on March 22, 1897.

13) _____ Maj. Lazaro Makapagal executed Bonifacio at Mt. Nagpatong on May 10, 1897.

14) _____ The Biyak-na-Bato Republic was inaugurated on November 1, 1897.

15) _____ Aguinaldo and 28 companions were exiled to Hongkong on December 27, 1898.

16) _____ The US battleship Titanic was blown off at Havana, Cuba on February 18, 1898.

17) _____ The naval fleet of Commodore Dewey defeated the Spanish fleet at Manila Bay on May 11, 1898.

18) _____ Emilio Aguinaldo returned to Cavite, from Hongkong exile, on May 29, 1898.

19) _____ Gen. Emilio Aguinaldo proclaimed the First Philippine Independence in Kawit, Cavite on June 21, 1898.

20) _____ The Filipino-American War started on February 4, 1899 triggered by a shooting incident at San Lorenzo Bridge.

4. *Multiple-Choice.* The *Multiple-Choice* examination uses structured questions that can measure simple knowledge to complex concepts. Assessments using multiple-choice questions can be answered quickly. They are very easy to check and the test result is always consistent. In many Nursing Colleges/Schools, the Multiple-Choice examination is commonly the preferred type of test given during midterm and final periods. Below is a typical example of Multiple-Choice test, designed as Part IV of the preliminary period examination in the college subject: "Philippine History."

IV. MULTIPLE-CHOICE
Direction: Choose and *encircle the letter* of the best answer.

1)   Mt. Mayon—the most beautiful of the Philippine volcanoes—is found in the province of:
    a.   Albay   c.   Pampanga
    b.   Batangas   d.   None of the above

2)   Mt. Taal—the smallest volcano in the world—is found in the province of:
    a.   Albay   c.   Pampanga
    b.   Batangas   d.   None of the above

3)   Mt. Pinatubo—which erupted on June 9, 1991—is situated in the province of:
    a.   Albay   c.   Pampanga
    b.   Batangas   d.   None of the above

4)   Earthquake visits the nation throughout the year very often, because the Philippines is located near the:
    a.   Pacific Ring-of-Fire   c.   Mainland Asia
    b.   Equator   d.   None of the above

5)   It is considered as the "Queen of the Philippine Trees," i.e. the:
    a.   Mahogany   c.   Ebony
    b.   Narra   d.   None of the above

6)   The pygmy water buffalo, locally named as Tamaraw, is found in the province of:
    a.   Palawan   c.   Mindoro
    b.   Bohol   d.   None of the above

7)   The tiniest mouse-deer in the world—locally called as Pilandut—is found in:
    a.   Palawan   c.   Mindoro
    b.   Bohol   d.   None of the above

8)   The smallest in the monkey family—called Tarsier—is found in:
    a.   Palawan   c.   Mindoro
    b.   Bohol   d.   None of the above

9)   It is considered as the "National Flower of the Philippines," i.e.:
    a.   *Dama de Noche*   c.   *Sampaguita*
    b.   *Ilang-ilang*   d.   None of the above

10) It is regarded as the "Queen of Philippine Orchids," i.e.:
    a.   *Dama de Noche*   c.   *Sampaguita*
    b.   *Ilang-ilang*   d.   None of the above

5. *Matching-Type.* The *Matching-Type* format is an effective way to test the learners' recognition of the relationships between words and definitions, people and place, events and dates, categories and examples, etc. Below is an example of the Matching Type test—Part V of the midterm period examination in "Philippine History."

V. MATCHING-TYPE

<u>Direction:</u>   Match Column B with Column A. Write the *letter only* of the correct answer before each number (under Column A).

A	B
1) Legazpi left Natividad, Mexico	a. June 24, 1571
2) Legazpi anchored near Cebu	b. Feb. 13, 1565
3) Legazpi-Chief Urrao's blood compact	c. Feb. 22, 1565
4) Legazpi landed in Limasawa	d. May 24, 1570
5) Legazpi landed in Bohol	e. May 19, 1571
6) Legazpi conquered Cebu	f. March 9, 1565
7) Date King Tupas was baptized	g. 1569
8) Legazpi moved base to Panay	h. March 21, 1568
9) Goiti and Salcedo captured Manila	i. April 27, 1565
10) Manila was made Philippine Capital City	j. Nov. 21, 1564
	k. March 16, 1565

6. *Essay Test.* The *Essay Test* is a free response type that measures the students' abilities to organize, integrate and interpret materials; and, express ideas or concepts in their own words. Essay Test is mostly given as a part of long examination. Students study harder when preparing for essay-type examinations. They focus on general concepts and interrelationships, rather than on specific details resulting in better understanding and performance. Some teachers give essay-type of test for short quiz, because it is easy to prepare. However, there is difficulty when checking the test, except if a standard marking rubric is used, e.g. "CGFN," where: *Content* is 50%; *Grammar* is 20%; *Format* is 15%; and, *Neatness* is 15%.

When an Essay Test is given as part of the long midterm/final examination, a specific weight should be designated to the test. In the example below, the Essay Test is just "Part VI" of the Midterm Examination in the subject, "Jose Rizal," and is assigned 15% in total weight of midterm/final examination grade.

V1. ESSAY TEST (15 points)
<u>Direction:</u>   In 200 words or less, choose one of the following topics and discuss:

1) "Dr. Jose P. Rizal's First Trip Abroad"
2) "Why is Rizal Selected as the Philippine National Hero?"
3) "Historical Background in the Writing of *Noli Me Tangere.*"
4) "Dr. Jose P. Rizal's Return from his First Trip Abroad."

Other Test Strategies.   There are other testing modes used by the teacher, especially for quizzes and short examinations. These testing procedures however are rarely used due to the longer period allotted to complete the examination; and, the possible subjectivity or bias in grading. In these types of tests, there is a need to develop a standard marking criterion (similar to the marking rubric for Essay Test) in order to be right, fair and just in grading the learners. The following are other test formats—sometimes given by the teacher for the purpose of quizzes or short tests, i.e.:

1. *Performance Test.*   In vocational and technical education, *Performance Test* is the most reliable measurement and evaluation used to determine the student's competency in *doing* a series of prescribed procedures, e.g. operating a machine; manipulating materials or equipment; designing models; reading blue prints or drawings; and, executing a series of steps in actual skill performance within an allotted amount of time. Performance Test is best administered to individual student, to assess the level of skills attained as required in the course objectives. It has solid relevance to work situations and provides a valid source of knowledge about the practical skills learned by individual student.

    Performance Test is seldom preferred in undergraduate studies because it is generally time-consuming and expensive in terms of needed materials, supplies and equipment. It is difficult to score—as there is no standard marking scheme that is simple, objective and reliable. It also creates interpersonal friction between the student and the teacher. This test is *not* always applicable to the content of most degree courses—except in special fields of health, science and education.

2. *Oral Test.*   The *Oral Test* is commonly used at the graduate level to assess the communication and interpersonal skills of the students relative to vital theories and concepts prescribed in the course. It is also being practiced very often in foreign language classes, where the aim is to test the competency of learners in the verbal or oral communication skills.

    In the secondary and undergraduate levels, oral examination is used in graded recitation, which is normally designated as a separate criterion for marking. Usually, 3-5 oral recitations are given within the preliminary, midterm and final periods (in every subject); and, the average recitation mark is credited as 5% to 10% in the total grade distribution. Oral Test is generally time-consuming and can result to unnecessary nervousness and embarrassment on the part of the student. It is highly subjective and is difficult to score also.

3. *Open-Book Test.*   The *Open-Book Test* is sometimes given by instructors to test the abilities of learners on how to use resources effectively in solving problems, e.g. preparing and writing reports and qualifying exercises. Open-Book Test is given more appropriately in the middle or latter part of the subject, when students have already learned the basic competencies needed in order to deal with more complicated theories, ideas, principles and concepts in the course. In general, the students who lack basic skills may waste too much time in scanning the pages of the reference book before attempting to answer the test question.

4. *Take-Home Test.* This type of test is commonly applied in the graduate level in the form of qualifying exercise or written report on a particular topic, with designated number of words to use (e.g. 2,000 words or less). This test allows the students to work at their own pace with access to reference books and materials. This strategy gives the students much longer time to do the test at home, without sacrificing the valuable minutes of the class period.

   In secondary and undergraduate levels, Take-Home Test is used, falling under home assignment—a separate criterion for marking. This test may be given 3-5 times within the preliminary, midterm and final periods. The average mark is credited 5% to 10% in the total grade distribution of a particular subject.

5. *Testing by Pairs.* In rare occasions, some instructors are conducting in-class *Testing by Pairs*, where designated partner-students work on a single essay topic or a free-response question, turning in one answer sheet at the end of the test. To save valuable class time, other teachers prefer giving this test in the form of home assignment and collect the answers during the following day only. This strategy aims to enhance peer learning process and to strengthen partnership and working cooperation among the students. In general, some intelligent members may be reluctant to share their grades with students of low-level intelligence. The teacher must give convincing explanation so that cooperative work can set in. Pairing of students should be assigned by the teacher according to his discretion; in some cases, it can be left to the choice of class members.

6. *Testing by Team.* This is another strategy in testing where groups of three to five students work at home as a team on a given conceptual problem or logical topic, submitting one group-answer only at a prescribed period. Similarly, this testing strategy aims to enhance peer learning activity and cooperative teamwork. *Testing by Team* is being done in the form of take-home examination, similar to group assignment projects. In forming the groups, the teacher may appoint the team leaders, who will select their respective team members in turn.

Learning Portfolios. A *Learning Portfolio* a cumulative collection of learner's work that describes annual growth and accomplishment. It is *not* a specific test but it can be graded similar to a Student Workbook, where the learners compile previous works in a particular subject for the duration of one school term. Originally, this exercise is most common in English composition classes only. Recognizing the impact in enhancing the learners' planning and organizing competencies, Learning Portfolio becomes a popular subject requirement today in other disciplines. Besides developing the abilities of the learners in productive planning and organizing, it also provides a comprehensive picture of the students' achievements. A Learning Portfolio can include sample composition drafts and revised papers, scores on pre-course/post-course exams, publication or journal entries, essay exams, advanced study recognition, attendance/awards in conferences, teacher's commendation, curriculum vitae and other works representative of the student's learning progress. Learning Portfolio is given before the final term ends. If the portfolio is to be graded, the teacher should use effective grading criteria (e.g. the CGFN rubric).

Assignment/Study Guide. In Social Science subjects, for every module or chapter, the teacher can design a number of relevant questions to highlight important knowledge and information relative to people, place, dates, events, things and others. These questions will be answered at home—as an *Assignment/Study Guide*—by the students on a separate notebook with a prescribed time to finish for checking. This guide can be allotted 5% to 10% in the average grade for a particular term. Below is an example.

MIDTERM PERIOD
Assignment Study Guide No. 1
(The Setting/Racial Stock/ Common Traits)

Chapter I. THE PRE-SPANISH PHILIPPINES

Direction: Answer the following questions briefly on a *separate* assignment notebook. Ten per cent (10%) of your midterm grades will be taken from 4x Assignment/Study Guide intended for the MIDTERM period.

1. How many islands consist of the Philippines? What is its total land area of the Philippines in square miles?
2. What are the three large ranges in the mountain system of Luzon? Which of them is considered as the longest continuous range?
3. What are the distinct ranges found in Mindanao? Which of them is the highest?
4. Name the river systems found in Luzon and give their importance. Where do you find the largest river system in the Philippines?
5. Name five of the most active Philippine volcanoes and describe their strategic locations.
6. How many statute miles is the length of Philippine coastline? Compare it briefly to other coastlines in the world.
7. Name 10 products being exported by the Philippines to other foreign countries.
8. How large is the Philippine forest in terms of square miles? What is the most famous of the Philippine hardwoods?
9. How many regions comprise the Philippines? Name ten cities and municipalities in the National Capital Region (NCR).
10. What are the foreign bloods—believed to have been running in the Filipino veins?
11. What are the traits common to Filipinos? Give three distinct regional traits as well.
12. Name five dominant tribes in the Philippines and specify their respective regions.
13. Discuss the *Migration* or the *Land Bridge Theory* concerning the early peopling of the Philippines. Who conceived this theory?
14. Explain the *Violent Earthquake Theory* of Dr. F. Voss.
15. Discuss the *Core Population Theory* of Prof. F. L. Jocano.

✓ VALUING. Do you agree that *hospitality* and *friendliness* are the *roots of all corruption* in the economic, social, and political systems of the Filipinos? Why or why not? Support your answer.

MODULE 12
REVIEW/SUMMARY/REINFORCEMENT

> The **review** procedure recalls, reorganizes and remembers the previously-discussed *theories, principles, ideas* and *concepts* (TPIC) in the lesson. **Summary** is the act of reemphasizing the vital TPIC—for transfer. **Reinforcement** is the act of depositing the valuable TPIC into permanent memory of learners for lasting productive use.

Review for Learning Transfer

Introduction.   The review of vital theories, principles, ideas and concepts (TPIC) taken during previous class meeting is a significant phase in any formal teaching-and-learning activity. It is the process of recalling, reorganizing and remembering those vital TPIC for eventual transfer and productive use. It evaluates if students had achieved the permanent learning of skill, method and social competencies that brings positive changes in learners.

Permanent learning transfer is not always an automatic by-product of one classroom discussion meeting. Learning transfer develops when enough time is given to learners to *review* or restudy the organized related experiences; repeat and re-emphasize the meaning of vital learning points; and, discover interrelationships among the TPIC being studied. In general, the review exercise triggers permanent learning.

Repetition Exercise.   The human memory has three stages in learning information. In general, students do not learn complex information or task in a single session. The mind cannot always remember, retain and apply new ideas, concepts and practices in one time classroom discussion or laboratory application. Mostly, the information is just temporary stored in the *surface memory* of learners and is often forgotten after a few seconds or minutes. Some selected items or pieces of information stored temporarily in the brain, which are forgotten in two days or a week's time, are considered to have stayed in the *transitory* or *short term memory* only. Repetition of information useful to learners results to learning— which is deposited in the *permanent* or *long term memory* of the brain.

Repetition exercise is based on the principle, that: "Information most often repeated are permanently retained." Constant repetition of drills and practices on vital TPIC enables information to become permanently stored in the long-term memory of learners. Such condition also allows recall of said information—even if a long time had lapsed after its registry. The permanency of learning storage and recall for use is greatly influenced by meaningful repetition: i.e. brief, but clear summary of the lesson using real objects, supported by learners' practical applications and the teacher's feedback. Review, summary, practical applications and feedback are the keys. For every repetition exercise, learning surely occurs. The teacher must review important TPIC for learners to redo the practice at "planned intervals," until learning of useful information becomes permanent.

Review Intervals. As earlier suggested, review must be done in appropriate or planned intervals. The theories, principles, ideas and concepts (TPIC) previously discussed and learned temporarily must be reviewed right away on the next class session meeting. The reason for this is to evaluate if relevant information/competencies are already stored permanently in the long-term memory of learners. During review, the teacher must be keen in reassessing if learning the previous lesson had ideally occurred. If learning is not achieved, then the teacher must perform further intensive review. Vital TPIC must be repeated, restated and reemphasized to make the students learn them. When positive learning is assured, then that is the only time when the teacher can proceed with the discussion of next lesson or topic.

The review exercise interval, or frequency of review, depends on teacher's evaluation and discretion. It is appropriately planned by the teacher, according to the need. A lesson must *not* be left-out unlearned. When a teacher jumps to a new topic without ensuring learners' learning of the vital TPIC of previous lesson, the logical succession of learning points will be disrupted. In general, subject syllabus is designed to contain a logical sequence of interrelated competencies to facilitate productive learning.

Intensive Review.   Any past lesson unlearned needs an *intensive review* to provide deep and thorough emphasis on significant TPIC that must be learned. As a rule, the more intense a subject is taught—the more intense learning is likely to happen. During intensive review, the learning points must be reemphasized in a clear, simple, concise and effective (CSCE) manner. The review must be supplemented with vivid, dramatic and exciting related learning experience for more impact. The teacher must also use real objects—similar to the first lesson discussion—because students learn more from the real thing than from imaginary substitutes. Also, enough time must be allotted to repeat actual demonstrations and applications by the students. Learners develop greater understanding of the tasks by performing them—rather than by being passive listeners to the teacher's lecture. In total, when learners do the tasks themselves, more immediate and dramatic learning occurs. Actual applications, with correct procedures in doing the tasks, create lasting impression on the long-term memory of the learners.

The following pointers summarize the logical steps when doing an intensive review of any past lesson unlearned from previous discussions, i.e.:

1. Stress the importance of learning the TPIC contained in the lesson.
2. Emphasize the main TPIC of the lesson in CSCE manner.
3. Use real objects as training aid, or project TPIC of the lesson in transparency.
4. Summarize the main points in CSCE way.
5. Point to each TPIC and ask learners about their comments on each.
6. Re-explain vague learning points very clearly (as noted).
7. Ask learners to summarize what they learned from the lesson covered.
8. Note: During intensive review, the teacher must take notes pertaining to students' difficulties in learning the lesson. These recorded notes can be useful information to adjust and simplify procedures for effective future lesson delivery.

Summary Procedures in Learning

Introduction. Summary of lesson is the time allotted for reflection and reemphasizing *theories, principles, ideas* and *concepts* (TPIC) that the teacher had previously discussed for the learners to learn. It is normally done before the end of every day's session. This exercise provides an opportunity to highlight all lesson TPIC and to assess if permanent learning has occurred. During the process, the teacher summarizes main TPIC. After the lesson summary, the question-and-answer portion follows. Relevant questions pertaining to previously-discussed TPIC are directed to the learners for practical answers. In many cases, the teacher assigns mark for every practical answer given by the learners—as part of their graded recitation.

Summary vs. Review. In lesson presentation, summary differs slightly from review. Summary is just an *end-part* in every lesson presentation process, while review involves repeating the *whole* process. Summary is always a part of any lesson—whether during *initial* topic presentation or during the *review* exercise. During initial lesson presentation, summary is done (in CSCE manner) to make the vital TPIC vivid to the memory of the learners. If the teacher notes that learning the TPIC has occurred, the lesson discussion can stop from there. However, it is always of vital importance to review lesson during the next meeting by summarizing vital TPIC for vivid understanding of information—so that permanent storage will result in the long-term memory of learners.

Summary Exercise. In evaluating if the learners have retained vital lesson TPIC, the teacher may give summary exercise, applying open-ended question in probing style where learners will use combination of logical and affective thinking process requiring comprehensive answers. The assessment of summary exercise is mostly done through question-and-answer. The learners' answers are marked accordingly and are recorded as graded recitation. If time allows, summary exercise can be given in the form of written quiz, which can be checked and marked by teacher, as part of the learners' graded quiz.

When there is only a limited time, summary quiz can be answered similar to a home assignment, to be collected during the next session. As the quiz assignment is submitted the following day, the teacher must be quick in browsing or reading the answers—to evaluate if there is still a need to redo another review/summary of past lesson. Below are suggested samples of probing questions that can be given to learners for evaluation of the summarized lesson, e.g.:

1. "What particular TPIC did you like best from the lesson? Explain how it will help you to improve your life as a future professional."
2. "What specific TPIC in the lesson did you dislike? Why?"
3. "What other related TPIC do you want to learn? Discuss.
4. "List down two most important TPIC that you learned from the lesson. In 200 words or more, discuss each TPIC and explain how they can help you improve your life. Refer to your notes/handouts."
5. "In your opinion, what specific TPIC—related to the lesson—was not discussed? Explain why it should be included and discussed as part of the lesson."

Motivation in Summary Exercise. One of the most important functions of the teacher is to prepare the physical, emotional, mental and sociological (PEMS) conditions of the learners in order to become ready for instructions and learning. Motivation gets the full CIA of learners and facilitates permanent learning.

There is no short-cut technique in motivation. It depends largely on the combined skill, method and social (SMS) competencies of the teacher during instructions—as observed by learners. Some learners are motivated by the teacher's *skill* in interpreting and explaining the TPIC of the lesson; others are inspired by the teacher's *method* in performing the TPIC practices in various ways; while many can be stimulated by teacher's emotional and *social* abilities—i.e. practicing/applying the values of respect, love, empathy and compassion (RLEC) to learners—inside and outside the classroom.

Undoubtedly, the values of RLEC to learners are very significant in teaching services; in similar manner, where the values of RLEC to clients are very critical in professional medical and nursing services. In teaching, RLEC to learners recognizes every learner regardless of worth. RLEC to learners is an effective emotion tool that motivates learners and thus, facilitating permanent learning transfer.

Motivation of learners is not done mainly at the beginning of the day's lesson. It should be done *continuously* by the teacher at every appropriate given opportunity (inside and outside the classroom). When lessons are presented to motivated students—learning takes place very easily. Hence, the teacher will not repeat, review, or summarize the topic anymore and will save time for other productive use.

The learning effect through motivation can be measured through behavioral reactions, as manifested by the learners. Some behavioral reactions indicative of positive learning effect through proper motivations are evidenced by learners, when they are:

1. Satisfied, happy and contented with their daily classroom learning activities.
2. Extending full contact, interest and attention (CIA) to the teacher during lesson presentation, discussion and demonstration.
3. Actively participating in classroom discussions and in performing practical and related learning experiences.
4. Maintaining harmonious social relations, i.e. practicing respect, love, empathy and compassion (RLEC) with one another, inside or outside the classroom.
5. Capable of solving difficult problems or tasks, with improved capability to understand, perform and master each problem or task completely.
6. Not feeling inferior or frustrated when advanced concepts are presented by the teacher for discussion; instead, they show eagerness and seriousness to learn.
7. Considers every learning experience as pleasant, with elements of hope and good feeling for future productive application.
8. Giving clear and correct answers for every oral question asked by the teacher and with marked self-confidence.
9. Getting high grades in every written examination of the class.
10. Able to show evidence of progress, or mark of achievement, with high degree of learning success.

Learning Reinforcement

Factors in Reinforcement.   In classroom teaching, *learning reinforcement* is the strategic act of strengthening the valuable ethico-moral theories, principles, ideas and concepts (TPIC) being discussed in the lesson—i.e. purposely for lasting storage in the permanent memory of the learner—for future and eventual productive use. It is also viewed as "the motive-satisfaction or reward which attends, and presumably strengthens, a stimulus-response connection being learned."[31] Learning reinforcement in teaching is generally influenced by four significant factors, i.e.:

1. *Motive.*   The teacher must be able to define in concise, simple, clear and effective manner the beneficial consequences of any such goal-directed activity. He/she must be able to penetrate into the internal condition of the learner to *arouse, direct* and *sustain* the intensity of drive/need/desire and efforts toward achieving the productive goals—which is the *main motive* to accomplish—for the personal and professional total developments of the learner.
2. *Stimulus.*   To sustain learner's drive/need/desire and efforts for a goal-directed motive, the teacher must apply or use some proven stimulating examples, e.g. events, cases, actual objects, principles, ideas, concepts, etc. that will considerably excite a positive response from the learner and thus stimulating a favorable positive change within the learner's personality.
3. *Response.*   The reaction or response of the learner—be it a positive or negative response—is often demonstrated on *how* the learner feels, thinks, talks or do some manipulative processes relative to the TPIC being learned. To ensure positive response, the teacher must be keen, competent and effective in *guiding* the learner through motivating, explaining, demonstrating and correcting substandard trials that will eventually lead the learner to further self-discovery and useful learning.
4. *Reward.*   Learning is further reinforced when a corresponding beneficial *return* or reward is given to a learner, as recognition for special accomplishment done. *Reward* to learner can be in any form of motive-satisfying object or event, e.g. high grades/marks, test-exemption, approval, security, or even food that will give intrinsic satisfaction to learner for his/her learning efforts and accomplishments.

In teaching, effective *reinforcement* results to learning, which eventually becomes a lasting behavioral modification. Effective reinforcement in learning is manifested by the continuous intensity of the learner's desire and efforts towards productive learning. The teacher is, supposedly, a competent and effective *learning reinforcer* that will increase the level of learning in a learner. If one learner did not learn—the teacher is *not* an effective learning reinforcer. If all the learners learn the valuable theories, principles, ideas and concepts contained in the lesson—the teacher, no doubt, is a competent, effective and productive learning reinforcer.

---

[31] Op. Cit. Frandsen, A. N.

REFERENCES

BOOKS:

Agoncillo, T. A. History of the Filipino People. Quezon City, Philippines. Garotech Publishing. 1990.

Anderson, M. B. Education For All: What are We Waiting? N. Y., USA. UNICEF New York. September 1992.

Archbishop Whealon, J., Imprimatur. Good News Bible (Catholic Edition). New York. Thomas Nelson, Publishers. 1979.

Barnhart & Barnhart, Eds. The World Book Dictionary. Chicago. Doubleday & Company, Inc. 1979.

Bishop, G. Innovation in Education. Hong Kong. Macmillan Publishers Ltd. 1986.

Bloom, B. S. (Ed.). Taxonomy of Educational Objectives. New York, USA. Longmans. 1956.

City & Guilds Examiners, Ed. Instructor Training Course 1: Theoretical Part. Austria. 1989.

Covey, S. R. Principle-Centered Leadership. New York, USA. Simon & Schuster. 1992.

Edelfelt, Roy A.. Careers in Education. Chicago, U.S.A. National Textbook Company. 1988.

Frandsen, A. N. Educational Psychology. New York, USA. McGraw-Hill Book Company, Inc. 1961.

Nault, W. H. et al., Eds. The World Book Encyclopedia. Chicago, USA. World Book–Childcraft International, Inc. 1979.

Smith, T., Ed. Complete Family Heath Encyclopedia. Great Britain. Dorling Kindersley Limited, London. 1990.

Vann, J. The Philippines and Its Public Enemy No. 1. Manila. Ten Star Books. 1991.

Zaide, S. M. The Philippines: A Unique Nation. Quezon City, Philippines. All-Nations Publishing Co., Inc. 1994.

WEBSITE:

http://www.suite101.com/content/ten. . . . Dec. 7, 2008.

http://www.suite.101.com/content/teach-students. . . Mar. 25, 2009

TEST BANK (SAMPLE)

IN

Main Ref.: Zaide, G. F. & Zaide, S. M. <u>Jose Rizal: Life, Works and Writings</u>. Quezon City, Philippines. All-Nations Publishing Co., Inc. 1994.

WANG-WANG UNIVERSITY (WWU)
0210 San Miguel, Manila

Marcelino D. Catahan, Ph.D.

1998

JOSERIZ-MIDTERM QUIZ 1 (MQ1)
(Prologue to Chapter 4)

I. IDENTIFICATION (2x point each)

Direction: Identify and write the correct answer to the following questions:

1. Four months before Jose Rizal's birth, a Russian Czar emancipated 22.5 million serfs to appease the discontentment of Russian masses. Who was this famous Russian Czar?
2. Eighteen days before Rizal's birth, a full-blooded Zapotec Indian was elected President of Mexico who resisted the invading French Army of Napoleon III. What was his name?
3. In Rizal's time, England was the world's leading imperialist power due to her invincible navy and magnificent army. Who was the ruler of England's during that era?
4. In 1858-1863, France conquered Vietnam and Cambodia. Later, France annexed Laos in 1893 and merged these three countries into a federation. Name the federation.
5. The Dutch drove away the Portuguese and the Spaniards from the East Indies in the 17th Century and colonized a vast/rich archipelago they named as the Netherland East Indies. Which country is it today?
6. An Asian country joined the scramble for territories in 1894 and grabbed Formosa and Pescadores from China. Later, she annexed Korea. Which country was this?
7. In early 1800s, Spain's *Siglo de Oro* (Golden Age) began to decline. From 1811-1825, about 14 colonies in Latin America had gained full independence. Which was the first country to gain independence?
8. Name the boastful and ruthless Spanish Governor-General in the Philippines who ordered the execution of GOMBURZA in February 1872.
9. The set of laws promulgated by the Christian Monarch of Spain that aimed to protect the right and welfare of the natives in overseas colonies.
10. In Hispanic Philippines the friars controlled religious, educational and political aspects of life. What term was given to this union of Church and State?
11. A compulsory service imposed by colonial authorities upon Filipino males—aged 16-60 years—in the construction of churches, schools, hospitals and in building roads and bridges for 40 days per year.
12. A sum of money paid to the government by well-to-do-Filipinos in order to get exemption from forced labor.
13. A term describing vast tract of agricultural land owned by Spanish Friars in Rizal's time.
14. Jose Rizal was born on moonlit night of Wednesday, between 11:00-12:00 P.M. in lakeshore town of Calamba, Laguna Province. Give his complete birthday.
15. Who was the baptismal godfather or *ninong* of Jose P. Rizal?

II. MULTIPLE-CHOICE

Direction: Choose the best answer (letters only).

1. Francisco Mercado Rizal studied Latin and Philosophy at:
   a. University of Santo Tomas
   b. Ateneo de Manila
   c. College of San Jose
   d. None of the above

2. Dona Teodora Alonzo Realonda was educated at the:
   a. College of Santa Rosa
   b. University of Santo Tomas
   c. La Concordia College
   d. None of the above

3. The great, great grandfather of Rizal on the father's side was a Chinese immigrant from Fukien City of Changchow who came to Manila in 1690. His name was:
   a. Domingo Tanco
   b. Domingo Chioco
   c. Domingo Juico
   d. None of the above

4. The great, great grandfather of Jose Rizal on mother's side was of Japanese ancestry, by the name of:
   a. Domy Ursua
   b. Eugenio Ursua
   c. Manuel Ursua
   d. None of the above

5. In Spanish Philippines, Rizal's family belonged to the town aristocracy, called:
   a. Principalia
   b. Aristocracia
   c. Illustrada
   d. None of the above

6. During Rizal's time Calamba—and all the lands around it—was owned by the:
   a. Augustinian Order
   b. Dominican Order
   c. Franciscan Order
   d. None of the above

7. At the age of eight the first formal schooling of Jose Rizal was in Biñan, under the tutelage of Maestro:
   a. Justiniano Montano Cruz
   b. Justiniano Aquino Cruz
   c. Justiniano Roco Cruz
   d. None of the above

8. The three martyr priests—GOMBURZA—were executed on order of Gov.-Gen. Rafael de Izquierdo on:
   a. January 17, 1872
   b. February 17, 1872
   c. March 17, 1872
   d. None of the above

9. In June 1872, Rizal matriculated at the Ateneo Municipal in Manila. At first he was denied admission by college registrar—Fr. Magin Ferrando—for being late and sickly. Rizal was reluctantly admitted through the intercession of:
   a. Manuel Xeres Burgos
   b. Manuel Roxas Burgos
   c. Manuel Quezon Burgos
   d. None of the above

10. The first professor of Jose P. Rizal at the Ateneo was:
    a. Fr. Jose de Venicia
    b. Fr. Jose Bech
    c. Fr. Francisco de Paula Sanchez
    d. None of the above

III. ENUMERATION (2x point each)

Direction: Enumerate the answers to the following questions:

01-05 = At least 5x cause of discontentment, or evil done by the Spaniards, that agonized the Filipino people during Dr. Jose P. Rizal's time.

o 0 o

JOSERIZ-MQ1 (ANSWER KEY)
(Prologue to Chapter 4)

I. IDENTIFICATION (2x point each)
Direction: Identify and write the correct answer to the following questions:

1. Czar Alexander II
2. Benito Juarez
3. Queen Victoria
4. French Indo-China
5. Indonesia
6. Japan
7. Paraguay
8. Gen. Rafael de Izquierdo

9. *Leyes de Indias*
10. *Frailocracia*
11. *Polo*
12. *Falla*
13. *Hacienda*
14. June 19, 1861
15. Fr. Pedro Casanas

II. MULTIPLE-CHOICE
Direction: Choose the best answer (letters only).

1. c
2. a
3. d (Domingo Lamco)
4. b
5. a

6. b
7. b
8. b
9. a
10. b

III. ENUMERATION (2x point each)
Direction: Enumerate the answers to the following questions:

01-05 = At least 5x cause of discontentment/evil done by the Spaniards that agonized the Filipino people during Dr. Rizal's time.

1. Instability of colonial administration
2. Corrupt officialdom
3. No Philippine representation to the Spanish Cortes
4. Human rights denied to Filipinos
5. No equality before the law
   Others:
   • Mal-administration of justice
   • Frailocracy
   • Haciendas owned by Friars
   • Racial discrimination
   • Guardia Civil
   • Forced labor

o O o

JOSERIZ-MQ2
(Chapter 5-7)

I. IDENTIFICATION (2x point each)
Direction: Identify and write the correct answer to the following questions:

1. Jose P. Rizal was 16 years old when he finished his studies at the Ateneo on March 23, 1877. What kind of degree did he obtain?
2. As an Atenean, the first poem written by Rizal was a felicitation on his mother's birthday in 1874. What was the title of the poem?
3. Jose was 16 years old when he experienced his first love. What was the name of the pretty Batangueña whom Rizal fell in love with?
4. In April 1877, Jose Rizal matriculated in the University of Santo Tomas. What course did he take up?
5. In 1878, the *Liceo Artistico-Literario de Manila* held a literary contest. In that particular contest, Jose P. Rizal won first prize for the best poem. What was the title of his winning poem?
6. In 1880, *Liceo Artistico-Literario de Manila* sponsored another contest. This time, Rizal participated in the drama category and won first prize again. What was the title of his winning drama?
7. During his first term at the UST, Rizal also studied at the Ateneo enrolling in a vocational course. He finished the course after a year but was awarded his title three years later. What title did he receive?
8. While at UST, Rizal founded a secret society of Filipino students to fight against arrogant Spanish students. The society members were called, "Companions of Jehu." What was the name of the society?
9. Shortly after losing Segunda Katigbak, Rizal paid court to a young woman in Calamba whom he described as "being fair with seductive and attractive eyes." In what name did Rizal call this girl?
10. In 1881, Rizal composed a poem entitled: "Al M.R.P. Pablo Ramon." Who was Fr. Pablo Ramon, to whom Rizal expressed his affection in this poem?

II. MULTIPLE-CHOICE
Direction: Choose the best answer (letters only).

1. Dr. Jose Rizal discretely left Manila (to study in Spain) on board the Spanish steamer *Salvadora* on:
   a. May 3, 1882
   b. May 13, 1882
   c. May 23, 1882
   d. None of the above

2. On May 9, the *Salvadora* arrived and docked at:
   a. Talim Island
   b. Colombo
   c. Singapore
   d. None of the above

3. On June 15, 1882, Rizal took a train at Marseilles, France—last lap of his trip to:
   a. Aden Africa
   b. Naples, Italy
   c. Barcelona, Spain
   d. None of the above

4. On the fall of 1882, Rizal left Barcelona following the advice of Paciano and moved to:
   a. Madrid
   b. Paris
   c. Berlin
   d. None of the above

5. On November 3, 1882, Rizal studied in Madrid enrolling at the:
   a. *Colegio Central de España*
   b. *Universidad de Madrid*
   c. *Universidad Central de Madrid*
   d. None of the above

6. In Madrid, Jose Rizal wrote a poem, which he declaimed in a Filipino New Year's Eve reception in 1882. The title of the poem was:
   a. "Un Recuerdo A Mi Pueblo"
   b. "Mi Piden Versos"
   c. "Colon Y Juan II"
   d. None of the above

7. In March 1883, Rizal joined a Masonic Lodge in Madrid, i.e. named as:
   a. *Acacia*
   b. *Solidaridad*
   c. *Le Grand*
   d. None of the above

8. On June 21, 1884, Jose P. Rizal was conferred by Universidad Central de Madrid the degree of:
   a. Philosophy and Letters
   b. Humanities
   c. Licentiate in Medicine
   d. None of the above

9. After Rizal's medical studies in Madrid, he specialized in ophthalmology in Paris under the guidance of:
   a. Dr. Adolf B. Mayer
   b. Dr. Louis de Weckert
   c. Dr. Rudolf Virchow
   d. None of the above

10. After acquiring enough experience in ophthalmology, Doctor Rizal left Paris on February 1, 1886 for:
    a. Spain
    b. Italy
    c. Switzerland
    d. None of the above

III. ENUMERATION (2x point each)
Direction: Enumerate the answers to the following questions:

01-03 = 3x reason why Rizal left UST
04-06 = 3x country Rizal saw on his way to Barcelona, Spain
07-10 = 4x Filipino contemporary that Rizal met in Spain/France

o 0 o

JOSERIZ-MQ2 (ANSWER KEY)
(Chapter 5-7)

I. IDENTIFICATION (2x point each)
Direction: Identify and write the correct answer to the following questions:

1. Bachelor of Arts
2. "My First Inspiration"
3. Segunda Katigbak
4. Philosophy and Letters
5. "A La Juventud Filipina"
6. "El Consejo de los Dioses"
7. "Perito Agrimensor"
8. *Compañerismo*
9. "Miss L"
10. Ateneo Rector

II. MULTIPLE-CHOICE
Direction: Choose the best answer (letters only).

1. a
2. c
3. c
4. a
5. c
6. b
7. a
8. a
9. b
10. d

III. ENUMERATION (2x point each)
Direction: Enumerate the answers to the following questions:

01-03 = 3x reason why Rizal left UST
1. Racial discrimination by Spanish students
2. Hostile Dominican Professors
3. Obsolete and repressive teaching method

04-06 = 3x country Rizal saw on his way to Barcelona, Spain
4. Singapore
5. Sri Lanka
6. Aden
    Others: Egypt/Italy/France

07-10 = 4x Filipino contemporary that Rizal met in Spain/France
7. Marcelo H. Del Pilar
8. Graciano Lopez Jaena
9. Mariano Ponce
10. Eduardo de Lete
    Others: Antonio/Maximo/Pedro Paterno & Trinidad/Paz/Joaquin Pardo de Tavera

o 0 o

JOSERIZ-MQ3

(Chapter 7-10)

I. IDENTIFICATION (2x point each)
Direction: Identify and write the correct answer to the following questions:

1. On February 1, 1886, Rizal left Paris for Heidelberg and worked at the University Eye Hospital under a German ophthalmologist. Who was this German expert?
2. At Heidelberg, Rizal was fascinated by the blooming flowers along the banks of Neckar River which inspired him to write a poem. What was the Spanish title of the poem he wrote?
3. From April 23 to June 25, 1886, Dr. Rizal was at Wilhemsfeld—a mountainous village near Heidelberg where he wrote the last few chapters of the *NOLI*. Who was the protestant pastor who hosted him?
4. On July 31, 1886, Doctor Rizal wrote his first letter in German to Prof. Ferdinand Blumentritt—the Director of Ateneo of Leitmeritz—enclosing a book entitled, *Aritmetica.* Who was the Filipino author of this book?
5. On August 9, 1886, Rizal left Heidelberg by train and reached Leipzig (August 14) where he attended some lectures in the university. What kind of lectures did he take in the university?
6. On October 29, 1886, Rizal left Leipzig for Dresden where he met the Director of the Anthropological and Ethnological Museum. Who was this Museum Director?
7. On November 1, 1886, Rizal left Dresden for Berlin. Here, he met a number of German scientists and scholars. One of them had written a book entitled, *Travels in the Philippines.* Who was this famous German Scientist?
8. In Berlin, Rizal led a methodical and frugal life. By day, he worked as assistant to the clinic of an ophthalmologist and at night, he attended lectures at the university. Who was this eminent ophthalmologist?
9. The winter of 1886 brought severe financial misery to Rizal in Berlin. Timely enough, a good friend—who was a scion of a rich Bulakeño family—came and saved him from further despondency. Who was this close friend, who was also accredited as the "savior" of *NOLI*?
10. Give the complete date when the *Noli Me Tangere*—the first book published by Dr. Jose P. Rizal—came off the press.

II. MULTIPLE-CHOICE
Direction: Choose the best answer (letters only).

1. On May 11, 1887, Dr. Jose P. Rizal and Dr. Maximo Viola began touring Europe. They left Berlin for Dresden and visited:
   a. Dr. Adolf B. Meyer
   b. Dr. Ferdinand Blumentritt
   c. Dr. Carlos Czepelak
   d. None of the above

2. On May 13, 1887, Doctor Rizal and Doctor Viola were at Leitmeritz and met:
   a. Dr. Adolf B. Meyer
   b. Dr. Ferdinand Blumentritt
   c. Dr. Carlos Czepelak
   d. None of the above

3. On May 19, 1887, Doctor Rizal and Dr. Maximo Viola were in:
   a. Leitmeritz
   b. Teschen
   c. Austria
   d. None of the above

4. On May 24, Rizal and Viola left Vienna for:
   a. Teschen
   b. Austria
   c. Lintz
   d. None of the above

5. From Rheinfall, Dr. J. P. Rizal and Doctor Viola crossed the frontier and stayed in a Swiss City (June 2-3), called:
   a. Schaffhausen
   b. Geneva
   c. Laussane
   d. None of the above

6. On June 23, 1887, Rizal and Viola terminated their tour and parted ways in:
   a. Schaffhausen
   b. Geneva
   c. Laussane
   d. None of the above

7. After their parting, Dr. Jose P. Rizal continued his tour to:
   a. Barcelona
   b. Madrid
   c. Italy
   d. None of the above

8. On July 3, 1887, Doctor Rizal boarded the steamer *Djemnah* for:
   a. Barcelona, Spain
   b. Naples, Italy
   c. Manila, Philippines
   d. None of the above

9. On the midnight of August 5, 1887, Rizal arrived in Manila aboard the steamer:
   a. *Salvadora*
   b. *Djemnah*
   c. *Haiphong*
   d. None of the above

10. Doctor Rizal finally returned to Calamba and saw his family on:
    a. August 5, 1887
    b. August 6, 1887
    c. August 7, 1887
    d. None of the above

III. ENUMERATION (2x point each)
Direction: Enumerate the answers to the following questions:

01-05 = 5x attacker of Dr. Jose P. Rizal's *NOLI*
06-10 = 5x Filipino gallant defender of Doctor Rizal's *NOLI*

o 0 o

JOSERIZ-MQ3 (ANSWER KEY)
(Chapter 7-10)

I. IDENTIFICATION (2x point each)
Direction: Identify and write the correct answer to the following questions:

1. Dr. Otto Becker
2. "A Las Flores de Heidelberg"
3. Dr. Karl Ullmer
4. Rufino Baltazar Hernandez
5. History and Psychology

6. Dr. Adolf B. Meyer
7. Dr. Feador Jagor
8. Dr. Karl E. Schweigger
9. Dr. Maximo Viola
10. March 21, 1887

II. MULTIPLE-CHOICE
Direction: Choose the best answer (letters only).

1. a
2. b
3. c
4. c
5. a

6. b
7. c
8. c
9. c
10. d

III. ENUMERATION (2x point each)
Direction: Enumerate the answers to the following questions:

01-05 = 5x attacker of Rizal's *NOLI*
1. Fr. Jose Rodriguez of Guadalupe
2. Arch. Pedro Payo of Manila
3. Fr. Gregorio Echavarria—UST Rector
4. Fr. Salvador Font
5. Gen. Jose Salamanca (Spanish Cortes)
   - Gen. Luis M. de Pando (Spanish Cortes)
   - Sr. Fernando Vida (Spanish Cortes)
   - Sr. Vicente Barrantes (Newspaperman)

06-10 = 5x Filipino Gallant Defender of the *NOLI*
6. Fr. Vicente Garcia
7. Marcelo H del Pilar
8. Graciano Lopez Jaena
9. Mariano Ponce
10. Dr. Antonio Ma. Regidor

o 0 o

JOSERIZ-MQ4
(Chapter 11-15)

I. IDENTIFICATION

Direction: Identify and write the correct answer to the following questions:

1. Give the exact date when Dr. Jose P. Rizal left Manila for his second trip abroad.
2. On Feb. 18, 1888, Rizal and Jose Maria Basa went to Macao (from Hongkong) on board the steamer *Kiu-Kiang*. Who was the Spanish spy that followed them?
3. On February 22, 1888, Rizal left Hongkong for Japan. After staying for six days in a Tokyo hotel, he was invited by the Secretary of the Spanish Legation to stay with them in the Legation Compound. Who was this Legation officer?
4. While in Tokyo, Doctor Rizal had a brief romance with a Japanese lady whom he fondly called as, *O-Sei-San*. What was her full name?
5. On April 13, 1888, Rizal continued with his travel. Where did he go this time?
6. The Japanese journalist whom Rizal befriended in the ship, on his way to U.S.
7. Doctor Rizal left New York on May 16, 1888—for what destination?
8. The Filipino patriot whom Rizal stayed with temporarily in London, in 1888.
9. The title of the book which Doctor Rizal annotated in London.
10. The family which gave board and lodging to Rizal at Primrose Hill, London.
11. The founder of *La Solidaridad* in Barcelona.
12. The first article of Dr. Jose P. Rizal in *La Solidaridad*.
13. A friend compatriot who requested Doctor Rizal to write a "Letter to the Young Women of Malolos."
14. Dr. Jose P. Rizal's destination after London.
15. The name of Doctor Rizal's girlfriend in London.
16. Dr. Jose P. Rizal's destination after Paris.
17. Title of the poem that Doctor Rizal wrote in Brussels.
18. The girlfriend of Dr. J. P. Rizal in Brussels.
19. The destination of Doctor Rizal after Brussels.
20. Dr. Jose P. Rizal's friend, who died in Madrid.

II. MULTIPLE-CHOICE

Direction: Choose the best answer (letters only).

1. Date when Dr. Jose Rizal wrote "Letter to the Young Women of Malolos," i.e.:
   a. February 21, 1889
   b. February 22, 1889
   c. February 23, 1889
   d. None of the above

2. In the "Letter to the Young Women of Malolos," Rizal urged the young women of Malolos to offer their sons in defense of the Fatherland, like a:
   a. Spanish mother
   b. German mother
   c. Spartan mother
   d. None of the above

3. Dr. Jose P. Rizal stressed in the "Letter to the Young Women of Malolos" that tyranny of some over others is possible due to:
   a. Cowardice and negligence
   b. Saintliness and obedience
   c. Kindness and ignorance
   d. None of the above

4. In his essay "The Philippines Within a Century," Rizal exposed the evil Spanish colonization of the Philippines and predicted the end of Spain's tyranny in:
   a. Asia
   b. South America
   c. Latin America
   d. None of the above

5. Doctor Rizal predicted too, that a great nation may someday dream of establishing foreign possession in the Pacific. This particular nation was:
   a. America
   b. England
   c. Germany
   d. None of the above

6. According to Dr. Jose P. Rizal, there was an ideal country—i.e. imagined only by Thomas Moore—where there existed universal suffrage, religious toleration and almost complete abolition of death penalty. The name of this country was:
   a. Utopia
   b. Cuba
   c. Puerto Rico
   d. None of the above

7. Rizal wrote a famous essay in defense of alleged laziness of Filipinos, entitled:
   a. "The Indolence of the Filipinos"
   b. "The Philippines within a Century"
   c. "Redemption of the Malays"
   d. None of the above

8. Doctor Rizal made a critical study of the causes why Filipinos did not work hard during the Spanish regime. His main thesis was:
   a. "Filipinos are not by nature indolent"
   b. "Filipinos hated the Spanish rule"
   c. "Filipinos prefer to gamble than to work"
   d. None of the above

9. The exact date when Dr. Jose P. Rizal left London for Paris was:
   a. March 19, 1889
   b. March 20, 1889
   c. March 21, 1889
   d. None of the above

10. In Paris, Doctor Rizal found difficulty to find a living quarter due to the Universal Exposition of 1889. Temporarily, Dr. Jose Rizal lived with a Filipino friend, i.e.:
    a. Valentin Ventura
    b. Maximo Viola
    c. Juan Luna
    d. None of the above

III. ESSAY (20x point)
Direction: In 400 words or more, write a summary of Doctor Rizal's second trip, i.e.:

"From Hongkong to London"

o 0 o

JOSERIZ-MQ4 (ANSWER KEY)
(Chapter 11-15)

I. IDENTIFICATION
Direction: Identify and write the correct answer to the following questions:

1. February 3, 1888
2. Jose Sainz de Veranda
3. Juan Perez de Caballero
4. Seiko Usui
5. U.S.A.
6. Techo Suehiro
7. London
8. Dr. Antonio Ma. Regidor
9. *Sucesos de las Islas Filipinas*
10. Beckett Family
11. Graciano Lopez Jaena
12. *Los Agricultores Filipinos*
13. Marcelo H. del Pilar
14. Paris, France
15. Gertrude Beckett
16. Brussels, Belgium
17. "To my Muse"
18. Susanne Jacoby
19. Madrid
20. Jose Ma. Panganiban

II. MULTIPLE-CHOICE
Direction: Choose the best answer (letters only).

1. b
2. c
3. a
4. a
5. a
6. a
7. a
8. a
9. a
10. a

III. ESSAY (20x point)
Direction: In 400 words or more, write a summary of Rizal's second trip, i.e.:

"From Hongkong to London"

(Note: This part of the quiz calls for free response/answer. It will be graded using the CGFN marking rubric or other marking criteria)

o 0 o

JOSERIZ-FINAL QUIZ 1 (FQ1)
(Chapter 15-20)

I. IDENTIFICATION (2x point each)

Direction: Identify and write the correct answer to the following questions:

1. Rizal's outstanding achievement in Paris was the publication of the annotated *Morgas's Sucesos . . .* in 1890. Who wrote the prologue in the annotated edition?
2. On January 28, 1890, Rizal left Paris for Brussels. Why did he move to Brussels?
3. Who was the Belgian girlfriend of Dr. Jose P. Rizal?
4. In August 1890, Doctor Rizal left Brussels for Madrid. Why did he go to Madrid?
5. The death of Doctor Rizal's friend in August 19, 1890 brought him another misery. Who was this friend who died in Barcelona?
6. About the end of August, Rizal almost had a duel with Antonio Luna in Madrid. Luna uttered unsavory remarks against the honor of a woman. Who was she?
7. In December 1890, Doctor Rizal received a letter from Leonor Rivera telling him about her marriage to an Englishman. Who was this Englishman?
8. Rizal also challenged to a duel a Spanish scholar/writer who wrote in *La Epoca* that Rizal's Family was ejected from Dominican lands in Calamba due to non-payment of rents. Who was this Spanish scholar/writer?
9. In Madrid, Rizal had another misfortune when he had a clash for leadership and supremacy with another Filipino reformer. Rizal eventually was elected to the post of *Responsible* but he abdicated his position. Why did he decline the post?
10. After Madrid, where did Dr. Jose P. Rizal go?

II. MULTIPLE-CHOICE

Direction: Choose the best answer (letters only).

1. The winter residence of the Boustead Family in Biarritz:
   a. Villa Boustead
   b. Villa Eliada
   c. Villa Nueva
   d. None of the above

2. Rizal's romance and marriage proposal to Nelly Boustead failed, because he:
   a. Refused to become Catholic
   b. Refused to give dowry
   c. Refused to become Protestant
   d. None of the above

3. In Biarritz, Rizal finished the manuscript of his book, i.e.:
   a. *Noli Me Tangere*
   b. *El Filibusterismo*
   c. *Sucesos de las Islas Filipinas*
   d. None of the above

4. Rizal finally published the *El Filibusterismo* on September 18, 1891 in:
   a. Brussels
   b. Biarritz
   c. Ghent
   d. None of the above

5. *El Filibusterismo* was the second published novel of Dr. Jose P. Rizal. Doctor Rizal dedicated this book to:
   a. The Fatherland
   b. The Filipino People
   c. GOMBURZA
   d. None of the above

6. The *El Filibusterismo* was considered by a number of known Filipino historians and writers, as a:
   a. Political Novel
   b. Romantic Novel
   c. Cultural Novel
   d. None of the above

7. Dr. Jose P. Rizal's wrote a third novel, which was not finished and published. According to research, Rizal began writing the manuscript in 1892. The title of the unfinished work was:
   a. *Kamandagan*
   b. *Makamisa*
   c. *Dapitan*
   d. None of the above

8. After publishing his second novel, i.e. *El Filibusterismo*, Dr. Jose P. Rizal decided to leave Europe for:
   a. Philippines
   b. Hongkong
   c. Singapore
   d. None of the above

9. Dr. Jose P. Rizal had a good friend in Hongkong, who helped him established therein, during the period of his stay. It was said that Doctor Rizal left a valuable collection of over 2,000 books with this friend. The name of Rizal's friend was:
   a. Jose Ma. Panganiban
   b. Jose Ma. Basa
   c. Jose Ma. Regidor
   d. None of the above

10. Another good friend, a Portuguese physician, also helped Dr. Jose P. Rizal in building up a wider Hongkong clientele in Ophthalmology. His name was:
   a. Dr. Lorenzo P. Marquez
   b. Dr. Lorenzo P. Ruiz
   c. Dr. Lorenzo P. Suarez
   d. None of the above

III. ENUMERATION (2x point each)
Direction: Enumerate the answers to the following questions:

01-05 = 5x Dr. Jose P. Rizal's writing in Hongkong
06-08 = 3x reason why Doctor Rizal returned to Manila
09-10 = 2x addressee of the letters that Doctor Jose P. Rizal left with a Portuguese friend in Hongkong—i.e. Dr. Lorenzo Marquez—for safekeeping and to be opened only after his death.

O 0 o

JOSERIZ-FQ1 (ANSWER KEY)
(Chapter 15-20)

I. IDENTIFICATION (2x point each)
Direction: Identify and write the correct answer to the following questions:

1. Dr. Ferdinand Blumentritt
2. High cost of living in Paris or social life in Paris hampering his writing of the *EL FILI.*
3. Petite Susanne Jacoby
4. To seek justice for his family and the Calamba tenants
5. Jose Ma. Panganiban
6. Nelly Boustead
7. Henry Kipping
8. Wenceslao Retana
9. To avoid disunity/bitterness among Filipinos
10. Biarritz, France

II. MULTIPLE-CHOICE
Direction: Choose the best answer (letters only).

1. b
2. c
3. b
4. c
5. c
6. a
7. b
8. b
9. b
10. a

III. ENUMERATION (2x point each)
Direction: Enumerate the answers to the following questions:

01-05 = 5x Rizal's writing in Hongkong
1. "Ang Karapatan ng Tao"
2. "A La Nacion Espanola"
3. "Sa mga Kababayan"
4. "Una Visita a la Victoria Gaol"
5. "Constitution of La Liga Filipina"

- "La Mano Roja"
- "Proyecto de Colonization del British North Borneo por los Filipinos"
- "Colonization du British North Borneo por de Familles de Iles Philippines"

06-08 = 3x reason why Rizal returned to Manila
6. To confer with Governor Despujol on "Borneo Colonization Project"
7. To establish *La Liga Filipina* in Manila
8. To prove Eduardo de Lete that he was not abandoning the country's cause

09-10 = 2x addressee of Rizal's letter left to Dr. L. P. Marquez for safekeeping
9. "To my Parents Brethren and Friends"
10. "To the Filipinos"

o 0 o

JOSERIZ-FQ2
(Chapter 21-25)

I. IDENTIFICATION (2x point each)

Direction: Identify and write the correct answer to the following questions:

1. On June 26, 1892, Rizal arrived in Manila (from Hongkong). On the same day he sought audience with the Governor-General in Malacañang. Why?
2. Who was the Governor-General with whom he talked to?
3. On July 3, 1892, Rizal founded a civic league aiming to unite, protect and defend Filipinos in the whole archipelago. What was the name of the civic organization?
4. The motto of the league was *Unus Instar Omnium.* Give the English translation.
5. On July 6, 1892, Rizal was arrested while conferring with Gov.-Gen. Despujol in Malacañang on the basis of an incriminatory leaflet which was allegedly found in Sister Lucia's pillowcase. What was the Spanish title of the leaflet?
6. Rizal was consequently jailed at Fort Santiago and on July 15, 1892, he was brought to the steamer *Cebu* for deportation to Dapitan. Who was the Spanish Commandant in Dapitan who received Rizal upon arrival on July 17, 1892?
7. Fr. Pablo Pastells—Superior of the Jesuit Society of the Philippines—sent a letter to Fr. Obach of Dapitan so that Rizal could live at the convent after meeting certain conditions. Rizal did not agree with the conditions and lived with Captain Carnicero instead. What was the main condition being required of Rizal?
8. Besides Fr. Obach of Dapitan and Fr. Jose Villaclara of Dipolog, Fr. Pastells sent Rizal's favorite teacher to Dapitan to persuade him to change religious views, but to no avail. Who was Rizal's favorite teacher at the Ateneo?
9. The Recollect Friars hired a spy who introduced himself to Rizal as a relative named, "Pablo Mercado" in order to have access on Rizal's correspondence and writings. What was the real name of the impostor?
10. On June 15, 1896, Andres Bonifacio sent an emissary to Dapitan to inform Rizal of the Katipunan's plan to launch a national revolution. Who was this emissary?

II. MULTIPLE-CHOICE

Direction: Choose the best answer (letters only).

1. The title of the poem Rizal wrote in Dapitan upon request of his mother—Dona Teodora Alonzo:
   a. "Himno a Talisay"
   b. "Mi Retiro"
   c. "El Canto del Viajero"
   d. None of the above

2. Rizal's friend who advised him to volunteer as a military doctor under the Spanish flag in Cuba:
   a. Capt. Ricardo Carnicero
   b. Dr. Pio Valenzuela
   c. Dr. Ferdinand Blumentritt
   d. None of the above

3. The Governor-General who approved Rizal's request to serve as a military doctor in Cuba:
   a. Eulogio Despujol
   b. Camilo de Polavieja
   c. Ramon Blanco
   d. None of the above

4. The length of Dr. Jose Rizal's exile in Dapitan was:
   a. 3 years and 13 days
   b. 4 years and 13 days
   c. 5 years and 13 days
   d. None of the above

5. On his way to Cuba, Rizal was arrested in Barcelona and was imprisoned at the prison-fortress, named:
   a. Malta
   b. Monjuich
   c. Said
   d. None of the above

6. On his way back to Manila as a prisoner, Rizal's friends—Dr. Antonio Ma. Regidor and Sixto Lopez—tried to rescue him in Singapore by means of a court order, called:
   a. *Writ of Certiorari*
   b. *Writ of Mandamus*
   c. *Writ of Habeas Corpus*
   d. None of the above

7. On Nov. 20, 1896, Rizal's preliminary investigation began under Judge Advocate:
   a. Col. Francisco Olive
   b. Col. Francisco Olivas
   c. Col. Francisco Olivares
   d. None of the above

8. On December 26, 1896, Rizal faced a military court consisted of seven army officers. The prosecutor who urged the court to give death penalty to Rizal was:
   a. Capt. Rafael Dominguez
   b. Lt. Enrique de Alcocer
   c. Capt. Fermin Perez Rodriguez
   d. None of the above

9. The Governor-General who approved Rizal's execution was:
   a. Eulogio Despujol
   b. Camilo de Polavieja
   c. Ramon Blanco
   d. None of the above

10. The exact date when Rizal was shot at Bagumbayan Field was:
    a. December 30, 1895
    b. December 30, 1896
    c. December 30, 1897
    d. None of the above

III. ENUMERATION (2x point each)
Direction: Enumerate the answers to the following questions:

01-05 = 5x Rizal's defense to prove he was not guilty:
06-07 = 2x visitor Rizal received at 5:30 A.M—December 30, 1896
08-10 = 3x person who walked on Rizal's side on his way to Bagumbayan Field

o 0 o

JOSERIZ-FQ2 (ANSWER KEY)
(Chapter 21-25)

I. IDENTIFICATION (2x point each)

Direction: Identify and write the correct answer to the following questions:

1. To seek pardon for his family
2. Gov.-Gen. Eulogio Despujol
3. *La Liga Filipina*
4. "One Like All"
5. *Pobres Frailes*
6. Capt. Ricardo Carnicero
7. Retract his religious errors
8. Fr. Francisco de Paula Sanchez
9. Florencio Namanan
10. Dr. Pio Valenzuela

II. MULTIPLE-CHOICE

Direction: Choose the best answer (letters only).

1. b
2. c
3. c
4. b
5. b
6. c
7. a
8. b
9. b
10. b

III. ENUMERATION (2x point each)

Direction: Enumerate the answers to the following questions:

01-05 = 5x Rizal's defense to prove he was not guilty
1. He advised Dr. Pio Valenzuela not to revolt
2. He did not correspond to radical/revolutionary elements
3. He could have escaped in Singapore
4. He could have escaped in Dapitan through a Moro vinta
5. He was not consulted by the revolutionists
   - The *La Liga Filipina* was just a civic organization
   - The *La Liga* did not live long
   - He did not know about the reorganization of the *La Liga*.
   - The *La Liga* was supplanted by the Katipunan

06-07 = 2x visitor Rizal received at 5:30 A.M.; Dec. 30, 1896
6. Josephine
7. Josefa (sister)

08-10 = 3x person who walked on Rizal's side on his way to Bagumbayan Field
8. Lt. Luis Taviel de Andrade
9. Fr. Estanislao March
10. Fr. Jose Villaclara

o 0 o

JOSERIZ-FQ3
(*Noli Me Tangere*)

I. IDENTIFICATION (2x point each)

Direction: Identify and write the correct answer to the following questions:

1. Give the exact date when *Noli Me Tangere* came off the press.
2. What is the English meaning of the Latin phrase, "Noli Me Tangere?"
3. To whom did Dr. Jose Rizal dedicate his famous novel *Noli Me Tangere*?
4. *Noli Me Tangere* begins with a reception given by Capitan Tiago at his residence in honor of a rich Filipino who returned from Europe. Who was this honoree?
5. Among the guests in the reception was a fat Franciscan Friar who was the parish priest of San Diego for 20 years. Who was this Franciscan Friar?
6. Another priest of the Dominican Order was present during the reception. He was the parish priest of Binondo. Who was this Dominican Friar?
7. In one European country, it was customary for a guest to introduce himself to the other guests, when no one could introduce him formally to the group. Ibarra imitated this custom at Capitan Tiago's reception. In what particular country did he learn this practice?
8. After dinner, Ibarra left the reception and returned to his hotel. On his way, the kind lieutenant of the Guardia Civil followed and told him the sad story behind his father's death. Who was this elderly kind Guardia Civil Lieutenant?
9. Who was the father of Crisostomo Ibarra and where did he die?
10. Ibarra found out from the grave-digger of San Diego cemetery that his father's corpse was removed from the grave and was thrown to the lake. On his way, he pounced upon the Franciscan Priest of San Diego—who said, 'Padre Damaso was responsible for the desecration of his father's grave.' Who was this Parish Priest?
11. One day, Crisostomo Ibarra visited *Pilosopong Tasio* who was writing something in hieroglyphics—for the future generation to read and to understand. What was Pilosopong Tasio expecting from the future generation to say, upon reading his writings? Explain your answer clearly.
12. In the fiesta of *San Diego de Alcala*, Ibarra was praying beside Maria Clara in the church when a man warned him to be careful during the laying of the schoolhouse cornerstone because there was a plot to kill him. Who warned Ibarra?
13. After laying the cornerstone, a lunch was held in a decorated kiosk attended by known residents of San Diego. In that gathering, Padre Damaso insulted the memory of Crisostomo Ibarra's father. Ibarra knocked down the fat Friar with his fist and was about to kill the Franciscan, had it not for the timely intervention of someone. Who stopped Ibarra from killing Padre Damaso?
14. What two consequences were brought about by Ibarra's attack to Padre Damaso?
15. To make things worse, Padre Damaso had asked Maria Clara to marry a young Spaniard—the cousin of Don Tiburcio de Espadaña and grandson of his brother-in-law. Who did Padre Damaso favor to become Maria Clara's husband?

II. MULTIPLE-CHOICE

Direction: Choose the best answer (letters only).

1. Don Rafael Ibarra defended a helpless boy from the brutality of an illiterate Spanish:
   a. Guardia Civil
   b. Tax Collector
   c. Friar
   d. None of the above

2. Don Rafael was imprisoned for killing a Spaniard. He was charged as heretic, meaning:
   a. Defending a boy to play as a hero
   b. Holding beliefs different from Catholic Church
   c. Revolting against Spain
   d. None of the above

3. Crispin allegedly stole money—died due to torture in the convent by the:
   a. Parish Priest
   b. Sacristan Mayor
   c. Guardia Civil
   d. None of the above

4. Elias, the rebellious character in *Noli* was educated at the:
   a. Jesuit College in Manila
   b. San Juan de Letran
   c. Ateneo de Municipal
   d. None of the above

5. Ibarra was imprisoned because his enemies engineered an attack on the Guardia Civil barracks—telling Ibarra was the mastermind. Elias helped Ibarra escaped, using a:
   a. Banca loaded with *zacate*
   b. Horse-driven carriage
   c. Horse-back ride
   d. None of the above

6. Maria Clara was forced to give the letter (of Ibarra) to the Spanish authorities in exchange of her late mother's letter that revealed that her father was:
   a. Capitan Tiago
   b. Padre Salvi
   c. Padre Sybila
   d. None of the above

7. Elias was wounded during the escape and managed to reach the forest where he met a boy weeping over his mother's dead body. The boy's dead mother was:
   a. Salome
   b. Sinang
   c. Andeng
   d. None of the above

8. Before Elias died, he looked towards the east and murmured, i.e.:
   a. *Not all were asleep in the night of our ancestors!*
   b. *I die without seeing the dawn brighten over my*
   c. *To die is to rest!*
   d. None of the above

9. Maria Clara did not marry the young Spaniard favored by Padre Damaso. Instead, she:
   a. Entered Santa Clara nunnery and became a nun
   b. Lived in Spain for the rest of her life
   c. Committed suicide
   d. None of the above

10. In original manuscript of *NOLI*, a Chapter was left unpublished for reason of economy:
   a. "In the Woods"
   b. "Goodbye, Salome"
   c. "Elias and Salome"
   d. None of the above

III. ENUMERATION (2x point each)

Direction: Enumerate the answers to the following questions:

01-05 = 5x characters in *NOLI* drawn by Rizal from actual living persons during that time

o 0 o

JOSERIZ-FQ3 (ANSWER KEY)
(Noli Me Tangere)

I. IDENTIFICATION (2x point each)
Direction: Identify and write the correct answer to the following questions:

1. March 21, 1887
2. "Touch Me Not"
3. "To My Fatherland"
4. Crisostomo Ibarra
5. Padre Damaso
6. Padre Sybila
7. Germany
8. Lt. Guevara
9. Don Rafael Ibarra/Prison
10. Padre Salvi
11. *Not all were asleep in the night of our ancestors!*
12. Elias
13. Maria Clara
14. Ibarra was ex-communicated; Engagement with Maria Clara was called off.
15. Don Alfonso Linares de Espadaña

II. MULTIPLE-CHOICE
Direction: Choose the best answer (letters only).

1. b
2. b
3. b
4. a
5. a
6. d (Padre Damaso)
7. d (Sisa)
8. a
9. a
10. c

III. ENUMERATION (2x point each)
Direction: Enumerate the answers to the following questions:

01-05 = 5x Character in *NOLI* drawn from actual living persons by Rizal

1. Maria Clara = Leonor Rivera
2. Ibarra & Elias = Jose Rizal
3. Pilosopong Tasio = Paciano
4. Padre Salvi = Padre Antonio Pernavieja of Cavite
5. Capitan Tiago = Capitan Hilario Sunico of San Nicolas
   - Dona Victorina = Dona Agustina Medel
   - Basilio/Crispin = Crisostomo Brothers of Hagonoy
   - Padre Damaso = Typical domineering friar—immoral, arrogant and anti-Filipino

o 0 o

JOSERIZ-FQ4
(*El Filibusterismo*)

I. IDENTIFICATION (2x point each)
Direction: Identify and write the correct answer to the following questions:

1. Give the date when *EL FILI* came off the press.
2. Give the city and the country where the *El Filibusterismo* was published.
3. To whom did Dr. Jose Rizal dedicate his famous *EL FILI*?
4. The story of *EL FILI* began on board a roundish-shaped steamer sailing upstream the Pasig River—from Manila to Laguna de Bay. In what name was the steamer called?
5. Among the passenger of the steamer was a rich jeweler who came from Cuba and who was an influential adviser-friend of the Governor-General. What was his name?
6. Included too, as a passenger, was Basilio. Basilio had gained prominence in the society as a promising medical student. Who was financing his college education?
7. Simoun's attempt to begin the armed uprising against the Spaniards did not materialize. At the last hour, he received tragic news on somebody he loved. What news did he get that brought him agony, thus failing to give the signal for the outbreak of the revolt?
8. Name the poet-nephew of Padre Florentino—the retired scholarly and patriotic Filipino priest; he was the lover of Paulita Gomez—niece of Doña Victorina.
9. Doña Victorina succeeded in convincing Paulita to marry Juanito Pelaez. On the occasion of the couple's wedding, Simoun gave them a beautiful gift. What was it?
10. Isagani, who had been rejected by Paulita, was outside the house where the wedding feast was being held. He was warned by a friend to go away because the lighted lamp would soon explode. Thinking about Paulita's safety, Isagani rushed into the house instead, seized the lamp and hurled it into the river where it exploded. Who was the friend of Isagani that divulged the secret of the lamp?

II. MATCHING-TYPE
<u>Direction</u>: Match Column-B with Column-A. Write the LETTER of the answer only.

	A		B
1.	Rich jeweler from Cuba		a. Capitan Tiago
2.	Niece of Dona Victorina		b. Don Custodio
3.	Anti-Filipino Spanish journalist		c. Padre Camorra
4.	A Filipino pro-Spanish Government Official		d. Isagani
5.	Parish Priest of the town of Tiani		e. Padre Irene
6.	Vice-Rector of the U. S. T.		f. Simoun
7.	The fiancé of Paulita Gomez		g. Paulita Gomez
8.	The patron of Basilio		h. Ben Zayb
9.	Nephew of Padre Florentino		i. Padre Sybila
10.	A friar-friend to UST Filipino students		j. Juanito Pelaez
			k. Padre Damaso

III. ESSAY (20x point)
<u>Direction</u>: In 400 words or more, write in brief the synopsis of:

El Filibusterismo

o 0 o

JOSERIZ-FQ4 (ANSWER KEY)
(*El Filibusterismo*)

I. IDENTIFICATION (2x point each)
Direction: Identify and write the correct answer to the following questions:

1. September 18, 1891
2. Ghent, Belgium
3. GOMBURZA: Frs. Mariano Gomez, Jose Burgos and Jacinto Zamora
4. *Tabo*
5. Simoun
6. Capitan Tiago
7. Death of Maria Clara at the Nunnery
8. Isagani
9. A lamp
10. Basilio

II. MATCHING-TYPE
Direction: Match Column-B with Column-A. Write the LETTER of the answer only.

1. f
2. g
3. h
4. b
5. c
6. i
7. j
8. a
9. d
10. e

III. ESSAY (20x point)
Direction: In 400 words or more, write in brief the synopsis of:

El Filibusterismo

(Note: This part of the quiz calls for free response/answer. It will be graded using the CGFN marking rubric or other marking criteria)

o 0 o

WANG-WANG UNIVERSITY (WWU)
0210 San Miguel, Manila

JOSERIZ FINAL EXAMINATION (Sample)

Student: _____ Date: _____
Instructor: _____ Time: _____
SEM/SY: 2nd Semester/2001-2002   Room No. _____

I. MODIFIED IDENTIFICATION

<u>Direction</u>: From the answer pool provided under each group, select the correct answer (letter only) for each number. Observe NO ERASURE policy.

1. The name of Dr. Jose P. Rizal's girlfriend in London.
2. Rizal's girlfriend—he fondly called O-Sei-San.
3. Doctor Rizal almost dueled with Antonio Luna because of this girl.
4. Jose Rizal's girlfriend who married an Englishman in 1890.
5. Dr. Jose P. Rizal's girlfriend in Brussels.

   a. *Nellie Boustead*
   b. *Gertrude Beckett*
   c. *Seiko Usui*

   d. *Suzanne Jacoby*
   e. *Consuelo Ortega y Perez*
   f. *Leonor Rivera*

6. Destination of Jose P. Rizal after leaving Tokyo in April, 1888.
7. Destination of Doctor Rizal after leaving New York on May 16, 1888.
8. Destination of Doctor Rizal after Brussels in 1890.
9. Destination of Jose Rizal after London (1889).
10. Destination of Dr. Jose Rizal after Hongkong (1892).

    a. *Manila*
    b. *San Francisco, USA*
    c. *Madrid*

    d. *Brussels*
    e. *Paris*
    f. *London*

11. The author of Republic Act No. 1425, a.k.a. the *Rizal Law*, requiring colleges and universities to teach the life, works and writings of Dr. Jose P. Rizal as a subject in tertiary degree courses.
12. The name of Filipino compatriot who accommodated Jose P. Rizal temporarily in his stay in London.
13. The name of the Secretary of Spanish Legation who invited Jose Rizal to live with them at the Legation in Tokyo.
14. The founder of the *La Solidaridad* in Barcelona.
15. The journalist who became a good friend to Rizal on Rizal's trip to USA.

    a. *Juan Perez Caballero*
    b. *Graciano Lopez Jaena*
    c. *Techo Suehiro*

    d. *Jose P. Laurel, Sr.*
    e. *Antonio Ma. Regidor*
    f. *Marcelo H. del Pilar*

16. The first poem Jose P. Rizal wrote in Tagalog at the age of eight.
17. The title of the book that Rizal annotated in London.
18. The first article of Rizal in the *La Solidaridad*.
19. The title of the poem that Rizal wrote in Brussels.

20. The civic league Rizal founded in Manila on July 3, 1892.
    a. *Los Agricultores Filipinos*
    b. *A Mi Musa*
    c. *Sucesos de las Islas Filipinas*
    d. *La Liga Filipina*
    e. *Sa Aking Mga Kababata*
    f. *Los Pobres Fraile*

21. Name of the Governor-General whom Rizal visited and talked to after arriving from Hongkong on June 26, 1892.
22. The Spanish Commandant who accommodated Dr. Jose P. Rizal in Dapitan.
23. The Father Superior of the Jesuit Society of the Philippines in 1892.
24. Jose P. Rizal's favorite teacher at the Ateneo.
25. Bonifacio's emissary to Dapitan on June 15, 1896.
    a. *Francisco de Paula Sanchez*
    b. *Ramon Blanco*
    c. *Eulogio Despujol*
    d. *Pio Valenzuela*
    e. *Pablo Pastells*
    f. *Ricardo Carnicero*

26. The date when *Noli Me Tangere* came off the press.
27. To whom did Doctor Rizal dedicate his *Noli*?
28. The date when *El Filibusterismo* came off the press.
29. To whom did Dr. Jose P. Rizal dedicate his *El Fili*?
30. The date when the *La Liga Filipina* was founded by Doctor Rizal.
    a. *September 18, 1891*
    b. *The Fatherland*
    c. *GOMBURZA*
    d. *July 3, 1892*
    e. *March 21, 1887*
    f. *July 15, 1892*

II. MULTIPLE-CHOICE (2x point)
<u>Direction</u>: Choose the best answer (letter only).

1. The poem which Dr. Jose P. Rizal wrote on the request of Dona Teodora while on his exile at Dapitan:
   a. *Himno A Talisay*
   b. *Mi Retiro*
   c. *El Canto del Viajero*
   d. *Mi Ultimo Adios*

2. He advised Doctor Rizal to volunteer as a military doctor in Cuba:
   a. Capt. Ricardo Carnicero
   b. Marcelo H. del Pilar
   c. Dr. Ferdinand Blumentritt
   d. Dr. Lorenzo P. Marquez

3. The Spanish Governor-General who approved Doctor Rizal's petition to serve as a military doctor in Cuba:
   a. Eulogio Despujol
   b. Camilo de Polavieja
   c. Ramon Blanco
   d. Valeriano Weyler

4. The duration of Dr. Jose P. Rizal's exile in Dapitan:
   a. 3 years and 13 days
   b. 4 years and 13 days
   c. 5 years and 13 days
   d. 6 years and 13 days

5. On his way to Cuba—to serve as a military doctor—Jose P. Rizal was abruptly arrested in Barcelona and was imprisoned at Fort:
   a. Malta
   b. Monjuich
   c. Said
   d. Chateau D'If

6. Before reaching Barcelona (and to Cuba) Dr. Jose Rizal's friend tried to save him in Singapore—through a court order, called:
   a. *Certiorari*
   b. *Mandamus*
   c. *Writ of Habeas Corpus*
   d. *Quo Warranto*

7. The Judge Advocate who investigated Doctor Rizal on November 20, 1896:
   a. Col. Francisco Olive
   b. Col. Francisco Olivas
   c. Col. Francisco Olivar
   d. Col. Francisco Olivarez

8. The Governor-General who approved Dr. Jose P. Rizal's execution was:
   a. Eulogio Despujol
   b. Camilo de Polavieja
   c. Ramon Blanco
   d. Valeriano Weyler

9. The exact date when Dr. Jose P. Rizal was shot at the Bagumbayan Field:
   a. December 30, 1895
   b. December 30, 1896
   c. December 30 1897
   d. December 30, 1898

10. He gave the title, "Mi Ultimo Adios" to Doctor Rizal's last-written poem:
    a. Fr. Francisco de Paula Sanchez
    b. Fr. Mariano Dacanay
    c. Fr. Vicente Garcia
    d. Fr. Pablo Pastells

III. ODD-ONE-OUT (2x pt.)
Direction: Write the letter of the option that does *not* belong to the group.

1. The famous ophthalmologists whom Doctor Rizal worked with in Europe:
   a. Dr. Ferdinand Blumentritt
   b. Dr. Louis de Weckert
   c. Dr. Otto Becker
   d. Dr. Karl E. Schweigger

2. Some avid attackers of *Noli Me Tangere*:
   a. Fr. Vicente Garcia
   b. Fr. Jose Rodriguez
   c. Fr. Gregorio Echevarria
   d. Fr. Salvador Font

3. Some brilliant defenders of *NOLI*:
   a. M. H. del Pilar
   b. Fernando Vida
   c. Graciano Lopez Jaena
   d. Mariano Ponce

4. The various places wherein Dr. Jose P. Rizal wrote the *Noli Me Tangere*:
   a. Madrid
   b. Paris
   c. Geneva
   d. Berlin

5. European scientists whom Doctor Rizal associated with in Germany:
   a. Dr. Adolf B. Meyer
   b. Dr. Carlos Czepelak
   c. Dr. Antonio Ma. Regidor
   d. Dr. Feador Jagor

6. Various pen names used by Dr. Jose P. Rizal:
   a. *Dimasalang*
   b. *Laong Laan*
   c. *Taga-Ilog*
   d. *P. Jacinto*

7. Dr. Jose P. Rizal's writings in Dapitan:
   a. *Mi Retiro*
   b. *The Philippines within a Century*
   c. *Himno A Talisay*
   d. *El Canto del Viajero*

8. Persons who knew about Rizal's first departure for abroad:
   a. Antonio Rivera
   b. Manuel T. Hidalgo
   c. Saturnina Mercado
   d. Leonor Rivera

9. The first article Jose P. Rizal wrote in Barcelona:
   a. *Noli Me Tangere*
   b. *Amor Patria*
   c. *Los Viajes*
   d. *Revista A Madrid*

10. The courses Rizal took in Manila:
    a. Medicine
    b. Philosophy and Letters
    c. Painting and Sculpture
    d. Surveying

11. Jose P. Rizal's reasons for going to London:
    a. To annotate Morga's *Sucesos de las Islas Filipinas*
    b. To improve his English
    c. To go on fighting for reforms
    d. To study ophthalmology

12. Rizal's disappointments in Madrid:
    a. Death of Jose Ma. Panganiban
    b. Death of Leonor Rivera
    c. Rivalry with Marcelo H. del Pilar
    d. Aborted duel with Antonio Luna

13. Rizal's writings in Hongkong:
    a. *Ang Karapatan ng Tao*
    b. *Amor Patrio*
    c. *A La Nacion Española*
    d. *La Mano Roja*

14. Reasons for Dr. Jose P. Rizal's return to Manila after the Hongkong stay:
    a. To see Gov. Gen. Despujol about the Borneo Colonization Project
    b. To establish the *La Liga Filipina* in Manila
    c. To assess the effects of *El Filibusterismo* in the Philippines
    d. To show Eduardo de Lete that he was not a coward

15. Doctor Rizal's defense to prove he was not guilty of treason:
    a. The La Liga was ONLY a civic organization
    b. He advised Dr. Pio Valenzuela not to revolt
    c. The *Katipunan* was founded while he was in Europe
    d. He could have escaped in Dapitan or Singapore, if he were guilty

IV. MATCHING-TYPE

<u>Direction</u>: Match Column-B with Column-A. Write LETTER only.

COLUMN-A	COLUMN-B
1. *Touch Me Not*	a. Padre Damaso
2. Hero of *Noli Me Tangere*	b. Padre Sybila
3. Maria Clara's real father	c. Simoun
4. Parish Priest of Binondo	d. *Noli Me Tangere*
5. Savior of Crisostomo Ibarra	e. Elias
6. Rich jeweler from Cuba	f. Capitan Tiago
7. Niece of Doña Victorina	g. Don Custodio
8. Anti-Filipino Spanish journalist	h. Padre Camorra
9. A Filipino pro-government official	i. Isagani
10. Parish Priest of Tiani	j. Padre Irene
11. Vice-Rector of the UST	k. Basilio
12. The fiancé of Paulita Gomez	l. Paulita Gomez
13. The patron of Basilio	m. Ben Zayb
14. The nephew of Padre Florentino	n. Padre Florentino
15. A Friar-friend to Filipino students	o. Juanito Pelaez
	p. Crisostomo Ibarra

V. ESSAY (5x pt.)

<u>Direction</u>: Answer the question below:

During Dr. Jose Rizal's trial, he presented 12 points in his supplementary defense to prove his innocence on the rebellion charges hurled against him. Write down the 12 points Doctor Rizal raised for his line of defense.

o 0 o

WANG-WANG UNIVERSITY (WWU)
0210 San Miguel, Manila

JOSERIZ FINAL EXAM KEY (Sample)

Date: _____   Time: _____

SEM/SY: 2nd Semester/2001-2002   Room No. _____

I. MODIFIED IDENTIFICATION

1. b		16. e	
2. c		17. c	
3. a		18. a	
4. f		19. b	
5. d		20. d	
6. b		21. c	
7. f		22. f	
8. c		23. e	
9. e		24. a	
10. a		25. d	
11. d		26. e	
12. e		27. b	
13. a		28. a	
14. b		29. c	
15. c		30. d	

II. MULTIPLE-CHOICE (2x point.)

1. b	6. c
2. c	7. a
3. c	8. b
4. b	9. b
5. b	10. b

III. ODD ONE OUT (2x point)

1. a	6. c	11. d
2. a	7. b	12. b
3. b	8. d	13. b
4. c	9. b	14. c
5. c	10. c	15. c

IV. MATCHING-TYPE

1. d	6. c	11. b
2. p	7. l	12. o
3. a	8. m	13. f
4. b	9. g	14. i
5. e	10. h	15. j

V. ESSAY (5x pt.)

During Dr. Rizal's trial, he presented 12 points in his supplementary defense to prove his innocence on the rebellion charges hurled against him, as follows:

1. He advised Dr. Pio Valenzuela not to rise in revolution.
2. He did not correspond to the radical, revolutionary elements.
3. The revolutionists used his name without his knowledge. If he were guilty he could have escaped in Singapore.
4. He bought lands in Dapitan and built a home, hospital and school. If he had a hand in the revolution, he could have escaped in a Moro vinta from Dapitan.
5. If he were the chief of the revolution, why was he not consulted by the revolutionists?
6. The *La Liga Filipina* was just a civic association—not a revolutionary society.
7. The *La Liga* died out when he was banished to Dapitan—it did not live long.
8. When *La Liga* was reorganized nine months later, he did not know about it.
9. The *Liga* did not serve the purpose of the revolutionists; otherwise they would not have supplanted it with the "Katipunan."
10. The bitterness in his letters was due to the persecution of his family in 1890.
11. His life in Dapitan was exemplary and could be attested by the politico-military commanders and the missionary priests in Dapitan.
12. His friends and associates knew that he opposed armed rebellion.

o 0 o

Appendix B: TEST BANK (SAMPLE)

IN

Main Ref.: Agoncillo, T. A. <u>History of the Filipino People</u>.
Quezon City, Philippines. Garotech Publishing. 1990

WANG-WANG UNIVERSITY (WWU)
0210 San Miguel, Manila

Marcelino D. Catahan, Ph.D.

1998

HISTORY-MIDTERM QUIZ 1 (MQ1)
(Pre-Colonial Philippines)

1. IDENTIFICATION (2x point each)
Direction: Identify and write the correct answer to the following questions:

1. The Philippines is an archipelago—i.e., "a group of many islands." Give the total number of islands and islets consisting of the Republic of the Philippines.
2. The group of islands comprising the Philippines are scattered in the Southwest Pacific Ocean, just a few degrees north of the Equator. What is the total land area of the Philippines in terms of square miles?
3. Which is the largest and most important island in the Philippines? What is the total land area (in square miles) of this particular island?
4. The second largest Philippine Island is locally referred to as: *Land of Promise*. It has a total land area of 38, 112 square miles. In what name is this island called?
5. The Muslim tribe-people are noted for being the fiercest lovers of freedom. What is the local name called to the Muslim Filipinos that live in Sulu?
6. The Ifugao rice terraces are considered as one of the *Eight Wonders of the World*. Where do you find the Ifugao rice terraces?
7. The longest continuous range, beginning at Baler, Quezon and crossing Isabela, Nueva Vizcaya and Cagayan Valley.
8. What is the name of the largest river system in the Philippines, which is found in the island of Mindanao?
9. The name of the largest lake in the Philippines; where do you find this lake?
10. The lowest spot in the world—37,782 feet deep—and is situated off the eastern shores of Mindanao.

II. MULTIPLE CHOICE
Direction: Choose the best answer. Write the letters only.

1. Mt. Mayon is considered as the most beautiful of the Philippine volcanoes and is found in the province of:
   a. Albay
   b. Batangas
   c. Pampanga
   d. None of the above

2. Mt. Taal—the smallest volcano in the world situated at the middle of a lake—is found in the province of:
   a. Albay
   b. Batangas
   c. Pampanga
   d. None of the above

3. Mt. Pinatubo—which erupted on June 9, 1991—is situated in the province of:
   a. Albay
   b. Batangas
   c. Pampanga
   d. None of the above

4. The earthquake visits the nation very often throughout the year, because the Philippines is located near the:
   a. *Pacific Ring of Fire*
   b. Equator
   c. Mainland Asia
   d. None of the above

5. There are more or less 3,000 varieties of trees suitable for lumber production. The most famous hardwood, considered as "Queen of the Philippine Trees" is called:
   a. Mahogany
   b. Narra
   c. ebony
   d. None of the above

6. The pygmy water buffalo, locally named as *Tamaraw*, is like a dwarf carabao which is most fierce and deadly. Tamaraw is found in the province of:
   a. Palawan
   b. Bohol
   c. Mindoro
   d. None of the above

7. The tiniest mouse-deer in the world, which is locally called as *Pilandut*, is found in the province of:
   a. Palawan
   b. Bohol
   c. Mindoro
   d. None of the above

8. The smallest in the monkey family—called, the *Tarsier*—is another wondrous sight for so many foreign tourists. This unique tiny monkey is found in:
   a. Palawan
   b. Bohol
   c. Mindoro
   d. None of the above

9. The Philippine flowers vary to more or less 10,000 species with different enchanting colors and delicate scents. Among these flowers, one is considered as the "National Flower of the Philippines," and is named:
   a. *Dama de Noche*
   b. *Ilang-ilang*
   c. *Sampaguita*
   d. None of the above

10. Another flower is regarded as the "Queen of Philippine Orchids" and is locally called as the:
    a. *Dama de Noche*
    b. *Ilang-ilang*
    c. *Sampaguita*
    d. None of the above

III. ENUMERATION (2x point each)
Direction: Enumerate the answers to the following questions:

01-05 = 5x most Dominant Tribe in the Philippines
06-10 = 5x Bornean Datu that settled in the Philippines, according to *Maragtas Code*

o 0 o

HISTORY-MQ1 (ANSWER KEY)
(*Pre-Colonial Philippines*)

I. IDENTIFICATION (2x point each)
Direction: Identify and write the correct answer to the following questions:

1. 7,107 Islands
2. 115, 707 Sq. Mi.
3. Luzon/ 43,308 Sq. Mi.
4. Mindanao
5. "Moros"
6. Banaue, Mt. Province
7. Sierra Madre Range or Pacific Coast Range
8. Rio Grande de Mindanao
9. Laguna de Bay
10. Philippine Deep

II. MULTIPLE CHOICE
Direction: Choose the best answer. Write the letters only.

1. a
2. b
3. c
4. a
5. b
6. c
7. a
8. b
9. c
10. d (Waling-Waling)

III. ENUMERATION (2x point each)
Direction: Enumerate the answers to the following questions:

01-05 = 5x Most Dominant Tribe in the Philippines
1. Tagalog
2. Ilocano
3. Visayan
4. Kapampangan
5. Pangasinense
   Others: Bicolano/Ibanag/Zambal

06-10 = 5x Bornean Datu that settled in the Philippines, according to *Maragtas Code*
6. Datu Puti
7. Bangkaya
8. Dumalugdog
9. Sumakwel
10. Lubay
    Others: Paiburong/Dumangsil/Balensusa/Paduhinog/Dumangsol

o 0 o

HISTORY-MQ2
(Pre-Colonial Philippines)

I. IDENTIFICATION (2x point each)
Direction: Identify and write the correct answer to the following questions:

1. The male attire of the ancient Filipinos was composed of upper and lower parts. Name the upper and lower traditional attire (in order) of a native Filipino.
2. The ancient Filipino male wore a headgear, a piece of cloth wrapped around the head. What is the local term for this headgear?
3. The ancient Filipino woman wore dresses consisting of the upper and lower parts. Give the traditional name for this upper and lower attire (in order).
4. Aside from the lower attire, a piece of red or white cloth was also being wrapped about the waist of ancient Filipino woman. What do you call this accessory piece?
5. The Visayans were considered as the most tattooed Filipinos. How were they called by the early Spanish writers?
6. Philippine society was divided into three classes. To what class did the richest and most powerful ancient Filipinos belong?
7. What do you call the middle class in the ancient Filipino social class structure?
8. It is the lowest class in the ancient Filipino social structure.
9. A stage in courtship where the young man served the girl's family in farm-works and other household chores, like chopping fire-woods or fetching water.
10. The stage of the courtship where the suitor's parents would come to the house of the girl to discuss with the girl's parents pre-marriage conditions/arrangements.

II. MULTIPLE CHOICE
Direction: Choose the best answer (letters only).

1. A kind of dowry obliged to the suitor's parents meant for the couple to be married as a form of security:
   a. *Bigay-kaya*
   b. *Bigay-suso*
   c. *Bigay-suhol*
   d. None of the above

2. A traditional treaty of friendship and alliance amongst Filipinos where the contracting parties drew blood from their arms, mixed it with wine in a cup and drank from it:
   a. *Ligawan*
   b. *Sanduguan*
   c. *Paninilbihan*
   d. None of the above

3. A self-sustained pre-colonial village or community consisting of 30-100 families ruled by a Datu or Chieftain:
   a. Barrio
   b. *Nayon*
   c. *Barangay*
   d. None of the above

4. A village member whose function is to announce the newly-promulgated written laws within the barangay:
   a. Village Elder
   b. Judge
   c. *Umalohokan*
   d. None of the above

5. The Ancient Filipinos had plenty of deities. The Chief Deity—equivalent to *Dios* of the Spaniards—was called:
   a. *Idiyanale*
   b. *Bathalang Maykapal*
   c. *Sidapa*
   d. None of the above

6. In ancient mourning tradition, members of certain tribes in Mindanao and Luzon become berserk due to death of their loved ones. The ancient term used to mean, "mourning for a dead woman" was:
   a. *Morotal*
   b. *Maglahi*
   c. *Laraw*
   d. None of the above

7. Upon the death of a person, the people made fires under the house to drive away evil spirits. An ancient term used to mean, "mourning for a dead man" is termed:
   a. *Maglahi*
   b. *Laraw*
   c. *Morotal*
   d. None of the above

8. There was a more formal observance of mourning for a dead chief of the tribe. The term used to mean, "mourning for a dead chief" was:
   a. *Maglahi*
   b. *Laraw*
   c. *Morotal*
   d. None of the above

9. It is an Ilocano dance where a group of dancers imitated a person as if being attacked by ants, by making such motions as scratching and jumping:
   a. *Balitaw*
   b. *Kinnalogong*
   c. *Kinnotan*
   d. None of the above

10. It was a small traditional Visayan guitar, which the Tagalog adopted later as the symbol of poetry:
    a. *Tambol*
    b. *Kudyapi*
    c. *Gangsa*
    d. None of the above

III. ENUMERATION (2x point each)

Direction: Enumerate the answers to the following questions:

01-05 = 5x negative trait common to Filipinos
06-10 = 5x foreign country that the pre-colonial Filipinos traded with

o 0 o

HISTORY-MQ2 (ANSWER KEY)
(Pre-Colonial Philippines)

I. IDENTIFICATION (2x point each)
Direction: Identify and write the correct answer to the following questions:

1. *Kanggan/bahag*
2. *Putong*
3. *Baro/saya*
4. *Tapis*
5. *Pintados*

6. Nobles
7. Freeman/*maharlika*
8. Slaves/*alipin*
9. *Paninilbihan*
10. *Pamamanhikan*

II. MULTIPLE CHOICE
Direction: Choose the best answer (letters only).

1. a
2. b
3. c
4. c
5. b

6. a
7. a
8. b
9. c
10. b

III. ENUMERATION (2x point each)
Direction: Enumerate the answers to the following questions:

01-05 = 5x negative trait common to Filipinos
1. Propensity for gambling
2. Fatalistic/*bahala na*
3. Sensitive
4. Extravagant
5. Lack of Discipline

Others:
- Lack of perseverance
- *ningas-cogon*
- Lack of initiative
- Jealousy/crab mentality

06-10 = 5x foreign country that the pre-colonial Filipinos traded with
6. China
7. Japan
8. Siam
9. Cambodia
10. Borneo

Others:
- Sumatra
- Java
- Old Malaysia

o 0 o

HISTORY-MQ3
(*The Spanish Period*)

I. IDENTIFICATION

<u>Direction</u>: Identify and write the correct answer to the following questions:

1. Give the exact date when Magellan left the port of San Lucar Barrameda, Spain to begin his expedition to Spice Island.
2. The other name for Spice Island.
3. The name of Ferdinand Magellan's parents.
4. The name of Ferdinand Magellan's father-in-law.
5. The leader of the mutiny that took place at Fort San Julian on April 1, 1520.
6. Two mutineers left by Magellan on the coast as they resumed their expedition.
7. The ship that got wrecked as they proceeded with the course/expedition.
8. The ship that deserted while they were negotiating the *Strait of All Saints*.
9. The pilot of the ship that deserted back to Spain.
10. An islet at the mouth of Leyte Gulf where Magellan landed on March 17, 1521.
11. The Chief of Masao, Butuan, Agusan del Norte who became a friend to Magellan.
12. The King of Cebu who also became a friend to Magellan.
13. The ship that successfully returned to San Lucar, Spain on September 6, 1522.
14. Spain sent five post-Magellan expeditions to the Philippines. The most successful (of these expeditions) was the fifth one. Who was the leader of the fifth post-Magellan expedition?
15. The date Manila was proclaimed as the Capital of the Philippines.
16. The Philippines was administered by Spanish Crown through the viceroyalty of Nueva España from 1572-1821. What is the name called to Nueva España today?
17. The Chief Executive of the Philippines during the Spanish era.
18. The Head of the Government for pacified province and district.
19. The Head of the Government for troublesome province and district.
20. The Administrator at the municipal level.

II. MULTIPLE CHOICE

<u>Direction</u>: Choose the best answer (letters only).

1. To check the power of the Governor-General and other royal officials in the Philippines, a policy was introduced by Spain, called the:
   a. *General Visita*
   b. *Specific Visita*
   c. *Residencia*
   d. None of the above

2. This was another check on the Governor-General and other royal officials, done from time to time by an investigator sent by the King of Spain to Manila:
   a. *General Visita*
   b. *Specific Visita*
   c. *Residencia*
   d. None of the above

3. It was an investigation done to a single official or a province in the Philippines by an investigator from Spain:
   a. *General Visita*
   b. *Specific Visita*
   c. *Residencia*
   d. None of the above

4. A large tract of arable lands owned by the friars and other loyal Spanish subjects:
   a. *Hacienda*
   b. *Frailocracia*
   c. *Polo*
   d. None of the above

5. A Spanish political philosophy where there is union of the State and the Church:
   a. *Hacienda*
   b. *Frailocracia*
   c. *Polo*
   d. None of the above

6. A kind of forced labor required from Filipinos—aged 16 to 60 years—to render service in government projects, e.g. building roads, bridges, churches, ships, etc.:
   a. *Hacienda*
   b. *Frailocracia*
   c. *Polo*
   d. None of the above

7. The persons who served in the government's "forced labor policy" were called:
   a. Slaves
   b. *Trabajadores*
   c. *Visitador*
   d. None of the above

8. A huge sum of money paid by rich Filipinos to the government to avoid/escape from serving the *polo*:
   a. *Falla*
   b. *Polista*
   c. *Buwis*
   d. None of the above

9. The affluent Spanish residents in the Philippines who were originally born in Spain were called as:
   a. *Español*
   b. *Peninsulares*
   c. *Insulares*
   d. None of the above

10. Locally-born Spanish residents in the Philippines were called as:
    a. *Español*
    b. *Peninsulares*
    c. *Insulares*
    d. None of the above

III. ENUMERATION (2x point each)

Direction: Enumerate the answers to the following questions:

01-05 = 5x economic achievement during the Spanish period
06-10 = 5x Early Filipino Revolt

o 0 o

HISTORY-MQ3 (ANSWER KEY)
(*The Spanish Period*)

I. IDENTIFICATION
Direction: Identify and write the correct answer to the following questions:

1. September 20, 1519
2. Moluccas
3. Ruy Magellan/Alda de Mesquita
4. Diego de Barbosa
5. Quezada
6. Cartagena/Fr. Sanchez dela Reyna
7. Santiago
8. San Antonio
9. Esteban Gomez
10. Homonhon Island
11. Rajah Kolambu
12. Rajah Humabon
13. Victoria
14. Miguel Lopez de Legaspi
15. June 24, 1571
16. Mexico
17. Gobernador y Capitan General
18. Alcalde Mayor
19. Corregidor
20. Capitan Municipal

II. MULTIPLE CHOICE
Direction: Choose the best answer (letters only).

1. c
2. a
3. b
4. a
5. b
6. c
7. d (*Polista*)
8. a
9. b
10. c

III. ENUMERATION (2x point each)
Direction: Enumerate the answers to the following questions:

01-05 = 5x economic achievements during the Spanish period
1. Introduction of new plants and animals from Mexico
2. Establishment of new industries
3. Opening of the Manila-Acapulco Trade/Galleon Trade
4. Tobacco Monopoly
5. Founding of Economic Society of Friends of the Country
   - Creation of the Royal Company of the Philippines
   - Opening of the Philippines to the World Trade

06-10 = 5x early Filipino Revolts
6. Lakandula/Sulayman Revolt (1574)
7. First Pampanga Revolt (1585)
8. Conspiracy of Maharlikas (1587-88)
9. Revolt against the Tribute (1589)
10. Magalat's Revolt (1596)
- Religious Igorot Revolt (1601)
- Revolt of the Irayas (1621)
- Tamblot Revolt (1621-22)
- Bankaw's Religious Revolt (1621)
- Pedro Ladia's Revolt (1643)

o 0 o

HISTORY-MQ4
(*Reform and Revolution*)

I. IDENTIFICATION
Direction: Identify and write the correct answer to the following questions:

1. The liberal Governor-General in 1869 who gave hope to middle class reformists in the Philippines.
2. The date when the Three-Martyr-Priests, i.e. Frs. Mariano Gomez, Jose Burgos and Jacinto Zamora (GOMBURZA) were executed through *garrote*.
3. The great reformist who was considered as the most prolific writer of Philippine Reform Movement.
4. The fortnightly official newspaper of the reform movement.
5. A civic league founded by Dr. Jose P. Rizal in Ilaya, Tondo—on July 3, 1892.
6. The date when the *Katipunan* or KKK was founded by Andres Bonifacio.
7. The password used by *Katipun* or associate (i.e. first grade members of KKK).
8. The password used by *Kawal* or soldiers (i.e. second grade members of KKK).
9. The password used by Bayani or patriotic (i.e. last grade members of KKK).
10. The traitor that divulged the secret of the KKK to Fr. Mariano Gil—Augustinian Curate of Tondo—on August 19, 1896.
11. The name called to the *Katipunan* faction of Emilio Aguinaldo.
12. The name called to the *Katipunan* faction of Andres Bonifacio.
13. The place where the *Magdalos* and *Magdiwangs* met on March 22, 1897 in order to solve their indifferences.
14. The follower of Aguinaldo who insulted Bonifacio—questioning his qualification to the post as elected Director of Interior.
15. Because of that insult, Bonifacio dissolved the meeting and annulled all approved resolutions. What was Bonifacio's function/position during that convention?
16. Who captured Bonifacio and his men following a skirmish at Indang, Cavite?
17. Who led the execution of the Bonifacio brothers at Mt. Nagpatong, Maragondon, Cavite on May 10, 1897?
18. The date when the *Biak-na-Bato Republic* was established by Aguinaldo.
19. The negotiator of the *Pact of Biak-na-Bato* signed on December 15, 1897.
20. The date when Aguinaldo and his companions left for Hongkong as part of the *Pact of Biak-na-Bato*.

II. MULTIPLE CHOICE
Direction: Choose the best answer (letters only).

1. The U.S. Battleship that blew-off at Havana Harbor, Cuba on February 18, 1898 which eventually started the war between America and Spain was:
   a. *Titanic*
   b. *Maine*
   c. *Nevada*
   d. None of the above

2. The *Battle of Manila Bay*—between Americans and Spaniards—was fought on:
   a. May 1, 1898
   b. May 2, 1898
   c. May 3, 1898
   d. None of the above

3. The Commander of the American Fleet that bombed Manila Bay on May 1, 1898:
   a. Gen. Arthur MacArthur
   b. Gen. Thomas Anderson
   c. Comm. George Dewey
   d. None of the above

4. The Commander of the Spanish Armada during the *Battle of Manila Bay*:
   a. Gen. Fermin Jaudines
   b. Adm. Patricio Montojo
   c. Gen. Basilio Augustin
   d. None of the above

5. Convinced by the Americans to continue his war activities against the Spaniards, General Aguinaldo returned to the Philippines from Hongkong exile on:
   a. May 19, 1898
   b. May 20, 1898
   c. May 21, 1898
   d. None of the above

6. As part of the secret negotiation between the Americans and the Spaniards, the *Mock Battle of Manila* was staged to save the Spanish honor; and, was fought on:
   a. August 11, 1898
   b. August 12, 1898
   c. August 13, 1898
   d. None of the above

7. Under a Dictatorial Government, Aguinaldo declared the Philippine Independence at Kawit, Cavite, on:
   a. May 12, 1898
   b. June 12, 1898
   c. July 12, 1898
   d. None of the above

8. The *Malolos Congress*—convoked by Aguinaldo on September 15, 1898 to frame a new Constitution—adopted and approved a constitutional draft, known as the:
   a. *Calderon Plan*
   b. *Paterno Plan*
   c. *Mabini Plan*
   d. None of the above

9. After the Treaty of Paris (Dec. 10, 1892) a proclamation of American intention to stay and rule the Philippines was made—known as the:
   a. *Benevolent Expansion*
   b. *Benevolent Conquest*
   c. *Benevolent Assimilation*
   d. None of the above

10. The Malolos Republic, a.k.a. First Philippine Republic, was inaugurated on:
   a. January 20, 1899
   b. January 21, 1899
   c. January 22, 1899
   d. None of the above

III. ESSAY (20x point)
Direction: In 400 words or more, write a synopsis of:

"The Filipino-American War"

o 0 o

HISTORY-MQ4 (ANSWER KEY)
(*Reform and Revolution*)

I. IDENTIFICATION
Direction: Identify and write the correct answer to the following questions:

1. Carlos Maria dela Torre
2. February 17, 1872
3. Dr. Jose P. Rizal
4. *La Solidaridad*
5. *La Liga Filipina*
6. July 7, 1892
7. *Anak ng Bayan*
8. GOMBURZA
9. Rizal
10. Teodoro Patiño
11. Magdalo
12. Magdiwang
13. Tejeros, Cavite
14. Daniel Tirona
15. Presiding Officer
16. Col. Agapito Bonzon
17. Maj. Lazaro Makapagal
18. November 1, 1897
19. Pedro Paterno
20. December 27, 1897

II. MULTIPLE CHOICE
Direction: Choose the best answer (letters only).

1. b
2. a
3. c
4. b
5. a
6. c
7. b
8. a
9. c
10. d (June 12, 1898)

III. ESSAY (20x point)
Direction: In 400 words or more, write a synopsis of:

"The Filipino-American War"

(Note: This part of the quiz calls for free response/answer. It will be graded using the CGFN marking rubric or other marking criteria)

o 0 o

HISTORY-FINAL QUIZ 1 (FQ1)
(*The American Period*)

I. IDENTIFICATION

Direction: Identify and write the correct answer to the following questions:

1. The capture of Aguinaldo at Palanan, Isabela marked the end of *Filipino-American War.* Give the date of Aguinaldo's capture.
2. The captured Revolutionary General who refused to take the oath of allegiance to the American flag which resulted to his exile in Japan.
3. The brave Revolutionary General from Batangas who surrendered to the Americans on April 6, 1902.
4. The last of the Revolutionary Generals that surrendered to the Americans on September 25, 1903 in the Bicol Region.
5. The first American Military Governor of the Philippines.
6. The last American Military Governor of the Philippines.
7. The first American Civil Governor of the Philippines.
8. The other name for the *First Philippine Commission.*
9. The other name for the *Second Philippine Commission.*
10. Who was the leader of the notorious *Pulahanes* of Samar that gave headaches to the Americans in 1905?
11. A law prohibiting the Filipinos from speaking or writing in support of Independence.
12. A law that imposed death penalty or life imprisonment to any person who was found to have engaged in banditry or robbing people of their cattle and properties.
13. A law passed in 1907 prohibiting the public display of nationalistic Filipino flags, e.g. the *Katipunan* flag.
14. The *Cooper Act*—first Congressional Law pertaining to Philippine governance—was passed by US Congress on July 1, 1902. In what other name was it better known?
15. The Speaker of the First Philippine Assembly—inaugurated on October 16, 1907?
16. Who was elected as the Majority Floor Leader of the First Philippine Assembly?
17. The first bill passed by the Assembly was an appropriation of P1 million for the construction of public schools. In what name was this law popularly known?
18. The American Governor-General of the Philippines, under Pres. Woodrow Wilson (Nov. 1912), who increased Filipino appointees in the government service.
19. On August 19, 1916, President Wilson signed a law declaring that independence would be granted to the Filipinos as soon as a stable government could be established in the Philippines. What was the name of the law?
20. The antagonistic Governor-General accused of meddling with the *Rey Conley Case* that led to the collective resignation of Senate President Quezon, Speaker Osmena and other Filipino Department Secretaries from the Council of State.

II. MULTIPLE CHOICE
Direction: Choose the best answer (letters only).

1. Gov.-Gen. Leonard Wood died on August 7, 1927 and was replaced by:
   a. Dwight F. Davis
   b. Frank Murphy
   c. Henry L. Stimson
   d. None of the above

2. The Ninth US Independence Mission in 1933, a.k.a. *OSROX Mission*, succeeded in securing passage of a bill known as the:
   a. Hare-Hawes-Cutting Bill
   b. Tydings-McDuffie Law
   c. Jones Law
   d. None of the above

3. The Twelfth Independence Mission in 1934—the most successful of the Philippine Independence Mission to Washington—was led by:
   a. Manuel Roxas
   b. Manuel Quezon
   c. Sergio Osmena
   d. None of the above

4. Following provisions of Tydings-McDuffie Law, the Filipinos elected 202 delegates to a Constitutional Convention on July 10, 1934. The eldest delegate elected was:
   a. Claro M. Recto
   b. Ruperto Montinola
   c. Teodoro Sandiko
   d. None of the above

5. The elected President of the 1934 Constitutional Convention was:
   a. Claro M. Recto
   b. Ruperto Montinola
   c. Teodoro Sandiko
   d. None of the above

6. On May 14, 1935, a plebiscite on the Constitution was held. For the first time in the history of the country, the Filipino women were allowed to:
   a. Hold government offices
   b. Vote during elections
   c. Organize women's league
   d. None of the above

7. In the first national elections under the new Constitution held on September 17, 1935, the elected Commonwealth President was:
   a. Emilio Aguinaldo
   b. Gregorio Aglipay
   c. Manuel L. Quezon
   d. None of the above

8. The Commonwealth of the Philippines was inaugurated with colorful ceremonies at the Legislative Building in Manila on:
   a. November 15, 1935
   b. November 15, 1936
   c. November 15, 1937
   d. None of the above

9. The first public school teachers under the American regime were called:
   a. *Ateneans*
   b. *Thomasites*
   c. *La Sallites*
   d. None of the above

10. According to historians, the *best legacy* that the Americans left the Filipinos was:
    a. Religion
    b. Education
    c. Culture

    d. None of the above

III. ENUMERATION (2x point each)
Direction: Enumerate the answers to the following questions:

01-05 = 5x of the *Seven Wise Men* of the 1935 Constitution
06-10 = 5x achievement of Pres. Manuel L. Quezon

o 0 o

HISTORY-FQ1 (ANSWER KEY)
(*The American Period*)

I. IDENTIFICATION

Direction: Identify and write the correct answer to the following questions:

1.	March 23, 1901	11.	Sedition Law
2.	Gen. Artemio Ricarte	12.	Brigandage Act
3.	Gen. Miguel Malvar	13.	Flag Law
4.	Gen. Simeon Ola	14.	Philippine Bill of 1902
5.	Gen. Wesley Merritt	15.	Sergio Osmena
6.	Gen. Arthur MacArthur	16.	Manuel L. Quezon
7.	Gov. William H. Taft	17.	Gabaldon Law
8.	Schurman Commission	18.	Francis B. Harrison
9.	Taft Commission	19.	Jones Law (1916)
10.	Nazario Aguilar	20.	Leonard Wood

II. MULTIPLE CHOICE

Direction: Choose the best answer (letters only).

1.	c	6.	b
2.	a	7.	c
3.	b	8.	a
4.	c	9.	b
5.	a	10.	d

III. ENUMERATION (2x point each)

Direction: Enumerate the answers to the following questions:

01-05 = 5x of the *Seven Wise Men* of the 1935 Constitution

1. Felimon Sotto
2. Manuel A. Roxas
3. Norberto Romualdez
4. Manuel C. Briones
5. Conrado Benitez
• Miguel Cuaderno
• Vicente Encarnacion

06-10 = 5x achievement of Pres. Manuel L. Quezon

6. Re-organization of the Government
7. Granting of women's suffrage
8. Creation of new chartered cities

9. Adoption of National Language based on Tagalog
10. Promotion of social justice
- Compulsory military training of able-bodied youth
- 1939 Official Census for the Philippines
- Improvement of Philippine economy
- Created Joint Preparatory Committee on Philippine Affairs
- Passed 3x amendment to the 1935 Philippine Constitution

o 0 o

HISTORY-FQ2
(*The Japanese Occupation*)

I. IDENTIFICATION
Direction: Identify and write the correct answer to the following questions:

1. The war in Europe that eventually led to World War II started in what year?
2. In what year did Japan begin her control over Korea?
3. In 1932, Japan invaded Manchuria and in the ensuing five years the Japanese conquered the whole country, which Manchuria was a part. Which was this country?
4. In 1940-41, Japan conquered Vietnam, Cambodia and Laos—former French Territories. In what name did the French call the federation of these three countries?
5. On July 26, 1941 because of the Japanese threat, Gen. Douglas MacArthur integrated fully the reserve and regular forces of the Philippine Army into the United States Army and formed the USAFFE. What is meant by the acronym USAFFE?
6. To neutralize the US Naval strength in the Pacific, Japan treacherously attacked Pearl Harbor while a negotiation was going on. Give the date of Pearl Harbor Attack.
7. A few days after Pearl Harbor Attack, the Japanese began landing in Northern Luzon. Give two places in Northern Luzon that were used as landing points by the Japanese?
8. To save Manila from being ravaged, Gen. Douglas MacArthur declared Manila as an *Open City*. Give the date when this declaration was made?
9. The major Japanese forces that landed in Lingayen (in the North) and Quezon Province (in the South) converged in Manila. Give the date of Manila's fall.
10. On February 20, 1942, President Quezon left Corregidor on a submarine. In what country did he take the plane that brought him to San Francisco, USA?
11. On March 11, 1942, Gen. Douglas MacArthur left Corregidor for Australia and the US. To whom did he entrust the USAFFE's command?
12. Before General MacArthur departed Australia for US, what promise did he pledge to the Filipino people?
13. Due to lack of food, medicines and ammunitions, the USAFFE got demoralized. Give the exact date of the "Surrender of Bataan."
14. As a result of the USAFFE's surrender, the prisoners were forced at gunpoint to march from Bataan to San Fernando Pampanga under the hot summer sun. In Pampanga, they were herded like animals and were transported by train to Capas, Tarlac. Historians recorded 22,155 Filipinos and 2,000 American soldiers perished in this march. In what name was this march called by Philippine historians?
15. With the fall of Bataan, the Japanese attack stepped up in Corregidor. Eventually, Corregidor surrendered. Give the date of the Fall of Corregidor.
16. Who was the Commander-in-Chief of the Japanese Imperial Forces?
17. On June 18, 1943 the KALIBAPI formed a Preparatory Commission for Philippine Independence (from Japan). What is meant by the acronym KALIBAPI?
18. On October 14, 1943, the Japanese-sponsored Philippine Republic was inaugurated. Who was inducted as President of the Philippines?
19. The Battle of Leyte Gulf was recorded as the greatest naval battle in History. When did the returning Americans re-take Leyte that eventually paved the way for the liberation of the entire Philippines?

20. When did General MacArthur proclaim the liberation of the entire Philippines from the Japanese Imperial Forces?

II. MULTIPLE CHOICE
Direction: Choose the best answer (letters only).

1. The Commander of the 14th Infantry Battalion operating in Northern Luzon:
   a. Col. Guillermo Nakar
   b. Gov. Roque Ablan
   c. Bado Dangwa
   d. None of the above

2. The Commander of a self-organized guerilla unit in Ilocos Norte:
   a. Col. Guillermo Nakar
   b. Gov. Roque Ablan
   c. Bado Dangwa
   d. None of the above

3. The leader of a guerilla unit operating in the Mountain Province:
   a. Col. Guillermo Nakar
   b. Gov. Roque Ablan
   c. Bado Dangwa
   d. None of the above

4. The leader of the guerilla unit operating in Pampanga, Tarlac and Nueva Ecija:
   a. Luis Taruc
   b. Wenceslao Q. Vinzons
   c. Eleuterio Adevoso/Salvador Abcede
   d. None of the above

5. The guerilla leader operating in the Bicol Region:
   a. Luis Taruc
   b. Wenceslao Q. Vinzons
   c. Eleuterio Adevoso/Salvador Abcede
   d. None of the above

6. The guerilla leader operating in Manila and Suburb:
   a. Luis Taruc
   b. Wenceslao Q. Vinzons
   c. Eleuterio Adevoso/Salvador Abcede
   d. None of the above

7. A guerilla leader operating in Samar and Leyte:
   a. Ruperto Kangleon
   b. Macario Peralta
   c. Tomas Cabili/Salipada Pendatun
   d. None of the above

8. A guerilla leader operating in Panay Island:
   a. Ruperto Kangleon
   b. Macario Peralta
   c. Tomas Cabili/Salipada Pendatun
   d. None of the above

9. A guerilla leader operating in Mindanao:
   a. Ruperto Kangleon
   b. Macario Peralta
   c. Tomas Cabili/Salipada Pendatun
   d. None of the above

10. Date of American bombing of Hiroshima, Japan:
    a. August 7, 1945
    b. August 8, 1945
    c. August 9, 1945
    d. None of the above

III. ESSAY (20x point)
Direction: In 400 words or more, discuss the subject:

"Japanese Influences Left in the Philippines"

o 0 o

HISTORY-FQ2 (ANSWER KEY)
(*The Japanese Occupation*)

I. IDENTIFICATION
<u>Direction</u>: Identify and write the correct answer to the following questions:

1. 1939
2. 1910
3. China
4. French Indo-China
5. United States Armed Forces in the Far East
6. December 7, 1941
7. Aparri/Vigan
8. December 26, 1941
9. January 2, 1942
10. Australia
11. Gen. Jonathan M. Wainright
12. *I shall return*
13. April 9, 1942
14. *Death March*
15. May 6, 1942
16. Gen. Masaharu Homma
17. *Kapisanang Lingkod sa Bagong Pilipinas*
18. Jose P. Laurel
19. October 26, 1944
20. July 4, 1945

II. MULTIPLE CHOICE
<u>Direction</u>: Choose the best answer (letters only).

1. a
2. b
3. c
4. a
5. b
6. c
7. a
8. b
9. c
10. d (August 6, 1945)

III. ESSAY (20x pt)
<u>Direction</u>: In 400 words or more, discuss the subject:

"Japanese Influences Left in the Philippines"

(Note: This part of the quiz calls for free response/answer. It will be graded using the CGFN marking rubric or other marking criteria).

o 0 o

HISTORY-FQ3
(*The Period of the Republic*)

I. IDENTIFICATION

Direction: Identify and write the correct answer to the following questions:

1. Who was proclaimed as the first President of the *Third Republic* at the inauguration of Philippine Independence on July 4, 1946?

2. Shortly after independence, the Philippines and US entered into a treaty whereby the Americans withdrew and turned over to the Filipinos "all possession, supervision, jurisdiction, control or sovereignty over the Philippines" with the exception of some selected US Naval Bases in the country. What was this treaty called?

3. The election of 1946 gave opportunity to the peasants to elect their political leaders. Who was elected as Congressman of Pampanga?

4. An act approved by the US Congress in October 1946 providing for an eight-year period of free trade relations between the US and the RP.

5. A term used to mean a pre-condition featured in the free trade agreement, where the Americans had the same rights as the Filipinos to dispose, exploit, develop and utilize all agricultural, timber and mineral resources of the Philippines.

6. In order to get the required three-fourths majority that would allow amending the Constitution, Roxas instigated Congress to unseat Luis Taruc and his Democratic Alliance colleagues. What were the grounds used for expelling them from Congress?

7. Besides Taruc and his colleagues, who were the two Filipino nationalists that voiced strong dissent on the parity amendment?

8. On April 15, 1948, Roxas succumbed to a heart attack after delivering a major speech at Clark Air Base, Pampanga. Who succeeded Roxas as President?

9. To bring back the outlawed *Hukbo ng Bayan Laban sa Hapon* (HUKBALAHAP or HUK) to the government's fold, President Quirino sent his brother to the hills to negotiate peace talks with Luis Taruc. Who was this brother of President Quirino?

10. In November 8, 1949 national elections, who was elected as President of the Philippines?

11. The Secretary of National Defense under Quirino Administration who used *policy of attraction* to win the HUK back to the government side.

12. He defeated Pres. Elpidio Quirino—his former boss—in the presidential race of November 10, 1953.

13. The date when Pres. Ramon Magsaysay met his mysterious death in an airplane crash on the slopes of Mt. Manunggal in Cebu.

14. NARRA was a program under Pres. Ramon Magsaysay, resettling about 8,800 families in 22 settlement projects. What is meant by the acronym NARRA?

15. FACOMA was another program during the time of Magsaysay that aimed to help farmers in marketing their produce. Give the meaning of the acronym FACOMA.

16. After the death of Pres. Ramon Magsaysay, who succeeded him in the presidency?

17. It is a policy adopted by Pres. Carlos P. Garcia that aimed purposely to stop foreigners from dominating the national economy.

18. He defeated Pres. Carlos P. Garcia in the elections of November 14, 1961.

19. An American ex-liberation soldier—who made multi-million fortunes from illegal business deals that caused the eventual downfall of Pres. Diosdado Macapagal.

20. A book containing names of private and government officials who had received large sums of money from Harry S. Stonehill.

II. MULTIPLE CHOICE
<u>Direction</u>: Choose the best answer (letters only).

1. He outlawed the HUKBALAHAP in March 1948:
   a. Pres. Manuel Roxas
   b. Pres. Elpidio Quirino
   c. Pres. Ramon Magsaysay
   d. None of the above

2. He granted *parity rights* to the Americans:
   a. Pres. Manuel Roxas
   b. Pres. Elpidio Quirino
   c. Pres. Ramon Magsaysay
   d. None of the above

3. He was considered as the *Father of Philippine Industrialization*:
   a. Pres. Elpidio Quirino
   b. Pres. Ramon Magsaysay
   c. Pres. Carlos P. Garcia
   d. None of the above

4. He was the first President who improved the condition of the barrio people:
   a. Pres. Elpidio Quirino
   b. Pres. Ramon Magsaysay
   c. Pres. Carlos P. Garcia
   d. None of the above

5. The first President who dressed in a *Barong Tagalog* during his inauguration:
   a. Pres. Elpidio Quirino
   b. Pres. Ramon Magsaysay
   c. Pres. Carlos P. Garcia
   d. None of the above

6. His government program centered on economic independence through *austerity*:
   a. Pres. Ramon Magsaysay
   b. Pres. Carlos P. Garcia
   c. Pres. Diosdado Macapagal
   d. None of the above

7. He reverted Philippine Independence from July 4th to June 12th:
   a. Pres. Ramon Magsaysay
   b. Pres. Carlos P. Garcia
   c. Pres. Diosdado Macapagal
   d. None of the above

8. He propagated the use of Filipino Language in government institutions:
   a. Pres. Ramon Magsaysay
   b. Pres. Carlos P. Garcia
   c. Pres. Diosdado Macapagal
   d. None of the above

9. He was the ninth in the hierarchy of Philippine Presidents:
   a. Pres. Ramon Magsaysay
   b. Pres. Carlos P. Garcia
   c. Pres. Diosdado Macapagal
   d. None of the above

10. He was the tenth in the hierarchy of Philippine Presidents:
    a. Pres. Ramon Magsaysay
    b. Pres. Carlos P. Garcia
    c. Pres. Diosdado Macapagal
    d. None of the above

III. ESSAY (20x points)
Direction: In 400 words or more, discuss the subject:

"The HUKBALAHAP Movement"

o 0 o

HISTORY-FQ3 (ANSWER KEY)
(The Period of the Republic)

I. IDENTIFICATION
<u>Direction</u>: Identify and write the correct answer to the following questions:

1. Manuel A. Roxas
2. Treaty of General Relations
3. Luis Taruc
4. Bell Trade Relations Act
5. Parity Rights
6. Electoral Fraud and Terrorism
7. C. M. Recto and J. P. Laurel
8. Elpidio Quirino
9. Judge Antonio Quirino
10. Elpidio Quirino
11. Ramon Magsaysay
12. Ramon Magsaysay
13. March 17, 1957
14. National Resettlement and Rehabilitation Administration
15. Farmers' Cooperative and Marketing Association
16. Pres. Carlos P. Garcia
17. "Filipino First"
18. Diosdado Macapagal
19. Harry S. Stonehill
20. "Blue Book"

II. MULTIPLE CHOICE
<u>Direction</u>: Choose the best answer (letters only).

1. a
2. a
3. a
4. b
5. b
6. b
7. c
8. c
9. c
10. d (Ferdinand E. Marcos)

III. ESSAY (20x points)
<u>Direction</u>: In 400 words or more, discuss the subject:

"The HUKBALAHAP Movement"

(<u>Note</u>: This part of the quiz calls for free response/answer. It will be graded using the CGFN marking rubric or other marking criteria)

o 0 o

HISTORY-FQ4
(Marcos to GMA)

I. IDENTIFICATION (2x point each)
Direction: Identify and write the correct answer to the following questions:

1. He defeated Pres. Diosdado Macapagal in the presidential election of November 5, 1965.
2. The bill signed into law by President Marcos on July 14, 1966 sending a Military Engineering Contingent to Vietnam "on the side of the Americans."
3. During the second term of President Marcos, military abuses were very rampant. On June 13, 1966, the Philippine Constabulary (PC) operatives massacred seven farmers in a village of Concepcion, Tarlac. How was this accident called in the annals of local history?
4. On May 21, 1967, the Philippine Constabulary killed 32 members of a fanatical organization right on the border of Pasay and Manila. In what name was the organization called?
5. The *Proclamation 1081* or Martial Law was declared by President Marcos in early 1970s because of deteriorating peace and order, rising criminality, rampant political unrest, etc. Give the exact date when the proclamation was issued.
6. The Constitutional Convention that had started before the Martial Rule continued meeting under the new regime. When the new charter was finished, Mr. Marcos presented it to a previously organized 26,000 Citizen Assemblies all over the country. What was the Filipino term/translation for Citizen Assembly?
7. The longest bridge in the Philippines between Samar and Leyte was constructed during the second term of Marcos. What name was called to this bridge?
8. Due to growing international pressure, Marcos signed Proclamation 2045—lifting the imposition of Martial Law. Give the date when this event happened.
9. Ferdinand Marcos succeeded in amending the 1973 Constitution through political maneuvering. A plebiscite was held on April 7, 1981 where the Filipinos unwittingly ratified the new 1981 Constitution. What provision was there in the new 1981 Constitution concerning the President's term of office?
10. On June 21, 1981, the first presidential election under the 1981 Constitution was held. Who won as President during that election?

II. MULTIPLE CHOICE
Direction: Choose the best answer (letters only).

1. Former Sen. Benigno S. Aquino, Jr.—the leading opposition to Marcos—returned home from a three-year exile in the US and was shot upon arrival at Manila International Airport on:
   a. August 22, 1983
   b. August 23, 1983
   c. August 24, 1983
   d. None of the above

182

2. According to the *National Movement for Free Elections* (NAMFREL), the winner of the presidential *snap election* held on February 7, 1986 was:
   a. Ferdinand E. Marcos
   b. Salvador H. Laurel
   c. Corazon C. Aquino
   d. None of the above

3. The *EDSA Revolt* or *People Power* ended the constitutional authoritarianism of Pres. Ferdinand Marcos. The revolt was staged from:
   a. February 22-25, 1984
   b. February 22-25, 1985
   c. February 22-25, 1986
   d. None of the above

4. The Constitutional Commission that framed the 1987 Constitution was appointed by Pres. Corazon C. Aquino consisting of:
   a. 48 members
   b. 58 members
   c. 68 members
   d. None of the above

5. The eleventh in the hierarchy of Philippine Presidents:
   a. Pres. Carlos P. Garcia
   b. Pres. Diosdado Macapagal
   c. Pres. Ferdinand E. Marcos
   d. None of the above

6. He was elected as President of the Philippines in the election of May 11, 1992:
   a. Pres. Diosdado Macapagal
   b. Pres. Ferdinand E. Marcos
   c. Fidel V. Ramos
   d. None of the above

7. He was remembered as the most-traveled President during his term of office:
   a. Pres. Corazon C. Aquino
   b. Pres. Ferdinand E. Marcos
   c. Pres. Fidel V. Ramos
   d. None of the above

8. He was ousted from his presidential office by *EDSA II* on January 20, 2001:
   a. Pres. Ferdinand E. Marcos
   b. Pres. Fidel V. Ramos
   c. Pres. Joseph E. Estrada
   d. None of the above

9. The fourteenth in the hierarchy of Philippine Presidents:
   a. Pres. Corazon C. Aquino
   b. Pres. Fidel V. Ramos
   c. Pres. Joseph E. Estrada
   d. None of the above

10. The fifteenth in the hierarchy of Philippine Presidents:
    a. Pres. Fidel V. Ramos
    b. Pres. Joseph E. Estrada
    c. Pres. Gloria M. Arroyo
    d. None of the above

III. ENUMERATION (2x point each)

Direction: Enumerate in successive/logical order "10x Philippine President beginning from Pres. Manuel A Roxas" of the Third Republic and up, i.e.:

1. Manuel A. Roxas (bonus 2x point)
2. . . . Up to No. 10.

o 0 o

HISTORY-FQ4 (ANSWER KEY)
(Marcos to GMA)

I. IDENTIFICATION (2x point each)
Direction: Identify and write the correct answer to the following questions:

1. Pres. Ferdinand E. Marcos
2. *Vietnam Aid Bill*
3. *Kulatingan Massacre*
4. *Lapiang Malaya*
5. September 21, 1972
6. *Kapulungan*
7. San Juanico Bridge
8. January 17, 1981
9. A 6-year tenure with indefinite number of terms
10. Pres. Ferdinand E. Marcos

II. MULTIPLE CHOICE
Direction: Choose the best answer (letters only).

1. d (August 21, 1983)
2. c
3. c
4. a
5. c
6. c
7. c
8. c
9. d (Gloria M. Arroyo)
10. d (Benigno Aquino III)

III. ENUMERATION (2x point each)
Direction: Enumerate in successive/logical order "10x Philippine President beginning from Pres. Manuel A Roxas" of the Third Republic and up, i.e.:

1. Manuel A. Roxas (bonus 2xpoint)
2. Pres. Elpidio Quirino
3. Pres. Ramon Magsaysay
4. Pres. Carlos P. Garcia
5. Pres. Diosdado Macapagal
6. Pres. Ferdinand E. Marcos
7. Pres. Corazon C. Aquino
8. Pres. Fidel V. Ramos
9. Pres. Joseph Estrada
10. Pres. Gloria M. Arroyo

o 0 o

Appendix C: **CURRICULUM VITAE**

1. PERSONAL DATA

- ❑ Name: MARCELINO DELA CRUZ CATAHAN
- ❑ Nationality: Filipino
- ❑ Date of Birth: June 3, 1938
- ❑ Marital Status: Married
- ❑ Address: 10 Angat St., NIA Village, Tandang Sora,

                        Quezon City 1116, PHILIPPINES

                        C/P No.: +639092185663

2. EDUCATION

- ✓ Pacific Western University (PWU). Los Angeles, California, USA. Doctor of Philosophy in Educational Administration. November 1992.
- ✓ Pacific Western University. Los Angeles, California, USA. Master of Education in Curricula and Instruction. May 1992.
- ✓ Technological Institute of the Philippines. Manila. Bachelor of Science in Industrial Education (BSIE). May 1965.
- ✓ Central Luzon School of Arts & Trades. Cabanatuan City. Automotive Technology. 1960.
- ✓ Central School of Arts & Trades. Cabanatuan City. Secondary Diploma. 1958.

3. UNPUBLISHED BOOKS/PAPERS

- ▪ *"Gusto Kong Maging Ama: Kalbaryo ng Isang OFW."* A book of poems on moral values written in Filipino. Quezon City. 2009.
- ▪ *"Santa Elena: Pagdulang sa Banal na Kurus."* Editor. A Tagalog Stage Play (*Arakyo*). Quezon City. 2004.
- ▪ "A Glimpse in Philippine History." A Teaching Guide in Philippine History. DLSU-CSB. Manila. 2004.
- ▪ "The Teaching of Research Methods in AMACC Computer-Related Courses: A Primer. AMA, Sta. Mesa, Manila. 2001.
- ▪ *"Gusto Kong Maging Ama: Kalbaryo ng Isang OFW."* A novel on moral values written in Filipino. Quezon City. 1996.
- ▪ "Touching the Minds: An Approach to Capacity Building of Educational Administrators." UNICEF-Somalia. 1994.
- ▪ "1994 Proposed Education Projects and Plan of Operations." UNICEF-Somalia.
- ▪ "Summary of Cooperation on Primary Education of UNICEF-Canadian Joint Task Forces." UNICEF-Somalia. 1993.
- ▪ "Touching the Minds: An Approach to Training of Trainers in Somalia." A Training Syllabus for Training of Trainers. UNICEF-Somalia. 1993.
- ▪ "Success in Vocational Training Administration at Vocational Training Center, Namibia." A Ph.D. project. Pacific Western University. L A., CA., USA. 1992.

- "Competent/Efficient Vocational Administrator: Key to Successful Manpower Development." A paper delivered at the ILO-MLMD Workshop. Namibia. 1992.
- "Curriculum: The Bible and Koran in Effective Training." A paper delivered at the ILO/MLMD Workshop in Namibia. 1992.
- "A Research Summary of the Demonstration of Professional Expertise." Pacific Western University, LA., CA., USA. 1992.
- "Vocational Training Programs at the Vocational Training Center Namibia." A Master's Qualifying Exercise. Pacific Western University. LA., CA., USA. 1992.
- "Training Curriculum: Touching the Minds." A Training Guide used in Staff Development Program. Vocational Training Centre Namibia (VTCN). 1991.
- "33 Original Quotes for Thought." VTCN-Namibia. 1990.
- "Training Curriculum: Refresher Workshop on Vocational Training." VTCN- Namibia. 1990.
- "Report: Refresher Workshop on Vocational Training." VTCN-Namibia. 1990.
- "Training Curriculum on Repair and Maintenance of Various Weighing Scales." Ministry of Health/UNICEF-Malawi. Malawi. 1988.
- "Measurement and Evaluation Procedures on Selecting Drivers." UNICEF-Malawi. Malawi. 1988.
- "Training Curriculum on Repair and Maintenance of Bicycle." Ministry of Health-UNICEF-Malawi. Malawi. 1988.
- "Report on Preliminary Assessment of Transport Facilities in and to Malawi Relative to Current Food Supply Situation." UNICEF-Malawi. 1987.
- "Instructor's Teaching Manual." A teaching guide for Automotive Instructors. ILO/Ministry of Labor, Project No. MLW/83/003. ILO-Malawi. 1987.
- "Student's Technical Guide." A learning guide for Automotive Candidate Entrepreneurs. ILO/Ministry of Labor, Project No. 83/003. ILO/Malawi. 1987.
- "Entrepreneurship Management and Leadership." A paper delivered at ILO/ Malawian Entrepreneurship Development Institute Workshop. Malawi. 1987.
- "Training Curriculum on Operations and Maintenance of Maize Mill and Huller." ILO/MEDI, Malawi. 1987.
- "Up Hargeisa Mountains." A collection of poems. Hargeisa, Somalia. 1983.

4. PROFESSIONAL REGISTRATION/MEMBERSHIP

- Lifetime Member. PWU Alumni Association. LA, CA., USA.
- Registered Secondary Teacher. Philippine Civil Service Commission. Manila.
- Registered Tradesman. Public Service Commission. Australia.
- Registered Teacher. Public Service Commission. Papua New Guinea.

5. PROFESSIONAL EXPERIENCE

- **Senior Lecturer-4 (Retired).** CSB-DLSU. Taft Avenue, Manila. 1998-2004.
- **Professor II (Part-time).** AMACC, Caloocan/Sta. Mesa, Manila. 1997-2003.
- **Education Consultant.** UNICEF-Somalia, East Africa. January 1993-April 1994.

Major Duties:

- Participate in the development of sectoral workplan. Ensure compliance to specific assigned objectives. Provide guidance and support to the staff.
- Design, prepare, implement and evaluate assigned programme or project. Analyze and evaluate data to ensure achievement of objectives and/or take corrective action when necessary to meet programme/project objectives. Assist in the development and/or introduction of new approaches, methods and practices in project management and evaluation.
- Meet with national and international agencies covering the management of programme or project. Participate in meetings with ministries responsible for programme; review and follow-up on implementation of recommendations and agreements.
- Undertake frequent field visits to monitor programme/project, as well as conduct periodic programme reviews with government counterparts. Propose or undertake action on operational procedures of project implementation and management. Provide technical assistance to government officials and other partner agencies in planning, implementation, monitoring and evaluation of programme/project.
- Prepare programme/project status reports required by/for management board, donors, budget review, programme analysis, annual reports, etc.
- Assist government authorities to plan and organize training programs. Identify training needs and objectives for the purpose of capacity building, programme sustainability, as well as promotion and advocacy.
- Prepare sectoral documents for Country Programme Recommendation (CPR) and Plan of Action, Country Programme Summary Sheet, etc.
- Contribute toward the preparation of Situation Analysis by compiling data, analyzing and evaluating information and writing chapters of the Analysis.
- Participate in the intersectoral collaboration with programme colleagues. Assist in developing appropriate communication and information strategy to support and/or advocate programme development.
- Coordinate the Operations and Supply staff on supply and non-supply assistance activities ensuring proper and timely UNICEF and Government accountability. Certify disbursement of funds; monitor and submit financial status report to Senior Programme Officer or Representative as required.
- Ensure the accurate and timely input of project information in computerized programme system and issuance of status reports for monitoring and evaluation purposes.

- ❖ **Training Director.** Vocational Training Center Namibia (VTCN). Namibia, Southern Africa. August 1990-December 1992.
- ❖ **Consultant.** UNIDO-Kenya. "Converting Kenya Industrial Training Institute into Kenya Entrepreneurial Training Institute." November 1989.
- ❖ **Curricula/In-Service Training Adviser.** Vocational Training Center Namibia. Windhoek, Namibia. June 1989-July 1990.
- ❖ **Consultant.** UNICEF-Malawi. "Training 174 Ministry of Health Officers in Repair and Maintenance of Weighing Scales" used in the nationwide UNICEF Health Programme. November-December 1988.

- ❖ **Consultant.** UNICEF-Malawi. "Evaluating UNICEF's Regular Drivers and Driver Applicants." August 1988.
- ❖ **Consultant.** UNICEF-Malawi. "Training 28 Cold Chain Technicians in Repair and Maintenance of Bicycles" used in the National Expanded Programme on Immunization (EPI). June-July 1988.
- ❖ **Consultant.** UNICEF-Malawi. "Internal and External Survey of Transport Facilities in Malawi." UNICEF-Malawi Food-Aid Programme. Dec. 1987.
- ❖ **Consultant.** ILO-Malawi Project No. MLW/83/003. "Developing the Curriculum for the Malawian Entrepreneurship Development Institute" (MEDI). 1986-1987.
- ❖ **Consultant.** ILO-Malawi Project No. MLW/83/003. "Upgrading the Capacity of MEDI Instructors in the art of Technical-Vocational Teaching." 1986-1987.
- ❖ **Workshop Supervisor/Instructor.** Cooperative for American Relief Everywhere (CARE). SOMALIA. July 1982-April 1984.
- ❖ **Technical Training Officer.** Staff Development & Training. Department of Works and Supply. Papua New Guinea. July 1976-April 1981.
- ❖ **Chief Auto-Electrician.** Plant & Transport Authority. Lae, Papua New Guinea. July 1975-December 1974.
- ❖ **Secondary School Teacher.** Ramon Avancena High School. Division of City Schools, Manila. July 1966-December 1974.

6. **KNOWLEDGE OF LANGUAGES**

- ➢ English: Can read, write, speak and understand easily
- ➢ Spanish: Can read, write and understand easily
- ➢ Portuguese: Can read, write and understand easily

7. COMPUTER LITERACY

- Windows/MS-Word 2007; Outlook (E-mail); MS-Power Point.

8. REFERENCES

- ❖ Dr. Gene R. Ward. Vice President, EDC. Honolulu, Hawaii. 875 Puuomaoo St., Honolulu, Hawaii, USA. 96825.
- ❖ Dr. Orlando G. Manuel. Director, Student Affairs. Nueva Ecija University of Science and Technology (NEUST). Cabanatuan City.
- ❖ Dr. Elizabeth Q. Lahoz. President, Technological Institute of the Philippines (TIP). 363 P. Casal St., Quiapo, Manila.
- ❖ Dr. Cristina Esquivel Saldivar. Dean, School of Multi-Disciplinary Studies (SMS). College of Saint Benilde (CSB-DLSU). 2544 Taft Avenue, Manila.
- ❖ Engr. Angelito C. Longos. Supervising Labor Enforcement Officer. Department of Labor & Employment. National Capital Region (NCR).

9. AWARD OF DISTINCTION (*One of the 20 Outstanding Awardees*)

- ✓ "2012 TIP OUTSTANDING ALUMNI AWARDS." **TIP 50th Anniversary Celebration.** Technological Institute of the Philippines (TIP, Manila). <u>For</u>: "his exemplary achievements in the field of education . . . as consultant in education to various countries through the *UNICEF*." February 11, 2012.

**2012 TIP MANILA OUTSTANDING
ALUMNI AWARDEES**

FRANCISCO C. AQUINO

Civil Engineering, 1966
for his exemplary achievements in corporate management in the United States, and for his dedication and commitment to his alma mater as the current President of the TIP International Alumni Association (TIPIAA)

MELITO A. BACCAY, Dr Eng

Civil Engineering, 1994
for his academic achievements in the field of civil engineering and for his success as researcher, nationally recognized young scientist, professor, institutional administrator, and practitioner in his field of expertise

REYNALDO A. CARPIO, PhD

Civil Engineering, 1983
for his exemplary achievements in corporate management and entrepreneurship as President of Grand Monaco Estate Developers, Inc. and in recognition of his various socio-civic involvement and corporate social responsibility endeavours

MARCELINO D. CATAHAN, PhD

Industrial Education, 1965
for his academic achievements in the field of education, and for his exemplary research and teaching endeavours in the field of vocational education and educational management, and for his outstanding achievements as cosultant in education to various countries through the UNICEF

PEDRITO M. CONDENO

Civil Engineering, 1967
for his exemplary achievements in professional engineering practice, and in corporate management and entrepreneurship as manufacturing supervisor, project manager, and vice president for engineering, and as President and Chairman of PEER Management Construct, Inc.

46 TIP 50ᵀᴴ ANNIVERSARY

(Note: The name of the author appears as second from below)

Figure 10. TIP 50th Anniversary Journal (Page 46)

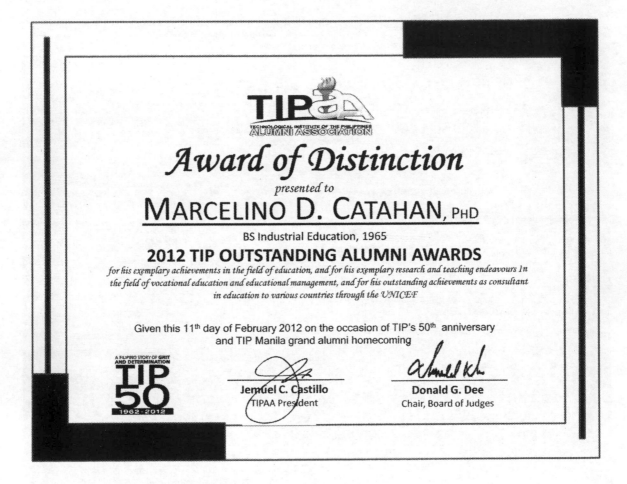

Figure 11. Award of Distinction Certificate

Figure 13. An Award of Distinction Plaque

ABOUT THE AUTHOR

Marcelino D. Catahan is a self-made man. He was fourth in the eleven children of a farmer's family in Cabanatuan, Nueva Ecija, Philippines. He was a self-supporting learner all the way—from high school to postgraduate studies. He obtained his bachelor's degree in industrial education in Technological Institute of the Philippines (TIP), Manila, in 1965. He finished MEd and PhD (educational administration) in Pacific Western University, Los Angeles, California, USA, in 1992, at age fifty-four.

Marcelino taught in Manila public secondary schools (1966–1974). He worked in Papua New Guinea as mechanical instructor/training coordinator in "Plant & Transport Authority" (1975–1980). His migration was influenced by two "special" sons—an autistic and a schizophrenic. Verily, he needed to save big money for their medical expenses. In 1980, he brought his family to California, USA. He supervised the boys' treatment at Stanford Medical Hospital at Palo Alto, California. But sadly, science effects up to a certain level only—the rest is left to God. With minimal progress, Marcelino's family went back to Manila in 1981.

Marcelino was a supervisor/instructor with "Cooperative for American Relief Everywhere" (CARE) in Somalia, 1982–1984. This began his more than twenty years stint in Africa. He was an ILO consultant in ILO-Malawi (1986–1988); curricula/in-service training adviser/assistant training director in "Vocational Training Center Namibia" (1989–1992); education consultant of UNICEF–Somalia (1993–1994), and education consultant of UNICEF–Mozambique (1994). He resigned in Mozambique to attend to his schizophrenic son, who attempted suicide.

For three years, Marcelino attended to his son's medication. In 1997, he went back to teaching. He was a social science professor in AMA Computer University, Sta. Mesa, Manila, and DLSU–College of St. Benilde at Taft Avenue, Manila, until his retirement in 2004.

The reactivation of primary education in Somalia—after disruption for more than ten years due to civil war—was an excellent feat of Marcelino. In recognition, he was awarded distinction as one of the "Twenty Most Outstanding Alumni" during the TIP's fiftieth anniversary celebration last February 11, 2012.

Printed in the United States
By Bookmasters